Corporate Environmental Management 1

D0755631

Corporate Environmental Management 1

Systems and Strategies

SECOND EDITION

Edited by Richard Welford

Earthscan Publications Ltd, London

First published in the UK in 1996 by
Earthscan Publications Ltd

Revised edition first published in the UK in 1998 by
Earthscan Publications Ltd

Copyright © Richard Welford, 1996, 1998

Reprinted 1999

A catalogue record for this book is available from the British Library

ISBN: 1 85383 559 5 paperback $\sqrt{}$
      1 85383 560 9 hardback

Typesetting and page design by PCS Mapping & DTP, Newcastle upon Tyne
Printed and bound by Biddles Ltd, Guildford and King's Lynn
Cover design by Andrew Corbett

For a full list of publications please contact:

Earthscan Publications Ltd
120 Pentonville Road
London N1 9JN
Tel: (0171) 278 0433
Fax: (0171) 278 1142
Email: earthinfo@earthscan.co.uk
WWW: http://www.earthscan.co.uk

Earthscan is an editorially independent subsidiary of Kogan Page Limited
and publishes in association with WWF-UK and the International Institute
for Environment and Development.

This book is printed on elemental chlorine free paper

Contents

Preface to the second edition

The second edition of this book updates each chapter to make it even more useful to managers, students and researchers. Like the first edition, it shows how business (and other institutions) can improve their environmental performance. The environment is a pressing issue and every person, every organization and every institution has an obligation and duty to consider ways to protect it and reverse the damage done to it over the past decades. This book examines the way in which business organizations can play their part in what has to be a concerted and international effort. However, in a modern pluralist society, businesses (and particularly big businesses) are granted large amounts of power. Along with other powerful institutions we should expect them to take a stance: to educate and lead workers and consumers rather than respond to their rather weak market signals.

With that in mind, this is very much a 'how to do' book, in that it tries to identify best practice, examines the key tools within the framework of corporate environmental management and provides the reader with references for additional reading. Where possible checklists, explanatory diagrams and summary charts have been provided to make the book accessible and useful. While we have not been uncritical about many of the developments in the field of corporate environmental management, it is intended that this book will be helpful to both students of the subject and practitioners in the field.

The book is divided into three (unequal) parts. The first part (Chapters 1 and 2) examines the general context of environmental management by considering the main drivers towards environmentalism and links between strategic management, competitiveness and environmental performance. Part 2 looks at the tools of corporate environmental management. In a detailed, critical and updated examination of environmental management systems and standards, environmental policies, guidelines and charters, environmental auditing, life cycle assessment, the measurement of environmental performance, and environmental reporting, this part of the book outlines, explains and examines the building blocks for success. This is all achieved within the framework of the systems based approach. Part 3 of the book takes the systems based approach a stage further in examining the case of small and medium enterprises and the management of local economic development from a local authority stance. The final chapter extends this systems based approach to a business based agenda for sustainable development.

Although practical in its approach, this book is different to the many 'do-it-yourself' guides which have appeared on the market in recent years. It provides a more holistic approach based on the development of environmental management systems. This systems based approach is much more likely to be successful than *ad hoc*, piecemeal initiatives and methodologies so often associated with other guides. Neither do we stress that corporate environmentalism is 'going green for profit' or 'cost reduction through environmental action'. Lower costs and higher profits may be a consequence of corporate environmental management. But in other circumstances the process may lead to higher costs and the need for higher prices. That is something we will have to learn to live with – the boundaries of business and of doing business are being redefined by environmentalism and we must adjust to these new demands. The environment is too big an issue to be seen only in narrow profit and loss, cost and revenue terms.

We must also recognize that this book provides only a start, the first stage towards creating a more sustainable and equitable future. Sustainable development has to be our ultimate aim and corporate environmental management techniques are necessary but not sufficient to attain sustainable development. The final chapter of this book points to the way ahead.

This book would not have been possible without the help and support of a number of people. As well as the contributors to the text I would like to thank a number of people who have all helped in their different ways. These include: Elaine White, Tina Newstead, Carmel Milner, Andy Gouldson, Linda Orwin, Andrew Young, Rowan Davies and Jonathan Sinclair Wilson, as well as all the other staff at Earthscan Publications. As ever, I recognize the love and support of Chris Maddison.

Richard Welford
August, 1998

About the Contributors

Richard Welford is professor of Corporate Environmental Management at the University of Huddersfield, UK and director of the Centre for Corporate Environmental Management. He is also professor of Sustainable Management at the Norwegian School of Management in Oslo. He has written widely on the subject of corporate environmental management, undertakes consultancy work and training for selected companies and organizations. He is a director of ERP Environment and member of the Eco-Power Trust. He is also editor of three leading academic journals: *Business Strategy and the Environment, Sustainable Development* and *Eco-Management and Auditing*. His mix of academic and practitioner experience make him one of the leading authorities on corporate environmental management.

David Jones is assistant professor in the Institute for Logistics and Transport, Copenhagen Business School.

Mark Shayler is design and environment advisor, Business Link, Bradford and District.

Donal O'Laoire is a director of EMA International, a Dublin based consultancy company.

Richard Starkey is a research fellow at the Centre for Corporate Environmental Management, University of Huddersfield.

C William Young is a research fellow at the Centre for Research on Organisations, Management and Technical Change, Manchester School of Management, UMIST.

Alan Netherwood works in the voluntary sector in Wales, promoting environmental awareness and action in communities.

Michael Brophy is an environmental consultant and project manager at EMA International in Dublin.

Part 1

The Context of Corporate Environmental Management

Chapter 1

Environmental Issues and Corporate Environmental Management

Richard Welford

INTRODUCTION

Since the 1960s, there has been a growing interest in the environment, or more specifically in the damage being done to the environment, in Europe and North America. This may have fluctuated in its intensity as other issues have also gained in importance, but those fluctuations have been around an upward trend. The process of European integration and the growth of international trade has brought the transnational nature of the environmental problem to the forefront. The hole in the ozone layer and global warming is the result of not one country's or one company's action but that of many. There is a role for individual governments and for intergovernmental agencies to put in place policies which begin to rectify the situation. There is also a role for the individual to re-evaluate his or her consumption patterns. This book, however, concentrates on what businesses can do to improve their environmental performance and together to contribute to the common good.

We have seen a rapid growth in environmental legislation and other policies such as the introduction of eco-taxes and levies. Such policies are likely to be further strengthened in the future and this will affect the way in which every business is run and the way in which managers must recognize their responsibility, not only to a company, but also to the environment in which it operates. Perhaps more importantly, many of the more recent initiatives on the environment, emanating from the European Commission, have been market driven and are voluntary. Collectively their impact is to demand that businesses take more responsibility for the environmental damage which they create and to approach corporate environmental management in a more proactive way.

The effects of different industrial sectors upon the environment vary enormously. At one end of the spectrum we might put the oil companies whose very business is environmentally damaging and at the other end we might put retailers and the service sector who have less of a direct impact on

the environment, although who, in most cases, could still make environmental improvements through recycling and improved transportation
policies. But there is still much confusion both for consumers and companies
about what constitutes an environmentally friendly product or operation, and
the 'green revolution' to date has provided few answers, although many
misrepresentations, particularly in the area of product marketing, have been
exposed.

Everything which consumers, companies and other institutions do will
have some impact on the environment. Even substances which in their final
form are environmentally benign may have been unfriendly in their
manufacture especially if that manufacture was energy greedy. They may
have been produced using non-renewable resources and may also pose
problems after they have been used and come to be disposed of. If we take
what is commonly called a 'cradle to the grave' view of products, where we
examine their environmental impact through their life-cycle from raw material
usage to disposal, then there are few, if any, products which will *not* have
some negative impact on the environment. The key question is therefore not
how we completely eliminate environmental damage, but how we reduce it
over time and how we achieve a state of balance such that the amount of
environmental damage done is repairable and therefore sustainable.

It is generally accepted that the world cannot go on using the resources of
the planet at the present rate. But there is a free rider problem at work.
Everyone thinks that something should be done, but many people just
assume that everyone else will do it, and since their individual impact is
minute it will not matter to the environment. The trouble is that when too
many people or firms think in that way then nothing is ever achieved. The
world has scarce resources and only limited capacity to deal with the pollution
caused through production and consumption. The ability to deal with that
pollution is also being reduced as we strive for further economic growth by,
for example, cutting down forests which help to control carbon dioxide
emissions.

Industry, particularly in the developed world, must increasingly take into
account the costs of the effect of its operations on the environment, rather
than regarding the planet as a free resource. In the past few companies have
counted the costs of the pollution which they discharged into the atmosphere,
and the debate has now turned to legislation aimed at forcing companies to
comply with certain standards and taxing firms which pollute. The so-called
'polluter pays principle' is now central to legislation. The implication here is
clearly that prices will rise for consumers as firms experience the increased
costs associated with environmental improvements. Less energy consumption
and more efficient use of resources are obvious targets for improvement and
should not conflict with industry's aims since their attainment can actually
reduce costs.

Many of the products now considered to be environmentally hazardous
were at the time of their discovery regarded as an invaluable resource. The
best example of this has been the use of chlorofluorocarbons in refrigerators
which have since been found to be a major ozone-depleting agent. Predicting
a product's long-term impact on the environment is a difficult process and,
until recently, has rarely been done. This will change as firms are forced to

consider cradle to grave management of their products and as we increasingly give the benefit of the doubt to the welfare of the planet, as demanded by the precautionary principle. Moreover, industry has a responsibility to ensure that its products are less harmful to the environment, and there is a need to push along a very steep environmental learning curve.

Governments across Europe and the European Commission have all been implementing increasingly stringent environmental legislation. There is even renewed debate within the European Union's Fifth Environment Programme (see below) regarding the provision of information about products and processes to the public. However, the statutory bodies which do exist with responsibility for monitoring the environmental performance of companies have limited resources and powers in most cases. Companies themselves have often, in the past, proven to be ignorant of current environmental legislation, particularly with regard to European Union environmental directives and legislation on issues such as waste disposal, air pollution and water quality. However, such ignorance is not an excuse for non-compliance. Moreover, non-compliance which can be attributed to negligence can not only result in fines but also occasionally in imprisonment for company directors.

In the USA the Environmental Protection Agency (EPA) is an independent environmental body with significant power. In 1980 the US Congress passed the Comprehensive Environmental Response, Compensation and Liability Act, better known as Superfund. Under the provisions of the Act, companies must report potentially toxic spills and releases greater than a clearly defined minimum. Violations of this are criminal offences with penalties of up to one year in jail and fines of up to $10,000. Superfund also deals with uncontrolled hazardous waste sites, where previous or present owners and operators of a site must help to pay for whatever remedial action is necessary. If the previous firm has gone out of business the EPA has often managed to obtain funds from companies which sent the waste there for treatment or disposal in the first instance.

SUSTAINABLE DEVELOPMENT

The ultimate aim of corporate environmental management must be to reach a situation where companies are operating in a way which is consistent with the concept of sustainable development. One key idea which lies behind the concept of sustainable development is that there is a trade-off between continuous economic growth and the sustainability of the environment. Over time growth causes pollution and atmospheric damage. Sustainable development stresses the interdependence between economic growth and environmental quality. It is possible to make development and environmental protection compatible by following sustainable strategies and by not developing the particular areas of economic activity that are most damaging to the environment.

The Brundtland Report, commissioned by the United Nations to examine long-term environmental strategies, argued that economic development and environmental protection could be made compatible, but that this would require quite radical changes in economic practices throughout the world.

They defined sustainable development as development that meets the needs of the present without compromising the ability of future generations to meet their own needs. In other words, mass consumption is not possible indefinitely and if society today acts as if all non-renewable resources are plentiful, eventually there will be nothing left for the future. But more importantly than that, mass consumption may cause such irreparable damage that humans may not even be able to live on the planet in the future.

The challenge that faces the economic system is how to continue to fulfil its vital role within modern society while working towards sustainable development. Compliance with the principles of sustainable development cannot be achieved overnight. However, both for entire economies and for individual businesses, there is hope that it can be achieved within the timescales which appear to be necessary if environmental catastrophe is to be avoided.

Sustainable development is made up of three closely connected issues:

1. **Environment:** The environment must be valued as an integral part of the economic process and not treated as a free good. The environmental stock has to be protected and this implies minimal use of non-renewable resources and minimal emission of pollutants. The ecosystem has to be protected so the loss of plant and animal species has to be avoided.
2. **Equity:** One of the biggest threats facing the world is that the developing countries want to grow rapidly to achieve the same standards of living as those in the North. That in itself would cause a major environmental disaster if it were modelled on the same sort of growth experienced in post-war Europe. There therefore needs to be a greater degree of equity and the key issue of poverty has to be addressed. But it seems hypocritical for the North to tell the South that it cannot attain the same standards of living and consumption.
3. **Futurity:** Sustainable development requires that society, businesses and individuals operate on a different timescale than currently operates in the economy. While companies commonly operate under competitive pressures to achieve short-run gains, long-term environmental protection is often compromised. To ensure that longer-term, inter-generational considerations are observed, longer planning horizons need to be adopted and business policy needs to be proactive rather than reactive.

The Brundtland Report concludes that these three conditions are not being met. The industrialized world has already used much of the planet's ecological capital and many of the development paths of the industrialized nations are clearly unsustainable. Non-renewable resources are being depleted, while renewable resources such as soil, water and the atmosphere are being degraded. This has been caused by economic development but in time will undermine the very foundations of that development.

The Brundtland Report calls for growth which is environmentally and socially sustainable rather than the current situation of unplanned, undifferentiated growth. This means reconsidering the current measures of growth, such as gross national product (GNP), which fail to take account of environmental debits like pollution or the depletion of the natural capital stock. While concern about the depletion of materials and energy resources has diminished since the 1970s there is nevertheless now concern surrounding the environment's capacity to act as a sink for waste. For example, bringing developing countries' energy use up to the level of that of the North would mean an increase in consumption by a factor of five. Using present energy generation methods the planet could not cope with the impact of sulphur dioxide and carbon dioxide emissions and the consequential acidification and global warming of the environment.

Sustainable development challenges industry to produce higher levels of output while using lower levels of inputs and generating less waste. The problem that remains is that while relative environmental impact per unit of output has fallen, increases in the absolute level of output, and hence environmental impact, have more than offset any gains in relative environmental efficiency.

THE CORPORATE RESPONSE TO SUSTAINABLE DEVELOPMENT

Companies are faced with the challenge of integrating environmental considerations into their production and marketing plans. There is always an incentive, however, for profit-maximizing firms seeking short-term rewards to opt out and become free riders (assuming that everyone else will be environmentally conscious such that their own pollution will become negligible). However, environmental legislation is increasingly plugging the gaps which allow this to happen and firms attempting to hide their illegal pollution are now subject to severe penalties. Even before such legislation comes into force, however, businesses should recognize that it is not only ethical to be environmentally friendly, but with the growth of consumer awareness in the environmental area, it will also be good business.

Firms clearly have a role to play in the development of substitutes for non-renewable resources and innovations which reduce waste and use energy more efficiently. They also have a role in processing those materials in a way which brings about environmental improvements. For many products (eg cars and washing machines), the major area of environmental damage occurs in their usage. Firms often have the opportunity of reducing this damage at the design stage and when new products are being developed there is a whole new opportunity for considering both the use and disposal of the product.

Given the internal and external demands to improve the environmental performance of a company, those companies that achieve high standards of environmental performance will benefit in a number of ways. In order to realize this competitive advantage, companies must seek to develop management strategies which will improve their environmental performance and address the environmental demands placed upon them by their stakeholders. By incorporating the increasingly important environmental dimension into the decision making processes of the firm, managers can seek to reduce costs and exploit the opportunities offered by increased public environmental concern within a dynamic marketplace. Such a strategy must be proactive and honest. It may also involve a degree of education and campaigning. But more than anything, it must be ethical.

EUROPEAN ENVIRONMENT POLICY AND REGULATION

The original Treaty of Rome was concerned with stimulating economic growth and contained no specific reference to the environment. Since then, however, European Union environmental policy has developed in line with general concern in Europe and the deteriorating environmental position in which Europe finds itself. By 1990, 160 pieces of environmental legislation had been passed covering pollution of the air and water, noise pollution, chemicals, waste, environmental impact assessment, the prevention of industrial accidents and wildlife protection.

However, few Member States have been able to fully enforce EU legislation. Denmark is probably the only country with a consistently good record; the Southern European countries having consistently bad records. Once again this highlights the emphasis often given to economic growth rather than environmental protection, with the primary aim of countries such as Spain and Portugal being the attainment of similar living standards to the rest of the Community.

The Single European Act gave environmental policy a boost by stating that there is not only a need for such legislation but that the laws should meet three key objectives:

1. Preservation, protection and improvement of the quality of the environment;
2. protection of human health; and
3. prudent and rational use of natural resources.

These objectives must be met by applying four principles:

1. Prevention of harm to the environment;
2. control of pollution at source;
3. the polluter should pay; and
4. integration of environmental considerations into other Community policies (all EU policies are now required to take the environment into account).

The Internal Market Programme has added a new note of urgency to environmental problems. The relationship between economic growth and the environment has returned to centre stage. Clearly, there exists a major opportunity with industrial and legislative restructuring to put into place the appropriate financial and regulatory mechanisms that would make the internal market environmentally sustainable. The extent to which this happens will be seen over time, but the Single European Act also provides the necessary constitutional basis for a forceful environmental response. Perhaps the strongest part of this is the requirement that policy makers should make environmental considerations a component of all the Community's other policies.

In 1992 the European Community's Fifth Environmental Action Programme was introduced. The first Environmental Action Programme in 1973 set out a number of principles which have formed the basis of environmental action in the EU ever since. The aims are clearly set out, stating that:

1. Prevention is better than cure.
2. Environmental effects should be taken into account at the earliest possible stage in decision making.
3. Exploitation of nature and natural resources which causes significant damage to the ecological balance must be avoided. The natural environment can only absorb pollution to a limited extent. Nature is an asset which may be used but not abused.
4. Scientific knowledge should be improved to enable action to be taken.
5. 'The Polluter Pays' principle; the polluter should pay for preventing and eliminating environmental nuisance.
6. Activities in one Member State should not cause environmental deterioration in another.
7. Environmental policies of Member States must take account of the interests of developing countries.
8. The EU and Member States should act together in international organizations and also in promoting international environmental policy.
9. Education of citizens is necessary as the protection of the environment is a matter for everyone.
10. The principle of action at the appropriate level; for each type of pollution it is necessary to establish the level of action which is best suited for achieving the protection required, be it local, regional, national, EU-wide or international.
11. National environmental policies must be coordinated within the EU without impinging on progress at the national level. It is intended that implementation of the action programme and gathering of environmental information by the proposed European environment agency will secure this.

(Source: Official Journal of the European Communities: C112 20.12.73)

The main activities of the EU in the environmental policy arena, until 1987, were centred on the application of nearly 200 command and control directives in areas as diverse as lead in petrol and aircraft noise. More recently, in realizing that environmental policy is of little use unless enforced, EU environmental policy has given increased emphasis to the improved enforcement of existing legislation. Emphasis has also shifted from the use of traditional command and control instruments in environmental policy to the application of economic market-based instruments such as the proposed carbon tax, and voluntary agreements such as the eco-labelling and eco-management and audit schemes. The aim of such measures is to encourage change in all sectors of industry and society, in a more general way than can be achieved through the use of tightly defined legislative instruments. The use of economic instruments and voluntary measures is seen as a complement to rather than a substitute for the more traditional application of command and control measures.

The EU view of the future of environmental policy and its interface with industrial development is clear. With some 370 million inhabitants, the European Union is the largest trading block in the world, and is therefore in a critical position to take the lead in moving towards sustainability. The Commission accepts that tighter environmental policy will impact on the costs of industry; however, increasingly, a high level of environmental protection has become not only a policy objective of its own but also a precondition of industrial expansion. In this respect, a new impetus towards a better integration of policies aiming at consolidating industrial competitiveness and at achieving a high level of protection of the environment is necessary in order to make the two objectives fully mutually supportive.

These views are given more substance within the Fifth Environmental Action Programme. While this Programme sets out the likely developments of EU environmental policy in a general sense, a number of specific measures relating to industry are included. Perhaps most importantly the commitment of the EU to strengthen environmental policy is underlined. The EU shares the view that urgent action is needed for environmental protection, and that many of the great environmental struggles will be won or lost over the next ten years. Further, it states that achieving sustainable development will demand practical and political commitment over an extended period and that the EU must exercise its responsibility and commit itself to that goal.

For industries and companies that are facing a rising tide of environmental legislation, it is essential that attempts are made to find out about and then positively address the legislative pressures which they are under. However, the Fifth Environmental Action Programme focuses not on new legislation, but on the improved enforcement of that which already exists. To some extent this should allow industry to take stock of the rapid increase in environmental legislation that has taken place in recent years and to focus on achieving compliance with existing legislation. Despite the stated objective to concentrate on the effective implementation of existing policy, there are many pieces of environmental legislation in the EU policy pipeline which are awaiting final adoption. Many of these measures have fundamental implications for business, and the need to track forthcoming legislation therefore remains essential.

Furthermore, the Maastricht Treaty and the Fifth Environmental Action Programme require that environmental policy should be fully incorporated into all other Community policies. Therefore while it may become easier to track the development of policies which are explicitly environmental, it will become more difficult to monitor the development of environmental policy throughout the activities of the Commission as a whole. The establishment of the European Environment Agency which will collect data and monitor compliance throughout the Community will help to disseminate information to all interested parties. In the meantime, the delay between the release of European legislation and its subsequent implementation in Member States offers vital planning time for those companies who monitor the development of European environmental policy in order to avoid the costs and exploit the opportunities which are undoubtedly generated.

The strategic significance of the EU's views cannot be overstated. By taking a long-term EU-wide perspective and accepting that industrial competitiveness is enhanced by tight environmental legislation, the policy framework within which all European companies must participate will reflect these views. Some companies, some regions and some nations will benefit. If the views of the EU are correct, the economic prospects of the Community as a whole will benefit and the environment will certainly benefit. However, at the company level, realizing these benefits will not be automatic, and strategic planning and proactive responses to the changing policy climate are imperative if success is to be secured. Information must be gathered, its implications assessed and the necessary action taken in a systematic and integrated way.

Tackling environmental problems always requires a concerted and cooperative effort, and in the EU success will depend on the extent to which Member States are politically committed to the environmental philosophy, and the extent to which they are willing to cooperate. The balancing of the economic growth/environment trade-off is likely to determine the Europe-wide success of any policies. But there also needs to be concerted and cooperative political motivations. There will be those who will argue, therefore, that the attainment of an effective and concerted environmental policy in Europe will require political and economic union. However the EU and national governments legislate over environmental protection and police offenders, significant environmental improvement will only be attained with the cooperation and commitment of producers.

CORPORATE ENVIRONMENTAL MANAGEMENT

Companies are beginning to realize that environmental issues need to be addressed for a number of reasons, including; consumer pressure, potential cost savings, legislation and ethics. There is therefore growing interest in the area of corporate environmental management. As environmental considerations are likely to be a source of quite profound changes in business practices, this book attempts to provide managers with the basis of a strategic plan for the environment. The first step must be to recognize the strategic advantage which corporate environmental management can bring and to ensure that commitment to environmental improvement exists in the business. The approach taken here is that once a company has decided to embark on a concerted effort to improve its environmental performance, it must build a comprehensive environmental management system within the organization.

In all parts of an organization a systems approach to attaining the goals of the enterprise is most likely to be successful. Failure to meet such goals is often a result of an ineffective system or alternatively, that although there was a system in place, there were gaps in it which allowed mistakes and errors to occur. No matter what the structure of the firm, be it an egalitarian cooperative or a strong vertical hierarchy, it is the lack of a comprehensive and effective management system which can often lead to failure. Inadequate management systems have been the cause of environmental damage and have cost firms and organizations heavily in terms of clean-up costs and damaged reputations. At the extreme we can think of disasters such as the *Exxon Valdez* oil spill and the Union Carbide explosion at Bhopal, where the environment became irreparably damaged in its turn due, at least in part, to inadequacies in systems which were supposed to prevent such disasters.

In environmental terms, at the core of the systems approach is the role of environmental management systems which companies enact through procedures which ensure that environmental performance is improved over time, and that environmental damage caused by accidents does not occur. Management systems aim to pull a potentially disparate system into an integrated and organized one. To that end, they cover not only management's responsibilities but the responsibility and tasks of every individual in an organization.

The arguments in favour of a systems based approach are clear. A fully integrated system which covers the totality of operations helps management and workers to see their place in the organization and recognize the interdependence of all aspects within it. Through establishing clear communications, information and reporting channels it should provide a clear and understandable organizational map laying out both responsibilities and reporting arrangements. This means that functions are less likely to be overlooked and gaps in the system will not occur.

An effective management system is therefore central to the avoidance of environmental degradation, in so much as it pulls together all the other tools and strategies for the avoidance of risks and provides a framework for a clear and focused approach to environmental improvement. The management system should be developed and implemented for the purpose of accomplishing the objectives set out in a company's or organization's policies, and these must include the avoidance of environmental damage. However, it must be noted that contemporary approaches to environmental management systems depend on the central objectives and targets being set by the company itself. This has been a source of some criticism and we return to this issue again in a review of environmental management systems standards.

The management system must have three main attributes. Firstly, it needs to be comprehensive, covering all the activities of the organization. Gaps must not occur in this coverage, since this is where errors and mistakes will occur and where accidents and disasters may happen. Every part of an organization must be involved in the implementation of the system and every person must recognize his or her responsibility for putting the system into practice.

Secondly, the system and procedures within it need to be understandable to everybody involved. If roles and duties are not specified in a clear way they may not be carried out. This will usually involve documenting the system, training people fully in their tasks and responsibilities, and periodically reviewing or auditing what is actually happening. It is a requirement that the system and all its elements are monitored, and that if the system breaks down it must be rectified quickly.

Thirdly, the system must be open to review and there must be a commitment to a continuous cycle of improvement in the operations of the firm and in the positive environmental attributes of the products or services it will produce. This continuous cycle of improvement can also be applied to the environment where firms should aim for an ultimate goal of zero–negative impact on the environment. Everybody has a role in the system and therefore participatory styles of management are usually superior to hierarchical ones.

Management pyramids often need to be flattened to allow for a freer flow of information from both top to bottom and bottom to top.

A central aspect of any management system will revolve around decision making. Modern management methods will highlight the need for flexibility and worker participation, and this ought to mean that decisions are taken further down any hierarchy which may exist. In arriving at decisions, the calibre and personal integrity of staff are of fundamental importance and each person in the organization needs to understand their role in decision making and the consequences of their actions. Decisions are often of a higher quality when they are participative and systems need to avoid giving single individuals too much power. It should also be noted that the quality of decisions will be closely linked to the availability of adequate education, and training programmes for all employees need to be built into organization-wide systems.

The commitment of senior management to the systems based approach is crucial, but real corporate change through a new environmental approach cannot be imposed from on high. It must be developed creatively with the inner commitment of the entire workforce. There is a need to consider new styles of leadership when implementing the management system and this must be informed by systems based thinking and acting. Workers must be valued in the system and involved in decision making through participatory styles of management.

Within the framework of the environmental management system there will be a need to develop an environmental policy, in order to regularly audit environmental performance and to report on that performance in some way. Many companies may consider the adoption of environmental management system standards as both a benchmark and a sign that they are improving their performance. Chapters of this book deal with each of these issues in more detail.

As this book progresses we argue that there is also a need to put greater emphasis on all the production processes of goods and services provided by the firm. Companies must recognize their wider responsibility and manage the entire life-cycle of their products. It is relatively easy for firms to target their internal systems and make changes to improve the environment. Insisting on high environmental standards from suppliers and ensuring that raw materials are extracted or produced in an environmentally conscious way provides a start. But the life-cycle approach should also extend to making every attempt to ensure that environmental damage done during use and disposal is kept at a minimum.

CONCLUSIONS

The environmental revolution has been gathering momentum since the 1960s and developed rapidly in the 1990s. Environmental considerations are likely to form an integral part of commercial normality and indeed competitiveness in the future. Definitions of business success are likely to include the assumption of zero–negative impact on the environment at the very least. A competitive advantage can be achieved not merely by keeping abreast of environmental developments, but also by initiating change within an organization and responding with new environmentally friendly products and production processes. Indeed, growing consumer awareness and environmental pressure groups are likely to ensure that firms which do not take action on the environmental front will lose market share. With increased competition, environmental management will provide firms with a competitive edge.

Governments will increasingly seek to make the polluter pay and one consequence of this is that some industries and products may simply disappear. But ultimately, the success of environmental improvement will be determined largely by the responsiveness of business. That is not to suggest that legislation is a bad thing; indeed it can act as the impetus to a firm thinking about instituting a proper environmental management system. In addition, increasing legislation and government expenditure to increase environmentally related expenditure might be seen as a win–win situation. It stimulates the economy without leading to the pollution problems often associated with growth. Moreover, a shift in expenditure from the military to the promotion of security on the environmental front is possible.

Corporate environmental management will increasingly be seen as a prerequisite for doing business. Firms will be expected to introduce environmental management systems into their operations. Indeed, legislative moves towards requiring firms to demonstrate that they are using the best available techniques and demonstrating the best practicable environmental option means that an environmental management system will be a necessity. The systems based approach has wider applications as well. As a tool for local development, for example, regional environmental management systems allow us to manage growth in a way which is consistent with the need to address sustainable development.

We must of course remember that corporate environmental management is a necessary but not a sufficient condition for sustainable development. In concert with the greening of industry, there are other areas where action is required. Poverty alleviation, population control, health crises, regional conflicts, inequality, famine and starvation, consumerism, political structures, the power of transnational corporations and a multitude of other issues all need to be tackled. This book deals only with corporate environmental management strategies but the reader is encouraged to think about these wider issues as well. It is hoped that this book can nevertheless make a small contribution to the enormous task of moving towards a sustainable future.

Chapter 2

Corporate Strategy, Competitiveness and the Environment

Richard Welford

INTRODUCTION

Corporate strategy has been driven by different forces in the past, by production pressures, personnel pressures, and more lately by information pressures. We see clear signs of corporate strategy being driven by environmental pressures (Welford, 1995). Major changes in corporate strategy are clearly visible due to the increased environmental concerns of stakeholders and the belief that being 'green' pays through cost reduction and increased market entry. This chapter examines some of the relevant theoretical literature in this field and examines how environmental management can increase competitiveness. In so doing it builds a basis for the more practical chapters which follow. This is a subject area which is still relatively underdeveloped, and given the paucity of literature, one intention of this chapter is to classify and provide a framework for past and current theories of corporate strategy and environmental pressures. We argue that not only are the existing sub-theories of corporate strategy (principally competitive advantage and competitive strategy) being slowly modified to include environmental problems and concerns, but they are also being broadened to incorporate the principles of sustainable development (Welford, 1995).

HISTORICAL OVERVIEW

Rachel Carson's *Silent Spring*, a book on the global problems of herbicides and pesticides written in 1962, heralded the arrival of the environmental era. The 1960s also saw the emergence of environmental economics as a separate branch of economics. During this period, it was felt that growth and development and protection of the environment could not go hand in hand. Hence most of the theories that developed during this period were anti-growth

(Pearce et al, 1990). It was in 1972 that the first Earth Summit was held, leading to the establishment of the United Nations Environment Programme (UNEP). During this decade, on the one hand, there were some environmental economists who were quite optimistic and felt that resources could never be completely exhausted (Pearce et al, 1990), and that the development of substitutes or technological changes like recycling, in order to conserve resources, was bound to take place. On the other hand, the Club of Rome's renowned *The Limits to Growth* (Meadows et al, 1979), concluded that even under the most optimistic assumptions, the world could not support the rate at which the world's population and economy were growing for more than a few decades.

The 1980s witnessed a shift in thinking. The concept of 'zero growth' was replaced by sustainable development, which essentially involves meeting the needs of the present without compromising the ability of future generations to meet their own needs (Bruntland Report, 1991). In other words, it means income generation while maintaining the (natural and man-made) capital base (Beaumont et al, 1993). Pearce, Markandya and Barbier's *Blueprint for a Green Economy* (1989), which showed how sustainable development might be achieved through market forces and regulations, was one of the first attempts to show that preservation of the environment and economic growth are not necessarily incompatible. This period also marked the rise to prominence of environmental organizations like Greenpeace and Friends of the Earth.

The 1990s, which saw the second Earth Summit in Rio de Janeiro (1992), might be regarded as the period of strategic action, both on the part of government and by some companies at the corporate level. In the 1970s, environmental management was regarded by companies with indifference and even hostility (Greeno et al, 1992), with the exception of a few such as 3M (Royston, 1979). More recently, leading companies have begun to regard environmental management as a strategic tool for gaining competitive advantage (Shrivastava et al, 1992). In most western countries governments, for their part, have increased the level of legislation affecting business with increased emphasis on the 'Polluter Pays' principle. In Europe there has also been an emphasis on the concepts of BATNEEC (best available techniques not entailing excessive costs) and BPEO (best practicable environmental option), which emphasize the importance of drawing a balance between economic growth and preservation of the environment. More recently there has emerged an expectation on the part of many stakeholders that companies should report on and be accountable for their environmental performance.

Thus the concept of zero growth and other steady-state theories that emerged during the 1960s and 1970s, which were anti-growth, have now been largely replaced by the concept of sustainable development. Moreover, theories of corporate strategy are also gradually being modified to incorporate environmental problems and concerns. However, there is still relatively little debate over whether a traditional corporate strategic planning approach within the traditional capitalist system (with all its financial and short-term constraints) can actually lead us towards sustainable development. Welford (1995) argues for a radical reappraisal of the way we do business for example. However, for the time being this problem is put aside.

THEORETICAL FRAMEWORK

Meima's (1994) categorization of the various environmental management paradigms that have emerged over the past few years into four groups, gives us an overall theoretical framework. His approach suggests that while there are some who perceive the environment as an anthropocentric moral/ethical issue, there are others who regard it as a means to gaining financial benefits. It is here that the concept of competitive strategies and competitive advantage comes in, and it is on this approach to the environmental challenge that this book will be focused. The third paradigm perceives environmental management as a function of quality (eg TQEM, ISO14001). The fourth approach to environmental management is determining ways in which industrial action can be made compatible with nature; for instance, by minimizing emissions, by reducing wastes at source etc. Although it is beyond the scope of this chapter we might also suggest a fifth (underdeveloped) category which takes the definition of the environment further, and deals with the achievement of wider principles of sustainable development including equity and futurity.

Simpson (1991) suggests that corporate responses to environmental pressures can be categorized into three main groups; the 'Why Mes', the 'Smart Movers' and the 'Enthusiasts'. The 'Why Mes' are the companies that have been forced to improve their environmental performance as a result of some well-publicized event. Some outstanding environmental accident acts as a catalyst and induces the company to take some action in the field. 'Smart Movers' are the ones that have been able to exploit the opportunity created by the arrival of the green consumer to gain competitive advantage. Heinz is an example of a company adopting such a strategy. The 'Enthusiasts' include companies like The Body Shop, that have moved beyond compliance, and have incorporated their environmental strategy into their overall business strategy.

Similarly, Steger's conceptual model (1990, in Roome, 1994) categorizes corporate strategies into four categories; indifference, offensive, defensive and innovative. Indifferent companies are those that have low environmental risk and even less environmentally-based opportunities for growth. Offensive companies are those that have considerable potential for exploiting environmentally-related market opportunities, and include companies that manufacture pollution control equipment etc. Those adopting a defensive strategy are companies like the chemical companies, which have high environmental risk and cannot afford to ignore environmental issues, or their very survival could be at stake. The innovators are those that have high environmental risk and also a lot of environmentally-based opportunities for growth.

In Roome's Strategic Options Model (Roome, 1992), there are five environmental strategies for companies, namely; non-compliance, compliance, compliance-plus, commercial and environmental excellence, and leading edge. These are referred to as; stable, reactive, anticipatory, entrepreneurial and creative in Ansoff's Strategic Posture Analysis (1990, in Ketola, 1993). The first three strategies are related to compliance with the environmental standards, as the name suggests. Compliance-plus implies looking beyond the existing standards and norms. It involves integration of the environmental management techniques with the entire management system of the company. Excellence and leading edge approaches view environmental management as good management, recognize the opportunities that have arisen as a result of the environmental revolution and strive towards state-of-the-art environmental management. Hence, it is through the adoption of excellence and leading edge strategies that a company can gain competitive advantage.

The difference between Steger's and Roome's models is that while Steger perceives corporate response to the environment as based on environmental risks and market-based opportunities, Roome argues that environmental pressures like legislation, constraints within the firm, and the ability of managers to bring about an organizational change in order to incorporate environmental issues, are equally important. James' framework (1992) is similar to that of Roome's. He believes that there are four categories into which companies can be divided, in accordance with the environmental strategy adopted by them. The first category is similar to Steger's indifference and Roome's non-compliance, where all environmental issues are simply ignored. Companies that do the minimum that is required by law fall in the second category. In the third category are companies that move beyond legislation and the last group consists of companies that use the environment as a tool for gaining competitive advantage.

Welford's (1994) categorization of the SME (small- and medium-sized enterprises) sector into four main groups is slightly different. The first group is referred to as the 'ostriches'. Companies that fall in this category not only assume that concern for the environment is a passing phase and that their impact on the environment is negligible, but also assume that their competitors feel the same and hence do nothing to conserve the environment. Then there are the 'laggards', companies that are aware of the environmental challenges facing them, but are unable to combat those challenges because of cost constraints, lack of trained manpower, lack of knowledge etc. The third group consists of the 'thinkers', companies that know that something should be done, but are still waiting for others to show the way forward. The 'doers' are the ones that have proceeded to put their thoughts into action.

Topfer (1985, in Bostrum et al, 1992) also divides companies into four categories, namely; resistant, passive, reactive and innovative. Companies that fall in the first category are the ones that view concern for the environment as a hindrance to their growth and do their level best to hinder the passing of environmental laws. Passive companies are like Steger's indifferent companies, who ignore the issue altogether. Roome argues that action taken by reactive companies has been triggered off by legislation, whereas Topfer sees it as a defensive move to catch up with the competitors. The last category, the innovators, are the same as Steger's innovators and Simpson's enthusiasts.

Pietilainen (1991, in Bostrum et al, 1992) has taken a different approach to classifying the various environmental strategies that can be adopted by an organization. Rather than classifying strategies in an ascending order of increased environmental responsibility, Pietilainen has identified the various strategic options that can be pursued by organizations simultaneously. One option available to companies is to improve market communication by highlighting a product's environmentally beneficial attributes and use it as an 'advertising gimmick'. The second strategic option is improving the existing manufacturing processes by using cleaner and more efficient technology. The third strategy is applicable to companies belonging to one particular industry, eg companies engaged in the manufacture of pollution abatement equipment, machines based on the conservation of energy and raw materials, waste reduction, recycling etc. The fourth strategy incorporates taking a long-term approach to the environment, basing the entire strategy and product mix on the environment, and carrying out research and development extensively.

Vandermerwe and Oliff's (1990) framework is based on a similar approach. In their framework, (see Figure 2.1), improving market communication, improving manufacturing processes, and carrying out research and development, are the three main options available to organizations. Thus environmental improvement will be driven by marketing and manufacturing innovations and ongoing research and development to support those innovations. Bansal (1993) provides us with a useful synthesis in an attempt to sub-categorize these three categories (see Table 2.1).

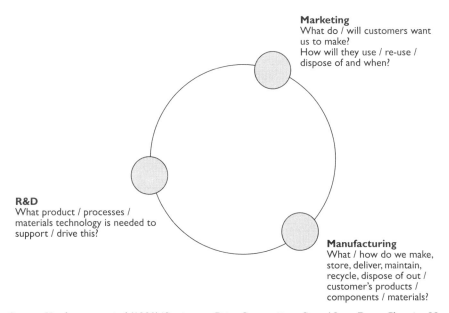

Marketing
What do / will customers want us to make?
How will they use / re-use / dispose of and when?

R&D
What product / processes / materials technology is needed to support / drive this?

Manufacturing
What / how do we make, store, deliver, maintain, recycle, dispose of out / customer's products / components / materials?

Source: Vandermerwe et al (1990) 'Customers Drive Corporations Green' *Long Range Planning* 23, 6, 10–16

Figure 2.1 Framework for green decisions

Table 2.1 Options for environmental improvement

Marketing

- Labelling own brand products for environmental enhancements
- Introducing a 'green' product line
- Landscaping and store design to make the external and internal environment safe and aesthetically pleasing
- Providing recycling points in car parks
- The publication and distribution of materials addressing general ecological issues

---

Environmental Management

- Removing CFCs from aerosols
- Replacing refrigerants when retired, with lower CFCs
- Reducing the use of CFCs in construction materials
- Energy reduction
- Ensuring that the claims made by manufacturers of ecologically friendlier product lines are substantiated
- Reducing the use of tropical hardwoods
- Recycling and reducing waste
- Using recycled paper
- Encouraging the reuse and recycling of carrier bags
- The use of unleaded petrol in the lorry and car fleet
- Reducing the amount of product packaging
- Adopting a corporate environmental policy
- Developing specific ecologically motivated targets and ensuring that they are being met
- Conducting environmental audits

Research and Development

- Engaging in scientific research with respect to ecological issues, eg research into CFCs
- Engaging in ecological research, like uncovering ways in which to reduce the impact of packaging waste
- Coordinating activities between other food retailers to reduce impact on the environment
- Applying pressure on suppliers of merchandized brands to change packaging
- Applying pressure on suppliers of own brands to use environmentally friendlier manufacturing processes
- Applying pressure on suppliers of merchandized brands to use environ-mentally-friendlier manufacturing processes

---

Porter's well-known framework (Porter, 1985) of the competitive forces that determine industry profitability, can be used to indicate the nature of competition with regard to the environment in any particular industry (Beaumont et al, 1993). The approach is summarized in Figure 2.2. Undoubtedly, the green revolution has been responsible for a number of new market entrants. For example, companies manufacturing greener and cleaner products have increased the threat of substitutes such as replacements for CFCs and aerosols etc. In addition, greening of industry strategies have brought about changed relationships between companies and their suppliers and buyers. And within some industries the environment has brought about new levels of competition and rivalry. The two by two matrix shown in Figure 2.3 sums up Beaumont, Pedersen and Whitaker's strategic environmental framework. It shows the various options available to companies for achieving competitive advantage.

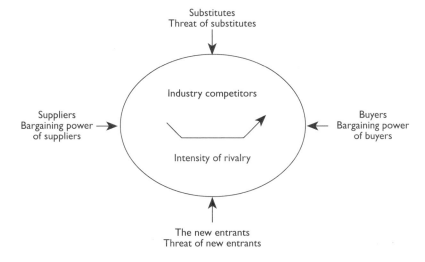

Source: Beaumont et al (1993) *Managing the Environment* Butterworth-Heinemann Ltd, Oxford

Figure 2.2 Industry structure analysis framework

Beaumont, Pedersen and Whitaker perceive corporations at six different levels, in accordance to their response to the environment. The first two levels are similar to Roome's non-compliance and compliance. The third level is referred to as 'corporate action', where management begins to regard environmental matters as important and takes a broader and a more long-term perspective of the environment. At the fourth level changes take place in the organization in response to environmental issues. The fifth level is 'supply chain action', where environmental matters become an integral part of the entire industry's supply chain. At the final level of 'business scope action', an organization expands its activities, using environmental issues to get ahead in business.

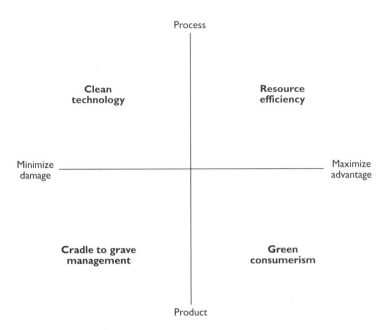

Source: Beaumont et al (1993) *Managing the Environment* Butterworth-Heinemann Ltd, Oxford

Figure 2.3 Alternative positions to achieve competitive advantage

Dodge and Welford have developed an environmental performance scale which has become known as the ROAST scale (Welford, 1995, see pp 21–22 for explanation) and is now being used by others to identify aspects of corporate environmental performance. It extends the traditional environmental categorizations to include sustainable development. In order to measure improving environmental performance Dodge and Welford argue that we need to define an ultimate goal towards which the organization must move. This goal may not be achievable but it will serve as an upper boundary of sustainable performance on a five point scale. This utopian form of organization is referred to as the 'transcendent firm'. This firm will have ideals very similar to those of deep ecology and will perform in a way which is completely consistent with sustainable development. Although the debate on a definitive definition of deep ecology and its comparison to sustainable development is far from settled, for simplicity Dodge and Welford consider the four pillars of the green philosophy and deep ecology to mix as one: ecology, grassroots democracy, social responsibility, and non-violence. It becomes quite obvious at this level of abstraction that human and animal rights, non-violent behaviour, ecological management and an emphasis on regionalism are all part of the same issue.

The least environmentally sensitive measure on the ROAST scale is represented by the 'resistant organization'; the firm's environmental performance would be represented by extremely resistive behaviour. Organizations would totally disregard ecological issues in their decision making. The prime and ultimate motive of the organization would be profit and the satisfaction of shareholders. The organization would contain strong, pervasive, negative environmental values. It would tend to reject any green arguments as the trite views of extremists and a few academics. Table 2.2 compares the extremes on the performance scale.

Table 2.2 Environmental performance scale extremes

Resistant organization	*Transcendent organization*
• Resists any green behaviour • Disregards green aspects in decisions • Willing to damage environment if beneficial to the organization • Negative environment values • Sees resources and nature for human profit and pleasure • Resists any green intellectual or philosophical argument as trite views of extremists	• Internalises sustainable development • Green criteria become paramount in decision making. • No decision will upset the ecological relationships • Environmental values take on an ideology associated with sustainable development • Human beings are not above nature and but with nature, all decisions must reflect the intrinsic values and interrelationships of other members of the biosphere

It is argued that an organization's performance can be categorized as lying somewhere between the resistant firm and the transcendent firm. The five point ROAST scale is therefore be represented by the following interval values:

R	Resistance (Stage I)	Total resistance to environmental values and rules. Organizations would be absolutely unresponsive and reactive to environmental initiatives.
O	Observe & comply (Stage II)	The organization observes environmental laws but actions reflect an unwilling attitude or lack of ability to comply. Actions are being enforced through legislation or court decisions.
A	Accommodate (Stage III)	Organization begins to adapt to change. Early indications of proactive and responsive behaviours. Actions are no longer based entirely on complying with environmental legislation; the organization begins to exhibit voluntary behaviour.
S	Seize & Preempt (Stage IV)	The organization voluntarily seizes and preempts its actions with environmental concerns. It proactively engages in setting the agenda. It is responsive to the many external stakeholders. The latter phases would display the attributes of sustainable development.
T	Transcend (Stage V)	The organization's environmental values, attitudes, beliefs and culture exhibit a total support for the

environment. The organization would proactively support and be responsive to all living things. It would act in a way which is fully consistent with sustainable development.

The ROAST scale can be useful in the classification of environmental performance responses from both external stakeholder groups and internal organizational functions, systems and activities. It integrates the deep ecology, social and business performance models of environmental performance. The scale, although it is a continuous spectrum, has been broken into five descriptive points for convenience. The extreme top end of Stage V represents near-perfect environmental performance reflecting the near-theological views of deep ecology. The voluntary environmental actions of the organization represented by Stages III and IV can be compared to the ideals of a more shallow ecology often typified by traditional approaches to environmental management. The organization displays a proactive and responsive attitude and stance as it moves from accommodating the greening agenda to seizing and preempting it.

At Stage V the firm transcends traditional commercial performance measures and adopts strategies consistent with ecological management and sustainable development. It becomes almost evangelical in its green marketing strategy and considers very carefully whether it is operating at an appropriate scale.

In summary we would suggest that while the frameworks developed by Steger, Roome, Topfer etc speak about competitive advantage, they do not specify the various strategies a company should adopt in order to become greener or to gain competitive advantage. Pietilainen, Vandermerwe and Oliff, Bansal and Beaumont, Pedersen and Whitaker have attempted to do this. Their frameworks, however, fail to indicate how competitive advantage and sustainability can be measured in the way which Dodge and Welford have described. These 'stage' models do provide us with an ability to categorise companies according to their environment-related behaviour. However, we must recognise that they are somewhat simplistic generalisations. Perhaps what is more important is to examine incentives for firms to move from one stage to the next. Here, a major driver will be 'competitive advantage'.

CORPORATE STRATEGIES FOR GAINING COMPETITIVE ADVANTAGE

We have argued above that while in the 1970s, environmental management was regarded by companies with little enthusiasm, more recently companies have begun to regard environmental management as a strategic tool for gaining competitive advantage (Shrivastava et al, 1992). This usually implies incorporating environmental management into the overall business strategy (Rushton, 1993; Bostrum et al, 1992). A study undertaken by Booz, Allen and Hamilton in 1991 of top executives in the chemical industry in the US, revealed that the leading chemical companies believe that an integrated and holistic approach to the environment is required in order to incorporate it into the overall business strategy (Rushton, 1993). This, in turn, requires the adoption of a proactive environmental strategy, as opposed to a passive or reactive strategy (Norcia et al, 1993; Little, 1991). This is equivalent to a shift from compliance to 'excellence' and 'leading edge' in Roome's Strategic Options Model (Roome, 1992). Thus according to Roome (1992), Norcia et al (1993), Little (1991) and Newman et al (1993), while a passive or a reactive strategy focuses on doing the minimum that is required by law, a proactive approach aims at moving beyond compliance, in order to gain an edge over competitors.

According to authors such as Taylor (1992) and Welford (1992) a proactive stance therefore requires total managerial commitment. It means incorporating environmental concerns into all the activities of the organization, like product quality, employee relations, and corporate image. Arthur D Little (1991) has adapted the traditional business value chain (Porter, 1985) to the environment in order to identify the various ways in which the internal performance drivers can contribute in the development of competitive environmental strategies (see Figure 2.4). Similar attempts have been made by James (1992, in Beaumont et al, 1993). Taylor's research (1992) shows that leading companies are using environmental pressures to improve operational efficiency, heighten corporate image and to develop new products and opportunities, and thus gain a competitive edge. This could mean a change in corporate culture, objectives, plans and even allocation of resources (Welford and Gouldson, 1993).

Roome (1994) regards change as essential for the growth and development of business in the 1990s, emphasizing the importance of environmental issues in business today. He feels that it is not sufficient simply to comply with the current legislation. According to Welford (1992) the first step must be the development of environmental management systems which promote quality and a commitment by the management as well as the employees to environmental issues. This would impact across all levels of business and would be a necessary (but not sufficient) step in the achievement of sustainability in businesses.

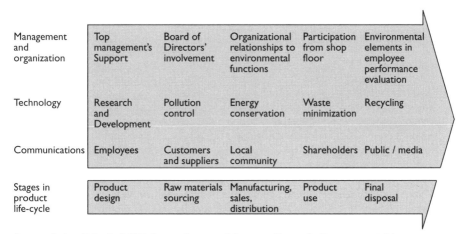

Source: Arthur D Little (1991) *Seizing Strategic Advantage* Centre for Environmental Assurance, London

Figure 2.4 The environmental value chain

Companies have begun to realize that 'green issues' or 'green management' is not a passing fad but is here to stay (Greeno et al, 1992). Consequently, they are now taking a more positive attitude to environmental regulations. Barrett (1991) claims that some companies have even begun to realize that they can influence the regulations that are introduced, in such a way as to increase competitive advantage. One way of doing this is by moving beyond compliance, in anticipation of future legislation and converting what might have become legislation into voluntary codes of conduct. Such a strategy enables a company to minimize the disruption caused by complying with new regulations, and to seize market opportunities. Besides, by spending now, one avoids having to spend much more at a later stage. For example, by developing its automobiles to meet the emission standards of the US market (Taylor, 1992), Mercedes-Benz was able to create a competitive edge over its European competitors. Similarly, Shell UK has started incinerating all its solid waste in accordance with US legislation, in anticipation of similar legislation in Europe in the near future.

Porter (1985) describes two main strategies for gaining competitive advantage – cost leadership and differentiation (see below). Little (1991) claims that both these strategies can be applied to the environment for gaining competitive advantage. Gladwin (1993) suggests that the theory of strategic choice can be applied to environmental management which, in other words, means an organization's search for different types of competitive advantage. Bostrum et al (1992) feel that there are a number of economic benefits from environmental considerations. A more effective use of raw materials in production results in diminishing costs for example, and a greener corporate image leads to an increase in market share. New market opportunities might also be created in the form of new products and technology. Some of the main constituents of competitive advantage are listed by Welford and Gouldson (1993), and can be seen in Figure 2.5.

In a nutshell, we might consider there to be five main environmental strategies that have been mentioned in the literature for gaining competitive advantage:

1. **'Excellence' and 'leading edge':** This implies moving beyond compliance, viewing environmental management as good management, seizing environmentally–based opportunities that have arisen as a result of the environmental challenge and striving towards state-of-the-art environmental management (Roome, 1992).

2. **Incorporation of the environmental management strategy into the overall corporate strategy:** This implies giving due weight and importance to environmental issues during the planning process and not just including it as an afterthought. As Little (1991) rightly points out, in many companies there is no intersection of the environmental management strategies and the overall corporate planning process. Moreover, quite often there is a conflict between the two. Welford and Gouldson (1993), Taylor (1992) and Newman et al (1992) feel that this should not happen. The organization's environmental policy, programmes and practices should be incorporated into all the activities of the business. Each and every aspect of an organization's environmental impact should be taken into consideration.

Source: Welford & Gouldson (1993) *Environmental Management & Business Strategy*, Pitman Publishing, London

Figure 2.5 The constituents of competitive advantage

3. **Line driven:** Environmental management ought to be regarded as a line function rather than a staff function. It has been seen in a number of companies that line managers hinder the environmental staff and are not themselves responsible for the company's environmental performance. This is not right. Line managers should be aware of their environmental obligations and should be fully accountable for the environmental performance of their particular operations.

4. **The short- vs long-term strategy:** Most companies tend to lay an emphasis on short-term gains and returns, thus discounting long-term environmental benefits like increases in the morale of the workers, goodwill, improvement in public image, avoidance of the cost of penalty, compensation etc. They look for short-term solutions and for an immediate financial payback on their investments. However, investments in the field of environment do not bring immediate returns and are evident only in the long run. Moreover, it may be much simpler and cheaper to clean up the existing process using end-of-pipe technology than to develop an entirely new process or product. However, Rushton (1993) and Royston (1979) point out that the opposite can also be true. In the long run, it may be more profitable to renew the entire production process than to clean up the existing process (Bostrum et al, 1992). Hence it pays to have a long-term environmental strategy.

5. **Effective communication:** Communication, as explained by Buhr (1991) and Grayson (1992), plays a significant role in maintaining good public relations and in achieving competitive advantage. For example, Norsk Hydro (Duff, 1992) was the first company in the UK to publish its externally audited environmental report. This exercise has greatly enhanced the company's green image in the eyes of its stakeholders.

COST LEADERSHIP AND DIFFERENTIATION

Porter (1985) identifies cost reduction and differentiation as key ways in which to achieve competitive advantage. Here, there is a win–win scenario available to companies in linking this sort of strategic thinking with environmental management practices.

Figure 2.6 illustrates the general approach taken here. We need to consider our general competitive factors and layer on top of this the environmental factors which are important. This leads us to the development of an environmental management strategy to improve competitiveness. Here we concentrate on costs and differentiation. The aims must be to reduce costs and to differentiate products (and company image) from those of the competitors. Both can be achieved, to some extent, through the use of environmental management tools. An important role for management will be to control, monitor and develop cost reduction and differentiation strategies.

Cost reduction is at the heart of maintaining competitiveness. But there are many environmental management techniques which can be employed which will also reduce competitiveness. For example, simply putting fewer inputs into an operation will reduce costs and increase both competitiveness and improve environmental performance.

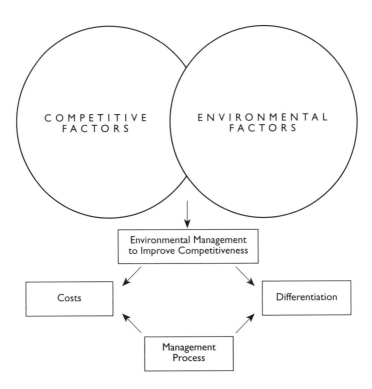

Figure 2.6 Improving competitiveness through environmental management

Table 2.3 Cost reduction strategies

Materials use	Reduce components
	Materials substitution
	Increase recyclability
	Reduce quantity of material/weight
	Supply chain pressure
	Product design/DFE/DFD
Energy usage	Fuel substitution
	Energy efficiency
Emissions and effluent	Reduce need for water
(including water usage)	recycling
	Reduce inputs
	Process redesign
	Process efficiency
	Identify markets for emission and effluent
Waste management	Redesign products and processes
	Reuse strategies
	Recycling
	Identify markets for waste
Distribution	Reduce packaging
(including packaging)	Substitute different materials for packaging
	Reduce transportation
	Increase fuel efficiency of vehicles
	Logistics planning
	Optimal loading of vehicles

In Table 2.3 and in Figure 2.7, we identify a number of ways in which a company can improve its environmental performance at the same time as reducing its costs. Here the emphasis is firmly placed on pollution prevention rather than end-of-pipe solutions because the former has the potential to reduce costs whilst the latter invariably increases costs. Whilst end-of-pipe technology serves a purpose it tends to be a reactive and somewhat expensive technique.

Much emphasis is placed on inputs into the production process including materials, energy, water and packaging. There are also pollutants and waste by-products to be managed. At the heart of the process we must also remember that distribution issues have quite an impact on environmental performance. Many companies are using supply chain and product stewardship initiatives to help them to improve their environmental performance and profile. this is an area which can also help to reduce costs and needs further investigation.

Differentiation relates to the ways in which a company and its products are perceived. In particular, it was emphasised earlier that an important part of differentiation was improving corporate image. Differentiation therefore requires a company to:

1. develop sound environmental performance;
2. engage in effective marketing and distribution strategies; and
3. communicate its performance to stakeholders.

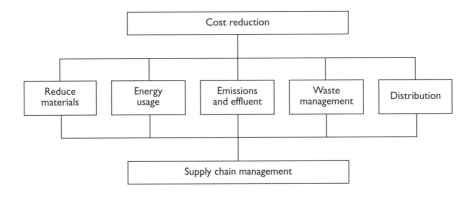

Figure 2.7 Cost reduction through environmental management

Sound environmental performance is based on having green products, green processes and green supply chains. Effective communication is based on a company's marketing capability and stakeholder accountability. Differentiation will also be aided by education, campaigns and project initiatives. These issues are summarised in Figure 2.8 and in Table 2.4 in more detail.

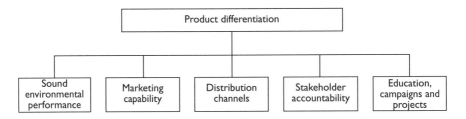

Figure 2.8 Key elements in product differentiation

BUSINESS STRATEGIES FOR SUSTAINABILITY

While many believe that competitive advantage rather than sustainable development motivates companies to improve their environmental performance (Irwin et al, 1992), there are others who have been quick to argue that competitive advantage and sustainability can actually go hand in hand. Throop et al (1993) advocate the use of clean technology, doing more than what is required by law, collective action and 'an environmentalist organizational culture', for attaining sustainable development. While collective action implies arousing the interest and involvement of the stakeholders as well as cooperation among the firms within the industry, an environmentalist organizational culture can be created by building up a knowledge base among employees, a personal belief and interest in the principles of sustainability by the management, developing adequate skills

Table 2.4 Differentiation strategies

Sound environmental performance	Green products
	Green processes
	Green supply chain
	Environmental management systems
	ISO certification
Marketing capability	Environmental reporting
	Product profiling and reporting
	Market segmentation
	Media management
	Sponsorship
	Environmentally-linked advertising
	Eco-labelling
	Packaging design
	Certification to standards
Distribution channels	Shorter supply chains
	Closer links with retailers
	Service networks
	Information provision
Stakeholder accountability	Environmental reporting
	Customer liaison
	Information
	Openness to concerns
	Transparency
	Social auditing
Education, campaigns and projects	Employee and supplier education/training
	Customer education
	Targeted campaigns
	Sponsorship
	Environmental projects
	Development projects
	Local community projects

and finally by evaluating performance along the abovementioned lines.

There are other approaches, however (see for example, the framework provided in the UN Report (1993) and Welford, 1995), that perceive competitive advantage and sustainable development as being two completely different managerial approaches to the environment. While strategies employed by the former are related to seizing environmentally-based opportunities for gaining competitive advantage, the strategies employed by the latter are oriented towards dealing with global issues like global warming, desertification etc. According to Welford (1995), environmental issues, widely defined, are too important to be regarded merely as a strategic tool for gaining short-term competitive advantage. While it is true that certain benefits of industrial action to preserve the environment, like cost reduction, are in keeping with the principles of profit maximization, companies must take a more ethical and long-term approach towards the environment. This means that the definition of competitive advantage must be broadened in order to incorporate the principles of sustainability in the absence of regulation. This can only be achieved if a holistic and an integrated approach is taken towards environmental management and has the support of top management.

Stikker (1992) has put forward ten commandments for moving towards a sustainable business. They include integrating environmental issues as the responsibility of top management, making environmental jobs a line function, taking a systems approach, reducing and substituting the use of non-renewable resources, eliminating wastes, monitoring environmental performance and setting up communication and information procedures on the company's ecological principles and environmental performance. A more comprehensive strategic framework for gaining competitive advantage and for moving one's business towards sustainability, has been given by Hutchinson (1992). Hutchinson argues that for formulating its environmental strategy, a company's external as well as internal environment must be analysed. The implications of environmental legislation, how market pressures like green customers and public opinion are impacting upon the business, and the various opportunities of becoming green – reduction in costs, new market opportunities in the form of new products and services – should be analysed. However, both of these approaches fail to take account of the non-environmental aspects of sustainable development such as equity and futurity.

At the same time, the environmental impact of all the activities of business, ranging from planning and public relations to manufacturing and distribution, should also be analysed – what are the wastes generated from each activity, the energy consumed for each activity, the impact on the community, so on and so forth. This information can then be analysed using SWOT (strengths, weaknesses, opportunities and threats) analysis. Hutchinson believes that this would enable the company to develop strategies, and to deal with 'the three dimensions of the environmental challenge', namely:

1. **Making the present impact acceptable:** A reduction in environmental impact can be achieved by identifying issues that require immediate action and by setting up realistic targets and future action plans.
2. **Identifying and realizing potential:** This can be done by minimizing pollution, reducing energy and raw material consumption, and exploring new business opportunities like developing new greener products or selling the old product in a new package which has an environmental appeal.
3. **Change to a sustainable business:** It is recognised in Figure 2.9 that, before a business can change to a 'sustainable business', it is essential that a strategic approach is taken towards the environment. To do this, first of all the staff at all levels of the organization should be involved. This can be achieved by creating environmental awareness and training. Secondly, the organization's culture should be changed and developed. Thirdly, cleaner and more efficient processes and technology should be developed (Irwin et al, 1992). Finally, an organization should have a clean public image. A number of stakeholders, ranging from employees to the investors, react favourably to this.

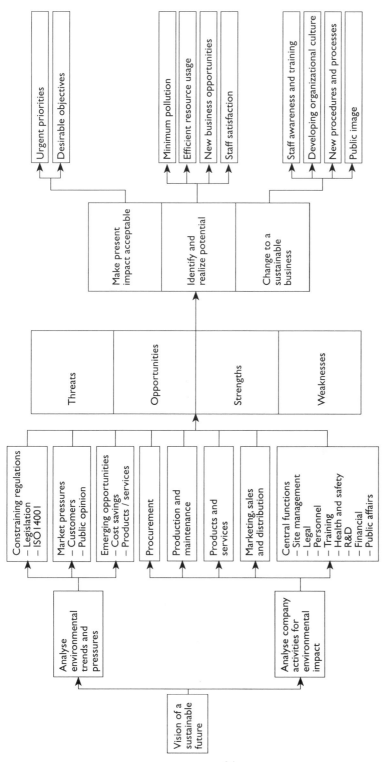

Figure 2.9 Strategic framework for environmental management

Source: Hutchinson, C (1992) 'Corporate Strategy and the Environment' *Long Range Planning* 25, 4, 9–21

CONCLUSIONS

There is little doubt that discussion of environmental strategy has increased substantially over the last two to three years. There have been many attempts, reviewed here, to analyse the strategy of companies and to propose workable ways forward which both maintain or increase profitability and provide for the improvement of corporate environmental performance (including competitiveness). It can be seen that the roots of such strategic analyses have much in common. But we must recognize that it is the majority of firms who are still operating at the levels associated with ostriches, resistors and laggards. Few are truly enthusiastic and innovative when it comes to environmental issues.

However, there is a far more fundamental criticism which might be made in the context of this chapter. This relates to whether strategic analysis and the strategic focus of many commentators will actually drive us towards sustainable development. On the one hand it might be argued that innovative strategic approaches will continually widen the definition of the environment to include equitable, social and future concerns, as consumers and governments become more critical and comprehensive in their thinking. On the other hand however, the strategic approach does not challenge the traditional model of the profit-centred industrial organization. It is therefore an extension of 'business-as-usual' paradigms. The achievement of sustainable development, to many, implies the need to challenge such paradigms and to fundamentally reassess the way we do business and the way in which we organize industry. Those debates are just beginning, but if they follow the speed of development of environmental strategy, it will not be long before we begin to have some rather more concrete answers. In the meantime, it seems to be agreed by most commentators that strategies associated with corporate environmental management, and integrating a systems based approach into those strategies, is the road down which we should head. To that end, the rest of this book deals with that subject area.

REFERENCES

Ansoff, H I (1979) 'The Changing Shape of the Strategic Problem' in *Strategic Management: A New View of Business and Policy Planning* Little, Brown and Co, Boston

Bansal, P (1993) 'A Proposed Framework for the Corporate Response to Ecological Pressures', DPhil Thesis, Templeton College, Oxford

Barrett, S (1991) 'Environmental Regulation for Competitive Advantage', *Business Strategy Review*, Spring 1991, 1-15

Beaumont, J R, Pedersen, L M and Whitaker, B D (1993) *Managing the Environment* Butterworth-Heinemann Ltd, Oxford

Bostrum, T and Poysti, E (1992) *Environmental Strategy in the Enterprise* Helsinki School of Economics, Helsinki

Bruntland, G H (1991) *Our Common Future* Oxford University Press, Oxford

Buhr, N (1991) 'The Environmental Audit: Who Needs It?' *Business Quarterly*, Winter 1991, 27–32

Duff, C (1992) Norsk Hydro's Environmental Report, *Long Range Planning*, 25 (4), 25–31

Gladwin, T (1993) 'The Meaning of Greening: A Plea for Organisational Theory', in *Environmental Strategies for Industry* Fischer, K and Schot, J (eds), Island Press, Washington DC

Grayson, L (1992) *Environmental Auditing* Technical Communications, Oxford

Greeno, J L and Robinson, S N (1992) 'Rethinking Corporate Environmental Management', *The Columbia Journal of World Business*, Fall & Winter

HMSO (1990) *This Common Inheritance* HMSO Publications, London

Hutchinson C, (1992) 'Corporate Strategy and the Environment', *Long Range Planning*, 25 (4), 9–21

Irwin, A and Hooper, P D (1992) 'Clean Technology, Successful Innovation and the Greening of Industry: A Case Study Analysis', *Business Strategy and the Environment*, 1 (2), 1–10

James, P (1992) 'The Corporate Response', in *Greener Marketing* (Charter, M (ed) Greenleaf Publishing, Sheffield

Ketola, T (1993) 'The Seven Sisters: Snow Whites, Dwarfs or Evil Queens? A Comparison of the Official Environmental Policies of the Largest Oil Corporations in the World', *Business Strategy and the Environment*, vol 2 (3), 22–33

Little, A D (1991) *Seizing Strategic Environmental Advantage* Centre for Environmental Assurance, London

Meadows, D H, Meadows, D L, Randers, J and Behrens, W W (1979) *The Limits to Growth*, 5th ed, Pan Books Ltd, London

Meima, R (1994) 'Making Sense of Environmental Management Concepts and Practices: A Critical Exploration of Emerging Paradigms', Proceedings of the 1994 Business Strategy and the Environment Conference, The University of Nottingham

Newman, J C and Breeden, K M (1992) 'Managing in the Environmental Era', *The Columbia Journal of World Business*, Fall & Winter

Norcia, V (1993) 'Environmental Performance and Competitive Advantage in Canada's Paper Industry', *Business Strategy and the Environment* 2 (4), 1–9

Pearce, D W, Markandya, A and Barbier, E B (1989) *Blueprint for a Green Economy*, 3rd ed, Earthscan Publications Ltd, London

Pearce, D W and Turner, R K (eds) (1990) *Economics of Natural Resources and the Environment Harvester* Wheatsheaf, London

Porter, M E (1985) *Competitive Advantage* The Free Press, New York

Porter, M E (1991) 'Green Competitiveness', *Scientific American*, April 1991

Roome, N (1992), 'Developing Environmental Management Strategies', *Business Strategy and the Environment*, Vol 1 (1), 11–24

Roome, N (1994) 'Business Strategy, R&D Management and Environmental Imperatives', *R & D Management* 24, 65–82

Royston, M G (1979), *Pollution Prevention Pays* Pergamon Press, Oxford, London

Rushton, B M (1993) 'How Protecting the Environment Impacts R&D in the United States', *Research Technology Management*, May–June 1993, 13–21

Shrivastava, P and Scott, H I (1992) 'Corporate Self–Greenewal: Strategic Responses to Environmentalism', *Business Strategy and the Environment*, 1 (3), 9–20

Simpson, A (1991) 'The Greening of Global Investment – How the Environment, Ethics and Politics are Reshaping Strategies', The Economist Publications, London

Smith, D (1992) 'Strategic Management and the Business Environment: What Lies Beyond the Rhetoric of Greening?' *Business Strategy and the Environment*, 1 (1), 1–9

Stikker, A (1992) 'Sustainability and Business Management', *Business Strategy and the Environment*, 1 (3), 1–8

Taylor, S R (1992) 'Green Management: The Next Competitive Weapon', *Futures* Sept 1992, 669–680

Throop, G M, Starik, M and Rands, G P (1993) 'Sustainable Strategy in a Greening World: Integrating the Natural Environment into Strategic Management', in *Advances in Strategic Management*, vol 9 (eds: Shrivastava, P, Huff, A and Dutton, J) JAI Press Inc, London, 63–92

United Nations (1993) *Environmental Management in Transnational Corporations, Report on the Benchmark Corporate Environmental Survey*, United Nations Publications, New York

Vandermerwe, S and Oliff, M D (1990) 'Customers Drive Corporations Green', *Long Range Planning*, 23 (6), 10–16

Welford, R J (1992) 'Linking Quality and the Environment', *Business Strategy and the Environment*, 1, 1

Welford, R J, and Gouldson, A P (1993) *Environmental Management and Business Strategy* Pitman Publishing, London

Welford, R J (1994) *Cases in Environmental Management and Business Strategy* Pitman Publishing, London

Welford, R J (1995) *Environmental Strategy and Sustainable Development: The Corporate Challenge of the 21st Century* Routledge, London

Part 2

The Tools of Corporate Environmental Management

Chapter 3

Environmental Management Systems

Alan Netherwood

INTRODUCTION

Many organizations have adopted environmental policies and carried out environmental audits or reviews in response to legislative pressures, green marketing opportunities, increased public pressure, ethical concerns and the commitment of local and central government to Agenda 21. However, if the commitments outlined in these policies and the recommendations made in reviews are to be honoured, these organizations will be faced with the problem of finding a systematic way of implementing commitments to environmental management within their existing organizational structure. Indeed, many organizations, having written their environmental policy and carried out an initial environmental review, find difficulty in translating recommendations into action. Sadgrove (1992, p215) states:

> *...there is often a gap between what companies aspire to and what they achieve. Environmental affairs is a case in point: inaction is a great problem. There is a danger that once an environmental audit is executed and the policy written, little will follow... Companies which lack a (management) system will 'cherry' pick their environmental activities: a bit of recycling here, some landscaping there. It does not add up to comprehensive environmental management.*

and Spedding et al (1993, p95) come to a similar conclusion:

> *Reviews alone cannot provide an organization with the assurance that its performance not only meets but continues to meet legislative and policy requirements.*

One tool which organizations are using to facilitate implementation of environmental policy is an environmental management system (EMS) which meets the need of organizations identified by Roome (1992), of 'planned and programmed change to support environmental management'. Even though the content, aims and objectives of environmental policies and the outcome of initial reviews may differ from sector to sector, there are common stages within an EMS that organizations use to try to ensure that the environment is considered in policy and processes. These stages are very similar to those present in Total Quality Management (TQM) Systems.

Environmental Management System standards such as the EU eco-management and audit scheme (1993) and the international standard ISO 14001 have been developed to provide organizations with a framework to implement an EMS within their organization and these standards are based upon the principles of TQM. However, just as there has been criticism of quality and TQM techniques, these standards and the EMS approach in general have been criticized in that they do not go far enough in environmental terms, that they are defensive, bureaucratic and do not provide an adequate framework to tackle urgent environmental issues and work towards sustainable management practices.

This chapter discusses the common elements found in organizational Environmental Management Systems, the links between EMS and TQM, common organizational factors which affect the development of an EMS and the limitations of EMS in achieving sustainable practices in organizations.

ENVIRONMENTAL MANAGEMENT SYSTEMS

An Environmental Management System is defined by the British Standards Institute (1994 p6) as:

> *the organizational structure, responsibilities, practices, procedures, processes and resources for determining and implementing environmental policy.*

Similar definitions are found in the EU eco-management and audit scheme and ISO 14001. Gilbert (1993) provides a useful summary of the guidelines and basic principles of environmental management by organizations such as the International Chamber of Commerce, the Business Council for Sustainable Development and the Confederation of British Industry, which summarize the basic stages of an organization's EMS:

- a policy statement indicating commitment to environmental improvement and conservation and protection of natural resources;
- a set of plans and programmes to implement policy within and outside the organization;
- integration of these plans into day to day activity and into the organizational culture;
- the measurement, audit and review of the environmental management performance of the organization against the policy, plans and programmes;
- the provision of education and training to increase understanding of environmental issues within the organization; and

- the publication of information on the environmental performance of the organization.

Gilbert (1993) pp 7–8

These stages of audit, measurement and review closely resemble elements of quality management systems which have been developed to ensure that the activities, policies and processes of organizations conform to specified quality requirements. These systems are used mainly between purchaser and supplier in contractual situations in which a purchaser is assured that the supplier has the necessary system in place to deliver a product or service. Quality management systems such as ISO 9000 are widely utilized, and compliance with these standards is independently assessed.

TQM Systems develop this concept by providing guidance for both the company philosophy and practices to ensure that they are developed and used efficiently to meet organizational objectives. TQM changes the focus of the organization from internal to external, measuring performance through customer satisfaction. In other words, the customer receiving the good or service is the final judge of the organization's performance. TQM requires that quality is the responsibility of everyone within the organization and that there is continual analysis, measurement and improvement of performance through a quality loop like the one shown in Figure 3.1.

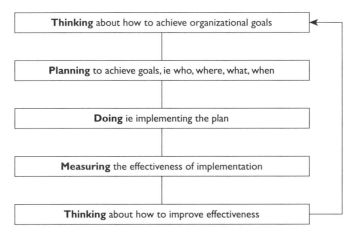

Figure 3.1 Total Quality Management loop

An organization can enter this quality loop anywhere as long as it follows the steps to improve performance on a continual basis. In order to facilitate this the organization should follow the procedure shown in Figure 3.2.

Many organizations which have written environmental policies and carried out environmental reviews have turned to this quality management approach to ensure that the commitments made in the policy, and the recommendations made after the environmental review, are implemented. In theory, the main link between EMS and TQM systems is that they both aim to achieve a continuous cycle of improvement through the commitment

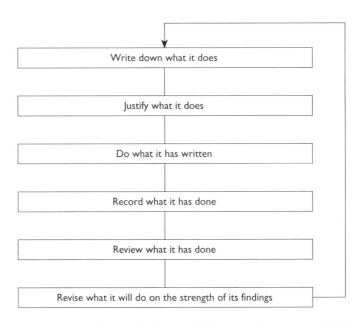

Figure 3.2 ISO 9000 cycle from Welford & Gouldson (1993)

of the whole organization. Welford & Gouldson (1993) argue that the EMS needs to mirror the TQM approach in dealing with the environment (in place of quality) at every stage of the production process, at both an internal and external level, and that EMS, like TQM, systems require effective commitment, planning, leadership, communications, organization, control and monitoring to succeed.

Spedding et al (1993) suggest that in the application of TQM to environmental issues, the customer is replaced by the environment and quality by environmental quality. Welford & Gouldson (1993) suggest that the TQM's ultimate aim for complete lack of defects can incorporate the concept of zero-negative impacts on the environment and that there are close parallels between aiming for TQM and cradle to grave environmental management.

In order for an organization to achieve environmental performance through a management loop such as this, it will need to define responsibilities for environmental management, deploy resources to ensure that action is taken on environmental issues, train staff to become aware of their environmental responsibilities, monitor environmental performance and audit and review the system of achieving environmental improvement. The basis of all of this activity is an organizational commitment to continual environmental improvement and an environmental policy, the first two stages of a typical environmental management system shown in Figure 3.3.

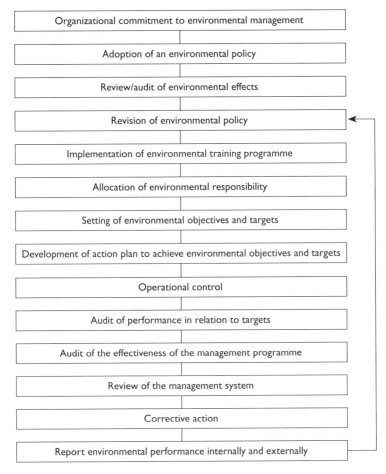

Figure 3.3 An Environmental Management System

Organizational Commitment to Environmental Management

The aims and priorities of all organizations differ, and the importance of the environment to those organizations will also vary. Despite these differences, the most successful EMS will be found where senior management commitment exists, because this facilitates the adoption of an environmental policy, and its subsequent translation into responsibility and action. This commitment should enable time, financial and other resources to be allocated to the environmental management process. However, in reality, many organizations find difficulty in ensuring this commitment, even when an environmental policy already exists. This may be due to the low priority of the environment when resources are allocated within departments, existing management pressures, and cynicism and apathy towards environmental issues.

Ledgerwood et al (1992) suggest that environmental managers, or those attempting to initiate an EMS within an organization, need to market the environment as an issue to senior management, outlining ways in which an EMS will benefit the enterprise and in a sense providing training to senior management on the relevance of the environmental agenda. Welford & Gouldson (1993) suggest that this commitment needs to be periodically and continually reinforced to ensure that environmental issues are not marginalized over the long term. In many organizations, commitment to the environment and knowledge of environmental issues may already be present at a high level, and in these cases the adoption and implementation of environmental policy may be less problematic.

Environmental Policy

An environmental policy formally outlines an organization's commitments to environmental management. In many organizations a general policy is developed before any environmental management activity and revised once more information about effects and performance is available; in others, a policy is developed only after an environmental review. Some organizations may develop a policy at a later stage, commonly when it is realized that the organization's environmental performance can only be tackled with adequate resources, which generally only a formal policy can secure.

Some policies take the form of a short statement, or a few bullet points, while others are lengthy policy documents specifying specific objectives and targets. Sadgrove (1993) outlines some of the common issues covered by organizational environmental policy:

- the organization's attitude towards the environment;
- the overall environmental goals of the organization;
- commitment to the audit and review of the organization's environmental performance;
- commitment to meet and surpass environmental standards;
- conservation of natural resources;
- minimization of the environmental effects of products, services and processes;
- commitment to provide a healthy workplace;
- commitment to liaise with the local community and society on environmental issues;
- commitment to train all staff and suppliers in environmental management; and
- specific commitments to areas such as energy, waste, land and water management

Sadgrove (1993) p 30

However, achieving implementation of these commitments may be problematic, especially within those organizations which have not adequately thought of the practicality of their implementation, in terms of the resources required and in terms of the difficulty of their incorporation into the organization's management structure. Ketola (1993) argues that environmental policies are not always drafted in the best possible way or by the best possible people and that policies may reflect the concerns of the organization at the time that they were created, but may not lend themselves to day to day environmental management over a period of time. Therefore, it is important that the policy is achievable, realistic and easily understood by both employees at all levels within the organization, and the public. Gray (1993) suggests that the policy should raise difficult and challenging questions regarding the organization's environmental performance.

There has been increasing criticism of organizations which develop environmental policies for marketing purposes, and the use of 'get out' clauses like, 'where it is financially and commercially viable' or 'practicable' alongside environmental commitments. However, it could be argued that whatever the content of the policy, it should make an organization more publically accountable, and is an essential basis for environmental improvement, responsibility and action within the organization, no matter how limited or shallow the policy commitments are.

Environmental Review

An environmental review provides a snapshot of the environmental performance of the organization in terms of the following types of issue; existing provision for environmental management, accident and emergency planning, communications, energy management, environmental effects, investment, legislative requirements, local communities, nature conservation, processes, purchasing, products, resource consumption, suppliers, transport, waste minimization and water management. The data produced from the review should enable realistic policies and recommendations to be developed which are relevant to the particular issues, impacts and objectives of the organization.

Obviously there is a great deal of variation in the content of environmental reviews depending upon the function, corporate ethics and culture of the organization. Some organizations may concentrate solely upon compliance issues and the way environmental issues affect the organization's economic performance, for example related to energy, water and waste management. Others may concentrate only upon direct effects to the environment, whereas others also consider service effects. The more proactive organizations may introduce the concept of ecological sustainability to this review stage, considering the organization's effect on global and development issues (Callenbach et al 1994, Welford 1993, Wheeler 1994).

The depth of an environmental review may vary between being a comprehensive review of all aspects of the organization's environmental performance with performance indicators identified and targets and objectives suggested, or just a preparatory review of the major significant environmental effects of the organization. Many reviews use environmental SWOT analysis but generally the depth and scope of the review, the methodologies and analytical tools used and the range of recommendations resulting from the exercise differ from organization to organization.

Many organizations use external consultants to carry out the environmental reviews, although this can have negative consequences in terms of translation of the review's findings and recommendations into action. Generally, reviews are carried out by internal departmental staff directed by an environmental coordinator, manager, or review team who analyse and report on the environmental effects of the organization. The review is a learning process for the organization and this internal approach can ensure a better understanding of environmental performance issues and how they can be effectively managed.

In terms of environmental policy formulation a preparatory limited review may be adequate in prioritizing environmental issues for an organization. However, it could also be argued that the deeper and more wide ranging the review, the more accurately, conscientiously and easily an organization will be able to set environmental priorities and objectives, draft or revise a realistic policy, and develop the environmental management system.

The findings of a review do not automatically translate into action, and it is at this stage that many organizations may find themselves struggling for both direction and resources, shelving the review findings because there is no mechanism to implement practical and structural environmental management initiatives. The findings of the review must therefore be incorporated into an EMS to facilitate action, improvement and performance measurement. This can be done by including clear recommendations and objectives based upon the review findings.

Training

The success of the EMS is very dependent upon training to encourage an understanding of the issues involved among employees, and to develop an understanding of their role and responsibilities within the greening process, as Roome (1992, p 15) suggests:

> *the improvement of managerial systems needs to recognize the value of building the belief and commitment of the workforce to an environmental policy.*

To enable the change in organizational culture that is required for a successful EMS, training can play a key role in increasing people's awareness of environmental issues, and achieving a certain level of understanding of issues such as energy and waste management techniques among all personnel. It is important that training takes place at all levels of the organization. It should include senior management who have key decisions to make on resourcing environmental management, middle managers who are affected by environmental issues on a daily basis and other staff who have influence on the processes and practices of the organization which affect the environment. Gilbert (1993) states that the establishment of an environmental training programme is essential in order to remove the suspicions about environmental management among personnel and to facilitate the change in management strategies necessary for environmental improvement.

Netherwood (1995) found that in many organizations the area of most inertia regarding environmental management was middle management. This suggests that they should be targeted specifically to disseminate information and train their operational staff in environmental management techniques. Other training methods include the use of external consultants, the skills of internal training units, workshops, videos and management manuals. Training should also encourage the feeling of ownership of the environmental management process among employees. The EMS is likely to function better if those involved feel that their contribution actually makes a difference, and that what they think about the organization's performance is fed back into the system and recognized.

Some organizations adopt voluntary environmental management training, while others find that compulsory training is necessary to involve employees in the EMS process. What must be considered in carrying out environmental training is the wide range of attitudes to the environment that will be present in the organization, and that the material should be pitched at the right level in terms of both understanding and radicality. Welford & Gouldson (1993) suggest that training should be an ongoing process and not just a one off exercise which is swiftly forgotten about by its participants. The training approach should continually reassert the importance of environmental issues to staff and affirm their own responsibilities to environmental management within the organization.

Allocation of Environmental Responsibility

Too often staff will deny responsibility for environmental issues, or 'pass the buck', even when an environmental policy exists. To ensure that the policy is implemented, clear management responsibilities need to be defined for all staff who are involved with the activities identified by the review as having environmental implications. According to Gilbert (1993) the ultimate aim should be the integration of environmental responsibilities into job descriptions and performance measurement.

Each member of staff should be clear about why they are carrying out environmental management responsibilities, which again emphasizes the importance of training to an implementing organization. This is particularly important so that the environment receives adequate time and attention from staff, and is not just placed at the bottom of their priorities. Ideally responsibilities should be allocated during workshops and departmental meetings which concentrate upon the implications of the environmental review, rather than being tagged on to the end of meetings with 'any other business'. Gilbert also indicates the importance of recording these responsibilities to ensure that they are not forgotten about (especially if they are infrequent), and also ensure that they are auditable, and that they are not lost in any restructuring or personnel changes.

The definition and documentation of the levels of authority associated with environmental management are also important at this stage of an EMS. The allocation of managerial authority enables the efficient resourcing and implementation of environmental management initiatives. For example, environmental managers may find that they have no power or authority to actually get things done without senior management approval, which seriously limits their effectiveness. The authority factor also has great implications for the status of environmental management within the organization in comparison to other management issues, which in turn affects the attitudes and subsequent success of the EMS process.

It is also important that there is some mechanism for ensuring that management are actually carrying out their environmental responsibilities. This can be done by defining a number of performance outputs derived from the responsibilities of each individual, for example the provision of documentation, or the provision of information to other staff, which also facilitate the later stages of the EMS concerning its audit and review. So, if the allocation of responsibility is carried out effectively then there will be clear lines of communication and no gaps in the organizational structure, areas where Welford & Gouldson (1993) suggest that the EMS frequently breaks down.

The Setting and Attainment of Objectives and Targets

Organizations need to define, from the environmental review, a set of objectives and targets which are realistic and attainable. They should be sufficiently short-term to be of some significance, and sufficiently long-term to enable effective measurement of environmental improvement.

The British Standards Institute, (1994, p 6) defines environmental targets as:

> *detailed performance requirements, quantified wherever practicable, applicable to the organization or parts thereof, that arise from the environmental objectives and that need to be set and met in order to achieve those objectives.*

Gilbert (1993) suggests that targets should be demanding in order to provide motivation, satisfaction and a sense of achievement when they are met. In practice it may be difficult to achieve this balance, however what Gilbert does suggest is that each individual concerned with environmental management throughout the organization should have a set of targets and goals to achieve. These can be set at workshops with representatives from every level of the organization, where all staff work together to work out what is achievable within a period of time, how this will be achieved, and how this will be measured and documented.

The objectives and targets should be easily understood by all staff, with appropriate timescales allocated to facilitate planning and implementation. However, many organizations find difficulty with developing appropriate environmental performance indicators, especially where the information on improved environmental performance is qualitative rather than quantitative. Whatever indicators of performance are identified, it is important that they are easily understood in terms of the relevant objectives and targets, and staff are able to work with them.

An action plan should be created to implement the review recommendations and to meet the objectives and targets. This should be well defined with appropriate procedures, responsibilities and measurement mechanisms identified. Gilbert suggests that this implementation programme can be created during the workshops to identify objectives and targets, and that programmes should be specific to departments. This programme should include:

- the identification of the environmental issue though the collection of appropriate information;
- the analysis of the issue to identify why is it a problem;
- the development of a solution to the problem;
- the implementation of the solution; and
- the review and documentation of the action taken.

Operational Control

Gilbert states that this part of the EMS should include a documented set of practices, procedures and systems which ensure that all environmental management activities and the attainment of the relevant objectives and targets are carried out under controlled conditions. In other words operational control is the measurement and verification of whether what's meant to be getting done is getting done, and the correction of procedures if this is not the case.

Clear documentation should facilitate this. This documentation should also ideally introduce employees to the EMS, clarify their responsibilities, indicate which records are to be kept up to date, and describe the procedures for carrying out environmental management activities. It should also facilitate training requirements, and provide the basis for the audit, review and evaluation of the EMS as well as provide an indicator to customers that the EMS is functioning properly. Many organizations develop a management manual to cover all of these functions and requirements

Audit of the Effectiveness of the Management Programme

This is a regular and systematic evaluation of the EMS in terms of its efficiency in achieving objectives and targets. This audit is on an organizational scale, looking at the organizational structure, environmental roles and responsibilities, the procedures to operate and administer environmental management, the activities and processes involved in environmental management, and the operating procedures and records which are being used to improve the environmental performance of the organization.

The audit can be carried out internally or externally, but a general requirement is that there is a degree of objectivity involved in the exercise, so the auditors will need to be independent of areas being audited within the organization. There can be problems with this stage of the EMS similar to those experienced during environmental reviews, in that there is a resistance to interference and a reluctance to be identified as an individual or department which is failing the organization. However, this stage of the EMS is not a managerial appraisal, but an appraisal of the EMS and its effectiveness in meeting organizational objectives, and implementing environmental policy.

Review of the Management System

This review, according to Gilbert (1993), should summarize the status of the EMS and current environmental performance, review internal and external pressures for change, and result in an action plan to facilitate further improvement in performance. To enable this the EMS review should include:

- the results of audits and assessments;
- progress of improvement;
- plans and programmes;
- action taken on non-compliance;
- overview of new and planned legislation;
- the performance of suppliers and partners;
- a review of public environmental issues;
- local community concerns;
- new environmental concerns; and
- conclusions and recommendations for amendment of the EMS

A final report on the EMS would generally include the identification of gaps and problems with the EMS, areas where tighter control limits could be implemented, areas where impacts could be reduced, the amendment of environmental objectives and targets, a review of the structure, staffing, systems and training in the EMS, and a set of new objectives and targets which are to be implemented.

Environmental Reporting and Environmental Statements

In some companies, and especially in local authorities, there is a genuine desire and feeling of responsibility to become more publically accountable regarding their environmental management practices. The site-based EU eco-management and audit scheme (EMAS) facilitates this accountability as it requires that an environmental statement is published which is independently verified. The statement should include:

1. A description of the environmental protection system
2. A description of the auditing system
3. A validated environmental statement including details of:
   - activities concerned
   - environmental problems associated with activities
   - inventories of emissions, waste, energy, raw materials
   - the company's environmental policy, programme and objectives
   - the company's environmental performance.

Gilbert (1993) p 183

48

Obviously this requirement has great implications for the organization if it wishes to register with EMAS in terms of being objective and honest about its environmental performance. It could be suggested that many organizations will decide to use the ISO14001 model for an EMS which does not require a validated statement or report, rather than undertake this final stage of the EMS loop.

However, there has been a great deal of activity in environmental reporting in companies in recent years. Whereas this is an encouraging trend, the honesty, selectivity and objectivity of these reports have often been questioned. The issues involved in assessing the quality of environmental reports are explored elsewhere in this book; however it could be argued that many organizations publish information about their EMS, mainly for public relations purposes, in the form of an environmental report which can often be short on fact about the organization's environmental shortcomings and concentrate on the organization's major environmental achievements.

STANDARDIZATION OF ENVIRONMENTAL MANAGEMENT SYSTEMS

Despite the fact that many organizations use these common steps to develop an EMS, there is a great discrepancy in the quality of the EMS in different organizations in terms of its ability to mitigate environmental impacts and integrate environmental management into the organization. The proliferation of environmental 'credentials', and lack of guidance on the development of the EMS within organizations has highlighted a need to ensure some quality standard in environmental management. In the last few years a number of voluntary environmental management schemes have been developed to try and ensure a certain quality for the EMS, and to encourage organizations to improve their environmental performance. The EU eco-management and audit scheme (1993) and ISO14001, the international standard for environmental management systems, are considered in greater depth elsewhere in this book, but in basic terms they provide a framework for organizations to begin identifying and quantifying their effects on the environment, and provide for a commitment to continuous improvement of environmental performance in participating organizations through an EMS. The management system steps used in these standards draw heavily on the TQM models already described.

The standards are voluntary and are designed to be externally verified by nationally accredited bodies, in a similar way as the quality standard ISO 9000. It is argued that organizations which register with the schemes, gaining the EMAS logo and ISO14001 accreditation, will experience market advantages, and a better relationship with regulatory authorities, investors and insurance companies, as well as experiencing financial benefits through a greater efficiency in the organization's management structure and in areas such as energy, waste and water management.

STRUCTURE OF THE ENVIRONMENTAL MANAGEMENT SYSTEM

There are common structures developed by organizations with EMSs which help to facilitate the coordination and communication among those involved in the environmental management process. An Environment Committee is often created which acts as the main decision-making level of the EMS. This generally includes key individuals at all levels and from all departments within the organization, ie senior and middle management, union representatives, shop floor workers, as well as personnel which already have some environmental responsibility, such as health and safety managers and energy managers. These committees aim to coordinate environmental activity, ensure effective communication to all levels of the organization and to act as an appropriate forum for problem solving. In essence these committees should act as the hub of the EMS by disseminating and receiving information, coordinating environmental activity and ensuring that policy is being effectively implemented.

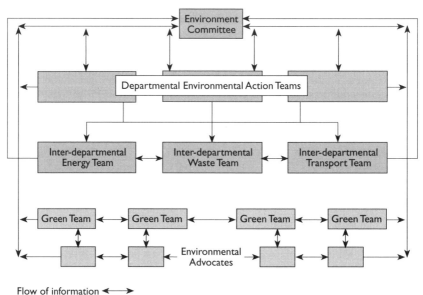

Flow of information ◄────►

Figure 3.4 A typical management structure for an EMS

Departmental environmental action teams are often developed which systematically record and act upon departmental environmental performance; in other words these are the teams within the organization which implement recommendations and work towards the achievement of environmental objectives and targets. These teams will often be made up of representatives from middle management and operational staff who have the greatest knowledge of the implications of environmental management activity. These teams generally feed back on their progress to the Environment Committee and have formal responsibilities within an EMS.

Inter-departmental teams are sometimes developed to tackle common environmental issues such as energy management, waste and transport, in order to obtain a corporate overview of the organization's environmental performance in these areas. These teams can also ensure effective dissemination of methods and techniques of environmental management across departments and provide a common basis for achieving targets and reporting. Generally they are made up of personnel who are particularly interested in the issue or are specialists in the field. Their tasks are often to collect information about particular environmental issues and provide recommendations that can be fed back into the EMS process.

Voluntary 'green' groups are frequently used within departments which are open to all employees to provide voluntary information and data on working practices. They aim to nurture a feeling of ownership of the environmental management process and are very often made up of environmental enthusiasts, or staff who are particularly concerned about the environmental performance of their particular workplace. Obviously due to their voluntary nature they occupy a less formal place within an EMS and therefore commonly receive no formal support. In many organizations it is felt, quite wrongly, that a voluntary green group is an adequate framework to use to implement the findings of the environmental review. Nevertheless, they can provide valuable information for the EMS, and enthuse (or alienate) other staff regarding the greening process.

Environmental advocates are often established within departments to disseminate information 'downwards' to employees from departmental action teams and the Environment Committee and 'upwards' through the same channel. It is essential that these type of people are present within the EMS structure as they provide a more informal avenue for 'bottom up' environmental initiatives, so that any individual can feel that their ideas and suggestions for environmental improvement will be heard by middle and senior management. Similarly, middle and senior management can be sure that their recommendations are understood at the grass roots of the organization. Environmental advocates can often act in an environmental training capacity (as can green groups) and are an important point of contact for the Environment Committee when they are considering attitudes to and awareness of environmental management activity in the organization.

It is important that at all stages of the EMS there is a lateral as well as a vertical flow of information throughout the management structure. Effective communication can ensure that departments, green teams and advocates are not reinventing the wheel when it comes to developing techniques for environmental management, and that in especially the larger organizations there is no compartmentalization or isolation of activity. Regular inter-departmental meetings at all levels of the management structure can facilitate this.

COMMON ORGANIZATIONAL FACTORS WHICH AFFECT EMS DEVELOPMENT

There is often a problem, however, with integrating these responsibilities and resource requirements into the existing management structure. In this respect, there are a number of external and internal factors which can commonly limit the effectiveness and development of the EMS within an organization.

Roome (1992) suggests that one of the main constraints on a successful environmental management strategy is 'the misjudging or mishandling of the process of organizational change'. Indeed, there are a number of factors which influence the development of an effective EMS within organizations, many of which have already been discussed in relation to the developmental stages of the environmental management loop. However, Netherwood (1995) suggests there are also factors which can benefit or more commonly hinder the development of an EMS, that may not be the result of inadequate planning, but are the result of economic and political factors and attitudes and culture inherent within the organization.

For example, the commitment of adequate resources to an EMS may be hindered due to the failure of middle and senior management to perceive the environment as being worthy of resource allocation in its own right rather than an add-on component of TQM systems, or a cheap marketing tool. When it becomes apparent that the environment will cost money within an organization, commitment can be swiftly withdrawn, policies can remain unfulfilled and promising environmental management initiatives can be curtailed. The EMS may also suffer from inertia resulting from stifling management practices, which affect all areas, not just environmental management. This inertia may be exacerbated by the fact that the environment is a new area and many middle and senior managers are averse to change, especially if this will add to their responsibilities.

It has been suggested that EMS and the standards will just add another layer of bureaucracy for the organization and put even greater pressure on limited management time, and that this will result in the relegation of environmental management responsibilities to the bottom of staff's lists of priorities. There may also be a problem with the status of environmental management within an organization, in that the environment can sometimes be associated with liberal and 'hippy' connotations, and it may be considered lightweight or even be treated as an area of ridicule by certain individuals or departments. Environmental management can also be regarded as non-essential in the short term and as an issue which can be addressed at leisure by an organization in the future.

Netherwood (1995) found that both internal and external economic influences can have negative (and sometimes positive) effects upon the initiation, development and resourcing of an EMS. At a corporate level, the commitments made in an environmental policy may be the first to be sacrificed if there is an increased pressure on limited resources. The EMS can very often be based upon ad hoc financial and staffing arrangements, especially in organizations which see the environment as a short-term trend. This can lead to inadequate resourcing of the EMS and consequently, low morale and apathy among those involved in the environmental management process. Subsequently, if the EMS process fails in a particular department or on a larger scale throughout the organization it will much more difficult to resurrect at a later stage when resources may become available. In local government, long-term resource planning for an EMS can also be difficult due to the fact that their annual budgets are controlled by central government and may differ from year to year.

Resourcing problems can also occur when organizations tag additional environmental responsibilities onto 'higher priority' areas such as health and safety management or quality management, instead of treating the environmental management as a distinct and important responsibility with its own separate budget. There can even be resource constraints in areas where there are potential financial benefits within the EMS, firstly due to competing demands for investment capital within an organization, and secondly due to the fact that often the budget which contains investment capital is separate from the area where the savings are likely to be met.

External political influences can also have a great influence upon the EMS both in local government, where the environment is seen as a vote-winning exercise, and also in business where there can be strong political connotations of environmentalism to certain industrial and business groups. Industrial and conservation lobbying groups can also affect the commitment of senior management to the greening process, and will therefore have consequences for the status and resources allocated to the EMS. In local government, there can be particular external political factors which affect the EMS, such as changes in political control of the council, and constraints put on authority spending by central government.

Netherwood (1995) also found that internal politics have an influence upon the EMS. Individuals can use the greening process for their individual gain, or likewise, block the process for their own ends. Alternatively, individuals may not want to be associated with radical, unpopular or bureaucratic management initiatives such as an EMS, and may withdraw or withhold support. However, others may see the greening process as a convenient political tool to facilitate a change in the corporate culture, management structure or personnel. There may also be problems experienced by newcomers to an organization who are given the task of implementing the EMS, in getting to grips with the red tape involved in the organization and learning the hidden rules for getting things done.

Many of the larger organizations, which have a considerable number of departments, staff, sites and functions may have a great deal of difficulty in coordinating an EMS. There may be a multi-speed system of environmental management within some organizations, with fragmented implementation both upwards and sideways through the management structure, leading to difficulties in managing both resources and inter-departmental politics, and difficulties in developing a corporate approach to environmental performance measurement. The EMS may also suffer as a result of organizational restructuring, or the promotion of other 'higher priority' programmes such as customer care initiatives, so that the environment gets pushed down the management agenda.

Problems can arise in departments which reach a threshold of environmental activity due to a lack of resources, or simply because there is little more to be done in practical terms. It is difficult in these situations to maintain the interest and enthusiasm for the EMS among staff, especially if progress is being delayed through senior management inertia regarding policy and resources.

There are many individual and personality factors that can affect the smooth running of the EMS. For example, resistance to outside interference, 'buckpassing', denial of responsibility, a disparity in motivation of those involved and the creation by individuals of 'logjams' and 'bottlenecks' in lines of communication within the EMS. Despite the need for effective leadership, there is also the problem of associating the EMS and the greening process with an individual, as this personification can cause barriers, especially where there are personality clashes in key areas, or there is cynicism about an individual's real reasons for their commitment to the environment. Some staff may feel threatened by the EMS either because they feel that they do not have the necessary knowledge or because they may feel that they are being personally investigated during the review and audit stages of the EMS. Many of these problems can be overcome by efficient allocation of responsibility, effective personnel management in gauging resistance to environmental management, and a knowledge of the organization to enable the right buttons to be pressed to facilitate change, training and the development of common ownership of the greening process.

There can be a great deal of entrenched cynicism towards environmental issues within organizations which even effective management and mandatory environmental training will not affect. It could be argued that organizations can act as a microcosm of society, where long-term environmental gains are sacrificed for short-term economic advantage and where there is a great deal of apathy towards environmental issues. Despite the need for cultural change within organizations to implement effective environmental management, it could be too much to ask of the EMS process and training to achieve a shift in corporate culture, as it can only go so far in changing the thought processes of each individual and may only achieve limited change in people's values in working towards a common environmental goal.

Obviously there will be more specific organizational barriers to Environmental Management Systems within different types of organization in different sectors, and there will be alternative solutions to these problems based upon political, economic, structural and individual factors.

CRITICISMS OF EMS, THE TOTAL QUALITY MANAGEMENT APPROACH AND EMS STANDARDS

Beside the organizational factors which can limit the effectiveness of EMS there are also problems with the EMS process and the EMS standards, if their ultimate goal is to mitigate environmental impacts and achieve sustainable practices within organizations. Sadgrove (1992) states that although the use of an EMS similar in character to a quality system makes things easier for managers who are already familiar with the concepts involved, similar criticisms can be made of EMS as TQM systems. For example, due to the fact that the organization sets its own environmental objectives and targets for improvement it can improve its environmental performance as little or as much, as fast or as slow as it likes. Shayler et al (1994) suggest that the targets an organization sets itself through an EMS might represent 'environmental tokenism rather than a solid commitment to decreasing environmental impact' (p 28). Therefore a self-regulated EMS does not guarantee significant improvements in performance, so in environmental terms it could be argued that EMSs are fundamentally flawed.

Spedding et al (1993) point out that there is a tendency for organizations to concentrate on satisfying the programme of achieving quality in TQM systems rather than the resulting achievement of quality. Welford (1993) suggests similarly, that the auditing process of the EMS is concerned mainly by the audit of the system rather than auditing environmental performance. Indeed, it could also be argued that TQM systems are about consistency rather than quality, and that an EMS will suffer from a similar drawback. Spedding et al (1993) suggest that few organizations believe that quality systems achieve tangible results, which subsequently undermines commitment. Similarly, it could be argued that there is a degree of apathy and cynicism towards the necessity and advantages of the EMS. Welford (1993) also identifies a similar problem in perpetuating the momentum of improvement and enthusiasm within an EMS.

Roome (1992) suggests further problems in the use of TQM as a basis for EMS in that he regards the achievement of an environmental ethic within an organization as being far more difficult than the nurturing of a concern for quality, and Welford (1993) suggests that the same thing will happen to the EMS standards that has happened to quality standards, ie the environment will be forgotten about once the standard is achieved.

Since, at the time of writing, the environmental management standards are still often in their first stages of implementation, speculation about their likely effects and efficiency are not based upon real world research, but upon the experiences of organizations using quality management techniques. However, there has been a great deal of criticism and debate about their value in terms of actually improving environmental performance and significantly reducing environmental impacts, and whether the systems approach is actually appropriate at all.

The EMS standards do not set specific limits upon energy or resource consumption, levels of emissions, or levels of performance, other than those based on national compliance, nor is there a requirement within their framework to tackle all of the organization's environmental effects. EMS and the standards only require a commitment to continual environmental improvement through the management system loop and do not aim for environmental protection. As Shayler et al (1994, p 28) state:

> the only requirement seems to be to demonstrate a capability for marginal environmental improvements within a self-determined framework of policies, targets, systems and assessment technologies.

Therefore, it is theoretically possible for an EMS to be developed by an organization and the standards satisfied, when the organization has an appalling record in environmental terms, by achieving minimum levels of compliance and demonstrating a commitment to continuous environmental improvement, however small that may be.

The EMS is seen in many sectors as being too bureaucratic, and there has also been criticism regarding the potential benefits of registering with the standards, and whether they will outweigh the costs. Netherwood (1995) found that organizations are put off the development of an EMS after the policy and review stages because of the financial costs and time involved, and because of the significant documentation requirements involved in the standards.

There is no doubt that many organizations will find the EMS standards useful as a motivating factor and as a framework to initiate environmental management and many see them as a toolbox to facilitate this. However, it is also apparent that an EMS based upon TQM systems does not provide guarantees or assurances to clients, shareholders and the public that organizational impacts are being minimized. It could also be argued that organizations will use the EMS standards as a marketing device, and as a smokescreen to pacify concerns regarding environmental performance, instead of as a catalyst for cultural change within the organization in order to provide real and significant improvements in environmental performance.

EMS AS A TOOL FOR SUSTAINABLE DEVELOPMENT

Roome (1992) states that sustainability requires managerially led, voluntary, organizational and managerial reform. However, it could be suggested that the majority of organizations would be unlikely to consider sustainable development issues voluntarily alongside their EMS, as many of them are already struggling to tackle their environmental problems. Even so, a small number of companies have adopted the principles of sustainable development within their EMS, and a growing number of local authorities are developing EMSs to deliver charters for sustainable development. Will the EMS model based upon TQM principles be able to deliver sustainable management practices?

The EMS can achieve improvements in environmental performance and has been widely regarded as one of the tools to work towards sustainability, yet there are strong doubts about their ability to deliver sustainable practices within organizations. What must be considered is, how far does an EMS take an organization towards sustainable management practices? Gray et al (1993) does define the role of an EMS in these terms: 'EMS may be a necessary condition for sustainability but is most certainly not a sufficient condition' (p 288), and Roome (1992, p 23) suggests that:

> *only strategies based on an integrated total EMS, and the introduction of environmental thinking and ethics into company practices, offer any real prospect of achieving pathways to environmentally sustainable action.*

Welford (1993) goes further in identifying the limitations of EMSs by suggesting that they are 'sub-optimal' if the ultimate objective of an organization is sustainable development, and states that the adoption of an EMS by organizations is not the adoption of sustainable development principles, which many organizations consider to be the case. Although he accepts that an EMS helps personnel to understand their position and responsibilities and the structure of environmental management within the organization, he suggests in a similar way to Callenbach et al (1993) that the EMS does not provide the 'paradigm shift' of organizational thinking regarding its environmental impacts in terms of global ecology and sustainable development concepts. It is also suggested by Welford that because EMSs are based upon a self-regulated rate of environmental improvement, sustainable practices will take a long time to achieve, except in the most forward thinking organizations.

The view of Callenbach et al is that traditional environmental management strategies such as EMS are not sustainable in that they tackle problems for the benefit of the organization and are not concerned with the effect of their policies and practices on a wide range of long-term global issues. It is suggested that they also fail to question the ideology of economic growth or the 'dominant corporate paradigm' and restrict radical action to solve urgent problems.

Callenbach et al suggest that the adoption of an Ecological Management System could achieve sustainable practices within an organization by being proactive and creative in dealing with environmental problems, while aiming to minimize social impacts and to be ecologically sound. They argue that these systems should also consider the place of the organization in a global sense and consider social, labour and cultural issues as well as environmental problems. The concept of Ecological Management Systems takes a less defensive and reactive approach to improving environmental performance within an organization than the types of EMS already described, in that they require a shift in values and culture within an organization from quantity to quality, to view the organization holistically, to view the world as a living system and to have ethical concerns for the well being of future generations.

Although these management systems may represent a theoretical example of best practice in environmental management and would represent a further step towards sustainable management in organizations, what must be questioned is their applicability in the real world, the likelihood of organizations adopting them, and the overall difference that their adoption would make to environmental problems on a wide scale. It could be argued that the required theoretical shift of values within an organization in considering its place within a global context, and the questioning the dominance of business in society must be placed within a realistic economic and political situation. As Gray et al (1993, p288) suggest:

> *The general concern in the West to develop 'greener' organizations is quite unlikely to come close to achieving sustainability except under the most restrictive and optimistic of assumptions.*

It could be argued that sustainable management practices are an unachievable goal for organizations. They can work towards sustainable management practices, but commentators seem doubtful of the suitability of EMS to enable this because of their voluntary and defensive nature, and it would seem that paradigm shifts in organizational thinking are unlikely to be derived through EMS due to economic, organizational and political necessities.

CONCLUSIONS

In reality every organization will take an individual approach to developing an EMS due to differing management structures, products, services and processes, priorities, and internal and external financial and political factors. However all EMSs will incorporate some method of planning, measurement and review. The adoption of an EMS within an organization will not necessarily raise environmental standards within the organization to a significant level, and may only address compliance issues, or an EMS may, in more proactive organizations, provide the stimulus for a major change in the corporate culture, to integrate environmental issues into every decision made.

However, one common factor determining the success of an EMS seems to be the degree of integration of environmental management responsibilities into the existing management structure. In this respect the development of an environmental policy and training is fundamental in ensuring that resources are allocated to the EMS, staff become environmentally aware, educated and responsible, and that practical improvements are made in an organization's environmental performance.

However, there is a definite weakness in the voluntary EMS approach based upon TQM principles in that it does not guarantee significant improvements in organizational environmental performance, let alone the achievement of sustainable management practices. The voluntary approach relies on the organization itself to set its own environmental targets, and unless there is a fundamental shift in the values and ethics of the organization towards environmental excellence the success of the EMS will be limited. As Gray et al (1993, p 299) states:

> *a faith in voluntary development of the mechanisms for environmental accountability...is misplaced.*

It could be argued that the EMSs would be far more efficient in mitigating environmental problems, and working towards sustainability if they were used in a stricter legislative climate, where mandatory EMSs were required by law, and specific environmental targets and objectives were set for organizations through legal requirements or in liaison with regulatory authorities. This would negate the need for a change in corporate culture from within and put the onus on external regulation and enforce change in the values and ethics of the organization. In order for this radical approach to be adopted on a national scale, a sympathetic and environmentally concerned political, legislative and economic situation would need to exist.

Legislation has another role to play especially in determining the long-term effects of organizations adopting EMSs. It could be suggested that one of the main motivations for organizations to undertake environmental management initiatives is compliance with legislation and not a sense of responsibility or wish to become 'sustainable'. If environmental legislation is tough then industry, business and other sectors react, so it could be argued that only legislation driven targets and objectives within organizations will lead to significant environmental improvements. This would ensure that environmental excellence would be an issue and aim for every organization, providing the basis for real environmental improvements at the organizational and sectoral level, while also providing a basis for strategic environmental management on a local, regional and national scale.

REFERENCES

British Standards Institute (1994) *British Standard for Environmental Management Systems: BS7750* BSI, London

Callenbach, E, Capra, F & Marbury, S (1993) *EcoManagement: The Elmwood Guide to Ecological Auditing and Sustainable Business*, Berret–Koehler Publishers, San Francisco

Commission of the European Communities (1993) *Council regulation (EEC) No1836/93 of 29 June 1993 amended proposal for a council regulation (EEC) allowing voluntary participation by companies in the industrial sector in a Community eco-management and audit scheme*, Official Journal of the European Communities L168/1–18 10 July 1993, Brussels

Gilbert, M J (1993) *Achieving Environmental Management Standards: a step by step guide to meeting BS7750* The Institute of Management, Pitman Publishing, London

Gray, R, Bebbington, J & Walters, D (1993) *Accounting for the Environment: The Greening of Accountancy Part II* Paul Chapman Publishing, London

ISO (1994) Committee Draft ISO/CD 14001, Environmental Management Systems

Ketola, T (1993) 'The Seven Sisters: Snow Whites, Dwarfs or Evil Queens: A Comparison of the Environmental Policies of the Largest Oil Corporations in the World', *Business Strategy and the Environment*, 2 (3)

Ledgerwood, G, Street, E & Therivel, R (1992) *The Environmental Audit and Business Strategy: A Total Quality Approach* Pitman Publishing, London

Local Government Management Board (1993) *A guide to the eco-management and audit scheme for Local Government* HMSO, London

Netherwood, A M (1995) 'Environmental Reviews and Environmental Management Systems: methodologies and organizational impacts' unpublished PhD thesis, Department of Environmental Management, University of Central Lancashire, Preston

Roome, N (1992) 'Developing Environmental Management Strategies' *Business Strategy and the Environment*, 1 (1)

Sadgrove, K (1992) *The Green Managers Handbook*, Gower, London

Spedding, L S, Jones, D M, and Dering, C J (1993) *Eco-management and eco-auditing: environmental issues in business* Chancery Law, London

Shayler, M, Welford, R & Shayler, G (1994) 'BS7750: Panacea or Palliative' *Eco-Management and Auditing* 1 (4)

Welford, R (1992) 'Linking Quality and the Environment: A Strategy for the Implementation of Environmental Management Systems' *Business Strategy and the Environment*, 1 (1)

Welford, R (1993) 'Breaking the Link Between Quality and the Environment: Auditing for Sustainability and Life Cycle Assessment' *Business Strategy and the Environment*, 2 (4)

Welford, R & Gouldson, A (1993) *Environmental Management and Business Strategy* Pitman Publishing, London

Wheeler, D (1994) 'Why ecological policy must include Human and Animal Welfare' *Business Strategy and the Environment*, 3 (1)

Chapter 4

The Standardization of Environmental Management Systems: ISO 14001, ISO 14004 and EMAS

Richard Starkey

This chapter provides details on the two international environmental management system standards:

- ISO 14001: Environmental management systems – Specification with guidance for use;
- ISO 14004: Environmental management systems – General guidelines on principles, systems and supporting techniques;

and on:

- EMAS – the European Community's eco-management and auditing scheme.

The first part of this chapter provides a brief introduction to environmental management systems and to the issue of standardization. This is followed by a brief history of environmental management system standardization and a discussion of ISO 14001, ISO 14004 and EMAS. The chapter concludes by looking at the reasons an organization might consider developing an environmental management system and at how many organizations have already done so.

WHAT IS AN ENVIRONMENTAL MANAGEMENT SYSTEM?

Before looking in detail at ISO 14001, ISO 14004 and EMAS, it will be helpful to establish what is meant by the term 'environmental management system'. Obviously an environmental management system is a kind of system relating to environmental management. So what is a system? And what is environmental management? A system can be thought of as 'a number of interrelated elements functioning together to achieve a clearly defined objective'. And environmental management can be thought of as 'the management of those activities, products and services of an organization which have (or can have) an impact on the environment'.

Hence we can say that an environmental management system consists of 'a number of interrelated elements that function together to achieve the objective of effectively and efficiently managing those activities, products and services of an organization which have (or can have) an impact on the environment'.

So what are the elements that make up an environmental management system? Many larger companies have had environmental management systems in place for a number of years. As each company has designed its system to meet its own particular needs, these systems have differed widely, ie they don't all contain the same elements. Since 1990 there have been efforts at the national, European Union and international level to standardize environmental management systems by setting out the various elements which such a system should contain.

Standards and Regulations: Who Produces Them and What Are They?

Standards are prepared by national, regional and international standards bodies. In the UK, standards are prepared by the British Standards Institution (BSI) – the world's first national standards body. Most European standards are produced by the European Committee for Standardization (CEN), with electrotechnical standards produced by the European Committee for Electrotechnical Standardization (CENELEC) and telecommunications standards produced by the European Telecommunications Standards Institute (ETSI). Most international standards are produced by the International Organization for Standardization (ISO), founded in 1947 and based in Geneva, Switzerland. ISO has a membership of approximately 130 standards bodies and has published in excess of 11,000 standards. International electrotechnical and telecommunications standards are prepared by the International Electrotechnical Commission (IEC) and the International Telecommunications Union (ITU) respectively.

As has been mentioned, the aim of the ISO standards and EMAS is standardization in the field of environmental management systems. Standardization is defined by ISO/IEC (1996) as the:

> *activity of establishing, with regard to actual or potential problems, provisions for common and repeated use, aimed at the achievement of the optimum degree of order in a given context.*

> *Notes*
> *1. In particular the activity consists of the process of formulating, issuing and implementing standards.*
> *2. Important benefits of standardization are improvement of the*

> *suitability of products, processes and services for their intended purposes, prevention of barriers to trade and facilitation of technological cooperation.*

The ISO definition of standardization makes clear that issuing standards is the primary means by which standardization is achieved. ISO/IEC (1996) defines a standard as a:

> *document, established by consensus and approved by a recognized body, that provides, for common and repeated use, rules, guidelines or characteristics for activities or their results, aimed at the achievement of the optimum degree of order in a given context.*

ISO 14001 is a specification standard whereas ISO 14004 is a guidance standard. According to British Standard BS 0 (BSI 1997), a specification is a detailed set of requirements to be satisfied by a product, material, process or system, indicating the procedures for checking conformity to these requirements. Specifications are written in such a way as to enable conformity to be verified by first party (supplier), second party (purchaser) or independent third party certifier. As its name suggests, a guidance document provides guidance rather than a set of verifiable requirements and is designed as an internal management tool.

Whereas ISO 14001 and ISO 14004 are standards, EMAS is a regulation. A regulation is one of the legislative instruments of the European Union. Article 189 of the Treaty of Rome (European Community, 1980) states that:

> *A regulation shall have general application. It shall be binding in its entirety and directly applicable in all Member States.*

This contrasts with a directive, which the Treaty states:

> *shall be binding, as to the result to be achieved, upon each Member State to which it is addressed, but shall leave to the national authorities the choice of form and method.*

The following passage from Hillary (1993) illustrates the reason that EMAS was issued as a regulation:

> *The text of the Regulation applies across the 12 Member States of the EC which means that a company applying the scheme in the UK will work to the same text as a company applying the scheme in Italy or Germany. Regulation status has thus created 'a level playing field'. No distortion or unfair competitive advantage can be achieved by companies working to different versions of the scheme, which could have been the case if the scheme had been a directive and each Member State had interpreted it into national law in a different way.*

A BRIEF HISTORY OF ENVIRONMENTAL MANAGEMENT SYSTEM STANDARDIZATION

In 1990, BSI was asked to consider the question of third party assessment of environmental performance. BSI had tackled the issue of quality using a systems approach producing the quality system standard BS 5750 (subsequently replaced by the ISO 9000 series of standards) and was of the opinion that environmental performance within organizations could be tackled using a similar approach, ie by the introduction of an environmental management system standard. BSI did some preliminary work on what it thought such a standard might look like and circulated its draft for comment. The business community showed interest in the idea of such a standard but was keen that it should be compatible with the quality management standard BS 5750. As a lot of time, money and effort had been spent putting quality management systems into place there was little enthusiasm for having to implement a new and separate set of procedures for environmental management.

Given the positive response from the business community, BSI decided to proceed with the development of an environmental management standard. The standard – BS 7750 – was published in March 1992 and was the world's first environmental management system standard. The standard was subjected to a 2-year pilot implementation programme involving almost 500 participants, including 230 implementing organizations, and was modified on the basis of the feedback obtained from the programme. The modified standard was published in January 1994.

At the same time that BSI began work on BS 7750, the European Commission was setting out its proposal for an eco-audit scheme. This proposal appeared in a discussion paper issued by the Commission in December 1990 and it was from this proposal that EMAS eventually emerged. The eco-audit scheme proposed in this paper was a mandatory scheme whereby companies from over 50 industrial sectors would be required to undertake annual environmental audits and publish a detailed environmental statement based on the audit results. However, by the time the scheme was published as a Commission proposal in the CEC's *Official Journal of the European Communities*, significant lobbying by industry, which claimed that the costs imposed by the scheme would make it uncompetitive with companies outside the Community, had resulted in it being changed from one requiring mandatory participation to one which industry would implement voluntarily. In addition, the requirement for annual auditing was changed to a requirement that 'the audit will be executed, or the audit cycle will be completed, as appropriate, at intervals no longer than 3 years' (CEC, 1993).

The Commission rewrote its proposal after taking into account the opinions of the European Parliament and Economic and Social Committee and, after further negotiation between the Member States, the scheme, now known as the eco-management and audit scheme (EMAS) was adopted by the Council of Ministers on June 29 1993. Article 21 of the Regulation states that it shall enter into force on the third day following its publication in the *Official Journal* (July 13 1993) and shall apply 21 months after publication. Hence the scheme became open to company participation in April 1995.

The environmental management system requirements in EMAS are very similar to those that were in BS 7750, reflecting the influence that the standard exerted on the drafting of EMAS. (This influence is hardly surprising as BS 7750 (1992 version) was the only environmental management system standard in existence when EMAS was being drafted.) In turn the 1994 version of BS 7750 was revised to make it compatible with EMAS (which as mentioned above was published in 1993).

1990 was also the year that activity relating to environmental management system standardization began on the international scene. Discussions in 1990 between ISO and the Business Council for Sustainable Development (BCSD) about the need for standardization in the field of environmental management led, in 1991, to the setting up of the Strategic Advisory Group on the Environment (SAGE), a joint ISO/IEC body composed of experts in this field. As a result of discussions that took place within SAGE, an ISO Technical Committee (TC 207) was set up, its scope being 'standardization in the field of environmental management tools and systems'. TC 207 first met in July 1993 and an initial work programme covering 25 items was established. It was agreed to set up subcommittees (SCs) to deal with:

- environmental management systems – SC 1;
- environmental auditing – SC 2;
- environmental labelling – SC 3;
- environmental performance evaluation – SC 4;
- life cycle assessment – SC 5; and
- terms and definitions – SC 6,

and to set up a working group to deal with environmental aspects in product standards – WG 1. Table 4.1 shows the items from the work programme that have been completed or are currently under preparation as of January 1998. For up-to-date news on standard preparation visit the TC 207 website at *http://www.iso.ch/meme/TC207.html.*

The work programme of SC 1 consisted of three items:

1. environmental management systems – specification with guidance for use (ISO 14001);
2. environmental management systems – general guidelines on principles and their application (ISO 14004); and
3. environmental management systems – guidelines on special considerations affecting small and medium sized organizations.

SC 1 divided itself into two working groups with WG 1 developing ISO 14001 and WG 2 developing ISO 14004. Both standards were published in October 1996, a development time of a little under three years, much less time than it normally takes to develop an international standard. One of the reasons that WG 1 was able to make such rapid progress was that it was able to use BS 7750 as a starting point for its discussions. The content of ISO 14001 is very similar to that of BS 7750, illustrating its influence on the development of the international standard. In 1996, SC 1 set up a task force to look at the experience of SMEs in implementing ISO 14001 and 14004 and is due to issue a report on its findings in mid-1998.

Table 4.1 The development status of the ISO 14000 series of standards

ISO International Standards	
ISO Guide 64:1997	Guide for the inclusion of environmental aspects in product standards
ISO 14001:1996	Environmental management systems – Specification with guidance for use
ISO 14004:1996	Environmental management systems – General guidelines on principles, systems and supporting techniques
ISO 14010:1996	Guidelines for environmental auditing – General principles
ISO 14011:1996	Guidelines for environmental auditing – Audit procedures: Auditing of environmental management systems
ISO 14012:1996	Guidelines for environmental auditing – Qualification criteria for environmental auditors
ISO 14040:1997	Environmental management – Life cycle assessment: Principles and framework
Draft International Standards (DIS)	
ISO/DIS 14020	Environmental labels and declarations – General principles
ISO/DIS 14021	Environmental labels and declarations – Self declaration environmental claims: Guidelines and definition and usage of terms
ISO/DIS 14024	Environmental labels and declarations – Type 1 environmental labelling: Guiding principles and procedures
ISO/DIS 14041	Environmental management – Life cycle assessment: Goal and scope definition and inventory analysis
ISO/DIS 14050	Environmental management – Vocabulary
Committee Drafts (CD)	
ISO/CD 14031	Environmental performance evaluation – Guidelines
ISO/CD 14042	Environmental management – Life cycle assessment: Life cycle impact assessment
ISO/CD 14043	Environmental management – Life cycle assessment: Life cycle interpretation
Working Drafts (WD)	
ISO/WD 14061	Guidance to assist forestry organizations in the use of ISO 14001 and ISO 14004 (future type 3 technical report)
New Proposals (NP)	
ISO/NP 14049	Environmental management – Life cycle assessment: Examples for the application of ISO 14041 (future type 3 technical report)

Source: ISO, 1998

In October 1994 the European Commission mandated CEN to produce, within 18 months, a European environmental management system standard, the requirements of which would be consistent with the environmental management system requirements of EMAS. The Commission issued this mandate as it realized that some companies would prefer to meet the environmental management system requirements of EMAS by becoming certified to an equivalent standard rather than meeting the requirements of EMAS directly.

The 1991 Agreement on Technical Cooperation between ISO and CEN (commonly known as the Vienna Agreement) states that:

> *Whenever the need to undertake new work...is identified in CEN, it is in accordance with its general policy to determine whether it is possible to give preference to the undertaking and completion of this work in time within ISO. (ISO/CEN, 1991, p3)*

CEN concluded that it could fulfil its mandate by adopting ISO 14001 as a European standard, which it did at the end of September 1996. When a European standard is issued, equivalent national standards must be withdrawn within six months of its issue date. Therefore BS 7750 and the other national EMS standards within Europe, ie:

- the Irish standard I.S. 310;
- the French standard X30-200; and
- the Spanish standard UNE 77-801(2)

were all withdrawn by March 1997.

ISO 14001

ISO 14001: Some Questions Answered

What is in ISO 14001?

The content of ISO 14001 is as follows:

- Introduction
- Clause 1: Scope
- Clause 2: Normative references
- Clause 3: Definitions
- Clause 4: Environmental management system requirements
- Annex A: Guidance on the use of the specification
- Annex B: Links between ISO 14001 and ISO 9001
- Annex C: Bibliography

What is the scope of ISO 14001?

According to Clause 1, ISO 14001:

specifies requirements for an environmental management system, to enable an organization to formulate a policy and objectives taking into account legislative requirements and information about significant environmental impacts.

To which organizations is the standard applicable?

ISO 14001 states in its introduction that 'it has been written to be applicable to all types and sizes of organizations and to accommodate diverse geographical, cultural and social conditions'.

In Clause 3, an organization is defined as:

company, corporation, firm, enterprise, authority or institution, or part or combination thereof, whether incorporated or not, public or private, that has its own functions and administration.

Why implement the standard?

This question is addressed in the introduction which states:

Organizations of all kinds are increasingly concerned to achieve and demonstrate sound environmental performance by controlling the impact of their activities, products or services on the environment, taking into account their environmental policy and objectives. They do so in the context of increasingly stringent legislation, the development of economic policies and other measures to foster environmental protection, and a general growth of concern from interested parties about environmental matters including sustainable development.

Many organizations have undertaken environmental 'reviews' or 'audits' to assess their environmental performance. On their own, however, these 'reviews' and 'audits' may not be sufficient to provide an organization with the assurance that its performance not only meets, but will continue to meet, its legal and policy requirements. To be effective, they need to be conducted within a structured management system and integrated with overall management activity.

What is the link between ISO 14001 and the ISO 9000 series?

The introduction to ISO 14001 states that it:

shares common management system principles with the ISO 9000 series of quality system standards. Organizations may elect to use an existing management system consistent with the ISO 9000 series as a basis for its environmental management system. The links between the subclauses of ISO 14001 and ISO 9001 are set out in two tables in Annex B.

Does ISO 14001 contain environmental performance requirements?

The introduction to ISO 14001 clearly states that it:

does not establish absolute requirements for environmental performance beyond commitment, in the policy, to compliance with applicable legislation and regulation and to continual improvement. Thus two organizations carrying out similar activities but having different environmental performance may both comply with its requirements.

ISO 14001 is a Five Step Process

The elements of ISO 14001 are organized around five steps (see Figure 4.1):

1. environmental policy;
2. planning;
3. implementation and operation;
4. checking and corrective action; and
5. management review.

Each step is briefly described below.

Environmental policy

An organization drafts a policy setting out its intentions in relation to the environment. A policy must contain commitments to:

- continual improvement;
- prevention of pollution; and
- complying with relevant environmental legislation and other relevant requirements.

ISO 14001 defines 'continual improvement' as:

> *the process of enhancing the environmental management system in order to achieve improvements in environmental performance in line with the organization's environmental policy.*

'Prevention of pollution' is defined as:

> *use of processes, practices, materials or products that avoid, reduce or control pollution, which may include recycling, treatment, process changes, control mechanisms, efficient use of resources and material substitution.*

Planning

The organization must then set itself objectives and targets relating to its three policy commitments and devise a plan to meet these objectives and targets.

Implementation and operation

Having devised its plan, the organization must then put in place the various elements necessary for its successful implementation and operation.

Checking and corrective action

Having implemented its plan, the organization must then check to see whether it has been successful in meeting its objectives and targets. If any have not been met, then corrective action must be taken. The entire management system must be periodically audited to see that it meets the requirements of the standard.

Management review

Management must periodically review the system to ensure its continuing effectiveness and suitability. Changes are made to the system as and when necessary.

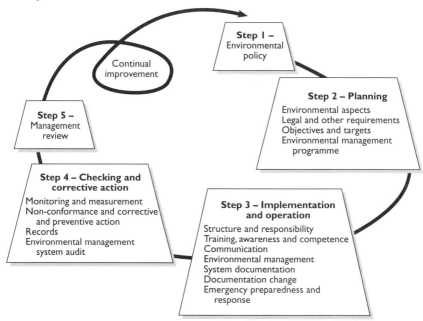

Figure 4.1 The five steps and the elements of ISO 14001

The Elements of ISO 14001

The various elements within each of the five steps are described below.

Environmental policy (Step 1)

As mentioned above, an organization's environmental policy must contain commitments to continual improvement, prevention of pollution and to complying with relevant environmental legislation. In addition the policy must:

- provide a framework for setting objectives and targets;
- be communicated to all employees; and
- be publicly available.

Planning (Step 2)

Environmental aspects

The first thing the organization must do is to identify what ISO 14001 refers to as 'environmental aspects'. These are defined as:

> *elements of an organization's activities, products or services which can interact with the environment.*

How does an organization go about doing this? ISO 14001 gives guidance on this matter in Annex A, stating that an organization should identify its environmental aspects by means of an environmental review (see Box 4.1). This review is the foundation upon which the rest of the management system

---

BOX 4.1 EXTRACT FROM ISO 14001 ANNEX A DESCRIBING AN ENVIRONMENTAL REVIEW

The review should cover 4 key areas:

a) legislative requirements;
b) an identification of significant environmental aspects;
c) an examination of all existing environmental management practices and procedures; and
d) an evaluation of feedback from the investigation of previous incidents.

In all cases, consideration should be given to normal and abnormal operations within the organization, and to potential emergency conditions.

A suitable approach to the review may include checklists, interviews, direct inspection and measurement, results of previous audits or other reviews depending on the nature of the activity.

The process to identify the significant environmental aspects associated with the activities at operating units should, where relevant, consider:

a) emissions to air;
b) releases to water;
c) waste management;
d) contamination of land;
e) impact of communities; and
f) use of raw materials and natural resources.

The process should consider normal operating conditions, shut-down and start-up conditions, as well as the realistic potential significant impacts associated with reasonably foreseeable or emergency situations.

Source: ISO, 1996a, p 7

---

is built and should be conducted as thoroughly as possible. Once its environmental aspects have been identified, the organization must establish which of them are significant, ie which of them have a significant impact on the environment.

Legal and other requirements

Given that the organization has made a commitment in its policy to comply with legal and other requirements, the organization must establish what these actually are. This is done during the environmental review (see Box 4.1).

Objectives and targets

In order to meet its commitment to legal compliance an organization must set itself the objective of identifying and correcting any non-compliance. In order to meet its policy commitment to continual improvement and prevention of pollution, the organization must set objectives and targets in relation to its significant environmental aspects.

Environmental management programme

Having set its objectives and targets the organization must now devise a programme for achieving them. The programme must state the time-frame in which the objectives and targets are to be achieved and identify the people responsible for achieving them.

Implementation and operation (Step 3)

The following elements are necessary to successfully implement and operate the plan (ie Step 2).

Structure and responsibility

The role, responsibility and authority of everyone involved with the EMS must be defined. Management must provide the resources necessary for the implementation of the EMS (which include human resources, technology and financial resources). The organization's management must appoint someone who is ultimately responsible for ensuring that the EMS is established, implemented and maintained in accordance with the requirements of ISO 14001.

Training, awareness and competence

All staff whose work may create a significant impact on the environment must receive the appropriate training. The organization must make them aware of:

- the importance of conformance with the requirements of the EMS;
- the significant environmental impacts of their work activities and the environmental benefits of improved personal performance; and
- their roles and responsibilities in the successful functioning of the EMS.

Staff performing tasks which can cause significant environmental impacts must be deemed competent to do so. (Competence is assessed on the basis of their education, training and/or experience.)

Communication

The organization must establish and maintain suitable procedures for communication between various parts of the organization regarding the EMS. It must also make provisions for receiving and responding to relevant communications about its EMS from external parties.

Environmental management system documentation

The organization must establish and maintain information – in paper or electronic form – to describe the elements of the management system and their interaction, and provide direction to related documentation.

Document control

The organization must establish procedures for controlling all the documents required by ISO 14001 to ensure, for instance, that they can be located and that they are periodically reviewed, revised as necessary and approved by authorized personnel.

Operational control

The organization is required to identify those of its activities that are associated with the significant environmental aspects that are covered in its objectives and targets. The organization then needs to produce documented operating procedures for these activities to cover situations where, if no procedures existed, the objectives and targets might not be met.

The organization must also establish procedures relating to the significant aspects of goods and services used by the organization. All relevant procedures must be communicated to suppliers and contractors.

Emergency preparedness and response

The organization must establish and maintain procedures:

- to identify potential accident and emergency situations;
- to respond to these situations should they arise; and
- for preventing and mitigating the environmental impacts that may be associated with them.

The organization must periodically test these procedures where practicable and review and revise them where necessary – particularly after the occurrence of accidents or emergency situations.

Checking and corrective action (Step 4)

Monitoring and measurement

The organization must establish and maintain documented procedures to monitor and measure on a regular basis those areas covered by the objectives and targets in order to see if the objectives and targets have been met. The organization must also establish and maintain a documented procedure for periodically evaluating compliance with relevant environmental legislation and regulations.

Non-conformance and corrective and preventive action

The organization must establish and maintain procedures for defining responsibility and authority for:

- investigating and handling instances of non-conformance with the
  targets and objectives it has set for itself;
- taking action to mitigate any impacts caused; and
- for initiating and completing corrective and preventive action.

The organization must implement and record any changes it makes to its
procedures as a result of any corrective and preventive action it undertakes.

Records

The organization must establish and maintain procedures for the identification, maintenance and disposal of its environmental records. These records
must include training records and the results of audits and management
reviews (see below).

Environmental management system audit

The organization is required to establish and maintain a programme and
procedures for periodic environmental management system audits to be
carried out. The audit seeks to determine whether or not the EMS conforms
with the requirements of the ISO 14001, and has been properly implemented
and maintained. The audit programme and procedures should cover:

- the activities and areas to be considered in audits;
- the frequency of audits;
- the responsibilities associated with managing and conducting audits;
- the communication of audit results;
- auditor competence; and
- how audits will be conducted.

Management review (Step 5)

The organization's management must periodically review the environmental
management system to ensure it continues to meet the needs of the organization. The review must address the possible need for changes to the
organization's policy, objectives and other elements of the environmental
management system in light of:

- the audit results;
- changing circumstances; and
- the organization's commitment to continual improvement.

The commitment to continual improvement and prevention of pollution will
mean that new objectives and targets will have to be set; and changing
circumstances, for instance the introduction of new products and processes,
will mean that new procedures need to be written and new roles and responsibilities designated.

ISO 14001: Self-declaration and Certification

ISO 14001 is a specification standard, ie it consists of a set of requirements for establishing and maintaining an environmental management system. By complying with these requirements an organization can demonstrate to the outside world that it has an appropriate and effective management system in place. One way in which an organization can demonstrate that it has met the requirements of the standard is by 'self-declaration'. This means that the organization checks its own compliance with the requirements. However an organization may feel that it carries more weight with the outside world if its compliance with the requirements of ISO 14001 is checked by an independent third party. This third party checking is known as 'certification'.

If an organization decides that it wants to become certified to ISO 14001, how can it be sure it is employing the services of a competent certifier? In order to be sure, the organization should ensure that the certifier is accredited. Each Member State within the EU has an accreditation body that can accredit certifiers. Accreditation is the procedure by which an accreditation body gives formal recognition that a certifier is competent to carry out certification activities. (To be deemed competent, a certifier has to comply with specific criteria laid down by the accreditation body.) The accreditation system for environmental management systems is set out in Figure 4.2.

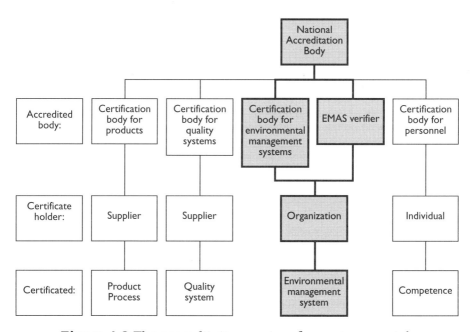

Figure 4.2 The accreditation system for environmental management systems

The accreditation body in the UK is UKAS, the United Kingdom Accreditation Service. UKAS is recognized by the UK government as the national body for providing national accreditation of certification bodies and of measurement and sampling. UKAS was formed in 1995 by a merger between the National Accreditation Council of Certification Bodies (NACCB) and the national Measurement Accreditation Service (NAMAS). The criteria used by UKAS to accredit certification bodies are set out in European Accreditation of Certification (EAC) Guide 5. The Guide (EAC, 1996) states that:

> *EAC brings together the national accreditation systems of seventeen European countries. It has already developed Guidelines for the accreditation of certification in the quality system, product and personnel fields. Some of its members have entered into a Multilateral Recognition Agreement under which they recognize the equivalence of each other's systems and the certificates of conformity issued by their accreditation certification bodies...*
>
> *With the development of the international standard for EMS, ISO 14001, underway, fifteen EAC members have been working on a common approach to the accreditation for certification in this field. Several of the members have based their input on the experience of accrediting certification to national EMS standards, such as BS 7750. The present Guidelines are the result of this work. Once EAC members have experience in their use, it is likely that they will enter into a Multilateral Recognition Agreement to recognize each other's work, based on common application of the Guidelines. Such an Agreement will involve Peer Review between the members to confirm that they are all implementing the Guidelines consistently. In time, this Agreement is likely to be managed as part of an overall Agreement between EAC members.*

ISO 14004

As mentioned above ISO 14004 is a guidance standard on environmental management systems. The standard sets out a five-step EMS model very similar to that in ISO 14001 and gives guidance on all the elements of the ISO 14001 system and also additional EMS topics. The guidance in ISO 14004 includes self-assessment questions on each EMS element together with a series of practical help sections based on industry experience of environmental management.

ISO 14004 provides useful guidance for an organization wishing to establish an EMS that conforms with the requirements of ISO 14001. It will also be useful for organizations who are interested in establishing an EMS but are not yet ready to, or do not wish to, establish an ISO 14001 system. (Note: ISO 14004 cannot be used for certification purposes as it contains guidance and not a set of requirements against which conformity can be assessed.)

THE ECO-MANAGEMENT AND AUDIT SCHEME (EMAS)

The contents of EMAS

EMAS consists of 21 articles and 5 annexes. These are listed and briefly described in Tables 4.2 and 4.3 below.

Article 1 of the Regulation states that EMAS is a 'Community scheme allowing voluntary participation by companies performing industrial activities ... established for the evaluation and improvement of the environmental performance of industrial activities and the provision of relevant information to the public ... The objective of the scheme shall be to promote continuous improvements in the environmental performance of industrial activities'.

Note: Whereas ISO 14001 can be used by all organizations, EMAS is open only to 'companies performing industrial activities'. 'Company' and 'industrial activity' are both defined in Article 2. A company is:

> *'the organization which has overall management control over activities at a given site'.*

An industrial activity is:

> *'any activity listed under sections C and D of the classification of economic activities in the European Community (NACE rev. 1) as established by Council Regulation (EEC) No 3037/90 with the addition of electricity, gas, steam and hot water production and the recycling, treatment, destruction or disposal of solid or liquid waste'.*

Article 3 of EMAS states that the scheme is open to companies operating on a site or sites where industrial activity is performed. A site is defined in Article 2 as:

> *'all land on which the industrial activities under the control of a company at a given location are carried out, including any connected or associated storage of raw materials, by-products, intermediate products, end products and waste material, and any equipment and infrastructure involved in the activities, whether or not fixed'.*

Note: Whereas a whole organization can be certified to ISO 14001, only sites can be registered under EMAS.

Article 3 outlines the entire EMAS process, listing the requirements that a company must meet in order for a site to become registered. A company must:

1 adopt a company environmental policy which must include 'commitments aimed at the reasonable continuous improvement of environmental performance';

Table 4.2 Eco-management and audit scheme articles (Hillary, 1993)

Article number	*Title and description of article*
Article 1	*The Eco-management and audit scheme and its objectives* Defines the scheme's aims and relationship with existing environmental laws
Article 2	*Definitions* Defines the 15 terms used in the Regulation, eg site, environmental audit, industrial activity and accredited environmental verifier
Article 3	*Participation in the scheme* Explains the elements a site must undertake to become registered on the scheme
Article 4	*Auditing and validation* Outlines who may conduct a site's internal environmental audit, how and at what frequency, and details accredited environmental verifiers' activities
Article 5	*Environmental statement* Lists the information required in a statement and explains simplified annual statements
Article 6	*Accreditation and supervision of environmental verifiers* Defines accreditation systems for environmental verifiers which Member States are required to establish
Article 7	*List of accredited environmental verifiers* Define frequency of lists and where they should be published
Article 8	*Registration of sites* Explains site registration and de-registration by the competent body
Article 9	*Publication of the list of registered sites* Defines how lists of registered sites should be published in the EC's Official Journal
Article 10	*Statement of participation* Defines where sites may use the statement
Article 11	*Costs and fees* Allows Member States to set up charges
Article 12	*Relationship with national, European and international standards* Explains under what conditions standards may be used in conjunction with the scheme
Article 13	*Promotion of companies' participation, in particular of small and medium-sized enterprises* States how Member States may promote company involvement in the scheme
Article 14	*Inclusion of other sectors* Defines under what conditions other sectors may be included
Article 15	*Information* Defines how Member States may promote and publicize the scheme

Table 4.2 *continued*

Article number	Title and description of article
Article 16	*Infringements* Gives Member States powers to act in cases of non-compliance with the Regulation
Article 17	*Annexes* States that the Annexes may be adapted before the Regulation's review date
Article 18	*Competent bodies* Defines and ensures the neutrality of the competent body
Article 19	*Committee* Sets up the structure and voting procedure for the Committee
Article 20	*Revision* Sets the time limit for the Commission review of the entire Regulation
Article 21	*Entry into force* Gives the dates when the Regulation enters into force and when it will apply in the Member States

2 conduct an environmental review of the site seeking registration;
3 introduce, in the light of the results from the review, an environmental management system applicable to all activities at the site;
4 carry out or arrange for a third party to carry out an environmental audit of the site;
5 set objectives aimed at continuous improvement of environmental performance in the light of the audit findings;
6 prepare an environmental statement specific to each site audited;
7 have the environmental policy, programme, management system, review or audit procedure and environmental statement(s) independently examined to verify that they meet the requirements of the regulation; and
8 send the validated statement to the competent body of the Member State where the site is located. (Article 18 requires each Member State to designate a 'competent body responsible for carrying out the tasks provided for in this Regulation'.) Once the competent body is satisfied that the site meets all the requirements of the regulation it will register the site. After registration the company must disseminate its environmental statement as appropriate to the public of the state where the site is located.

Note: Like ISO 14001, EMAS specifies requirements for an environmental management system but, as can be seen from the above, it also requires the publication of an environmental statement and independent verification of compliance with the requirements of the regulation. These three elements are examined in more detail below.

Tabel 4.3 Eco-management and audit scheme annexes (Hillary, 1993)

Annex number	Description of annex
Annex I	Details the requirements for a company's environmental policy and a site's environmental objectives and programmes, environmental management systems similar to BS 7750 and good management practices
Annex II	Details the requirements concerning site environmental auditing, its methodology, coverage and frequency
Annex III	Details the accreditation criteria for environmental verifiers and their functions and actions during verification
Annex IV	Shows four examples of the statement of participation with its graphic symbol which may be used to advertize participation in the scheme
Annex V	Lists the information that needs to be supplied to the competent body in an application for registration on the scheme

Environmental management system

The term 'environmental management system' is used somewhat ambiguously in the regulation. As already mentioned, Article 3 requires the formulation of an environmental policy followed by an environmental review, the introduction of an environmental programme and management system and then an environmental audit. Here an environmental management system is referred to as one of a number of components that make up the overall environmental management framework. However in Annex 1 the term is used to describe all aspects of environmental management, including 'the establishment and periodical review, and revision as appropriate of the company's environmental policy, objectives and programmes...'. In other words, the environmental management system is the overall environmental management framework. In this chapter the term is used in this latter sense.

The environmental management system requirements of 14001 and EMAS are very similar. Table 4.4 lists the subclauses of ISO 14001 and the sections of EMAS that cover the various management system elements. The requirements of ISO 14001 have been recognized under EMAS as corresponding to certain of the management system requirements of EMAS.

Recognition of ISO 14001 under EMAS

Article 12 of EMAS states:

> *1. Companies implementing national, European or international standards for environmental management systems and audits and certified, according to appropriate certification procedures, shall be considered as meeting the corresponding requirements of this Regulation provided that:*
> *(a) the standards and procedures are recognized by the Commission...*

Table 4.4 ISO 14001 subclauses and part of EMAS covering
various EMS elements

System Element	ISO 14001	EMAS
Environmental management system	4.1	Annex 1 part B
Preparatory environmental review	Annex A3.1 – guidance only	Article 3 paragraph b Annex I part C
Environmental policy	4.2	Annex I part A and D
Environmental aspects/effects	4.3.1/4.3.2	Annex I part B3 part D2/3
Objectives and targets	4.3.3	Annex I part A4
Environmental management programme	4.3.4	Annex I part A5
Organization and personnel	4.4.1/4.4.2/4.4.3	Annex I part B2 part D11
Manual and documentation	4.4.4/4.4.5	Annex I part B5
Operational control and emergency preparedness	4.4.6/4.4.7	Annex I part B4 part D6/7/8
Monitoring and corrective action	4.5.1/4.5.2	Annex I part B4
Records	4.5.3	Annex I part B5
EMS audits	4.5.4	Annex I part B6 Annex BII
Management reviews	4.6	Annex I part B1
Environmental statement	Not applicable	Article 5

Source: DNV, 1997

> *(b) the certification is undertaken by a body whose accreditation is recognized in the Member State where the site is located.*

On 16th April 1997 the European Commission (CEC, 1997a) recognized the requirements of ISO 14001 as corresponding to certain of the environmental management system requirements of EMAS. There are other management system requirements in EMAS for which there is no corresponding requirement in ISO 14001. Therefore if a company with an ISO 14001-certified EMS wishes to register a site or sites under EMAS there are certain additional management system requirements that need to be met. Guidance on the changes that need to be made to an ISO 14001 system to register it under EMAS has been published by CEN (CEN, 1997).

In another Decision issued on the same date (CEC, 1997b) the Commission recognized the EAC guidelines for the accreditation of certification bodies for environmental management systems (EAC Guide 5) as constituting appropriate certification procedures under Article 12 of EMAS.

Environmental statements

Article 5 requires companies to prepare an environmental statement following the initial environmental review and following the completion of each subsequent audit or audit cycle for every site participating in the scheme.

The statement must be designed for the public and written in a concise, comprehensible form. Technical material may be amended.

> *The environmental statement shall include, in particular, the following:*
> a) *a description of the company's activities at the site considered;*
> b) *an assessment of all the significant environmental issues of relevance to the activities concerned;*
> c) *a summary of the figures on pollutant emissions, waste generation, consumption of raw materials, energy and water, noise and other significant environmental aspects, as appropriate;*
> d) *other factors regarding environmental performance;*
> e) *a presentation of the company's environmental policy, programme and management system implemented at the site considered;*
> f) *the deadline set for submission of the next statement;*
> g) *the name of the accredited environmental verifier.*

The environmental statement must also draw attention to significant changes since the previous statement.

A simplified environmental statement must be prepared annually in intervening years, based as a minimum on the requirements set out in c) above and drawing attention where appropriate to significant changes since the previous statement. These simplified statements require validation only at the end of the audit or audit cycle.

Verification of compliance with EMAS requirements and accreditation of verifiers

Article 4 of EMAS states that:

> 'the environmental policies, programmes, management systems, reviews or audit procedures and the environmental statements shall be examined to verify that they meet the requirements of this Regulation, and the environmental statements shall be validated, by the independent accredited environmental verifier, on the basis of Annex III'.

Annex III lays out the requirements concerning the accreditation of verifiers and the function of the verifier.

Article 6 requires Member States, in accordance with the requirements of Annex III, to 'establish a system for the accreditation of independent verifiers and for the supervision of their activities'. As well as being the UK's accreditation body for ISO 14001 certifiers, UKAS is also the UK accreditation body for EMAS verifiers. UKAS use EAC Guide 5 plus an EMAS supplement (UKAS, 1996) as accreditation criteria as together these cover in detail the general principles set out in Annex III of EMAS.

Differences between ISO 14001 and EMAS

The main differences between ISO 14001 and EMAS are set out below.

- ISO 14001 is applicable worldwide, whereas only EU Member States can participate in EMAS.
- ISO 14001 is a standard whereas EMAS is a regulation.
- A whole company, a specific site or a specific activity can be certified to ISO, whereas only individual sites can be registered under EMAS.
- ISO 14001 is applicable to all organizations, whereas only companies performing industrial activities specified in the EMAS regulation can participate in EMAS.
- EMAS contains a requirement for an initial environmental review whereas there is no such requirement in ISO 14001 (guidance on conducting such a review is provided in Annex A).
- ISO 14001 only contains requirements for an environmental management system, whereas EMAS:
    - contains requirement for an environmental management system;
    - requires a firm to produce an environmental statement; and
    - requires that a firm's EMS and statement be independently verified.

EMAS Revision

Article 20 of EMAS states that:

> *Not more than five years after the entry into force of this Regulation, the Commission shall review the scheme in the light of the experience gained during its operation and shall, if necessary, propose to the Council the appropriate amendments, particularly concerning the scope of the scheme and the possible introduction of a logo.*

The Commission is currently involved in drafting a revision of EMAS. This draft will be discussed by the European Parliament and the Council of Ministers and EMAS 2 is expected to emerge in the year 2000. It is expected that ISO 14001 will constitute the environmental management system requirements of EMAS 2, with additional requirements in place regarding environmental performance, legal compliance and communicating with stakeholders. An EMAS logo is being proposed which companies can use when making claims about their activities, products and services provided that these claims are covered in the environmental statement and have been validated by the verifier.

REASONS FOR ESTABLISHING AN ENVIRONMENTAL MANAGEMENT SYSTEM

ISO 14001 and EMAS set out the elements that any viable environmental management system needs to contain. By becoming certified to ISO 14001/verified to EMAS, a company is committing itself to putting these elements in place and to being periodically audited by a competent third party to check that each element is properly in place. Obviously there are costs involved in setting up such a system and these include:

- staff time spent establishing and maintaining the system;
- payment of consultants, if used to help establish the system; and
- payment of ISO 14001 certifier/EMAS verifier.

A firm should consider establishing an environmental management system if it believes that the benefits of doing so will outweigh the costs. Some of the benefits that can arise from establishing an EMS are set out below (Starkey, forthcoming).

A Cost Effective Approach

An EMS takes a systematic approach to environmental management. The environmental review highlights all the areas of the firm where improvement in performance is possible and a firm can then assess which of these are likely to be cost effective. The firm can then set targets that benefit both itself and the environment. A number of companies have made substantial cost savings by developing an environmental management system.

Targets Not Just Set But Met

An EMS not only requires firms to set themselves targets but ensures that these targets are met. A firm must devise a management programme for achieving its targets, ensure that the resources are available for it to be carried out, monitor its environmental performance to check it has met its targets and take corrective action if it finds it has not.

Procedures in Place to Ensure Legislative Compliance

As well as bringing about a continual improvement in environmental performance, an EMS enables a firm to ensure it is complying with relevant legislation and regulations. The environmental review identifies all the legislation and regulations with which the firm should be complying and the firm must then establish procedures for checking compliance and for taking corrective action should it discover instances of non-compliance.

CASE STUDY 1: VAUXHALL MOTORS (BSI, 1998)

Having invested enormously in technical development to minimise the environmental impacts of its products, Vauxhall Motors recognised the need for management systems in its factories to be equally focused on best environment practice. Since implementing ISO 14001 and EMAS at its Ellesmere Port factory in the UK, the company has not only reduced its environmental impacts, but also benefited from significant financial savings and a motivated workforce with a greater environmental awareness.

The 400-acre site has a workforce of about 4000. As well as manufacturing components for other GM sites in Europe, the US and South America, the factory produces engines and about 120,000 cars and vans per year for the UK and worldwide exports. Utilities usage is a large expenditure at the factory, so the company has implemented monitoring and targeting programmes as a framework for the workforce to take ownership of resource use, and then optimise it. This in turn has resulted in huge financial savings which include:

- reducing its annual electricity costs of £4 million by £240,000 or 6 per cent.
- Eliminating air leaks further reduced the annual electricity bill by £105,000.
- Reduced gas consumption of 5 per cent on an annual bill of £530,000.
- The payback period on the investment to make this saving was approximately seven months.
- Improved water-use efficiency, resulting in annual savings of 5 per cent, with a ten month payback period on the investment to produce the savings.
- Waste minimisation and recycling produced annual savings of about £75,000.

Vauxhall Motors is registered to both EMAS and ISO 14001. Vauxhall's Ellesmere Port factory in Cheshire installed extra measuring equipment with a dramatic effect, reducing its consumption of electrical energy and water. The factory spends about £4 million per year on electricity, so Vauxhall adopted a means of sub-metering to encourage individual sections of the factory to take responsibility for their own fuel use.

The factory installed 33 meters and linked to a centralised, computerised database for energy consumption, which is updated and reviewed every 24 hours. As a result, the electricity consumption in the vehicle assembly area of the factory was reduced by 6 per cent in just six months.

The factory applied a similar strategy to water and gas, producing enormous savings in both areas. In the case of gas, Vauxhall installed meters for each piece of gas-burning equipment. Although this cost a relatively large amount for the meters, the savings of 5 per cent which they generated – through a better control of gas consumption – meant a payback for the investment in well under a year, after which the extra metering meant large net savings.

Vauxhall says that the benefits of certification were apparent from early on. According to Ken Davies, Communications Manager at Ellesmere Port, 'Managing the environmental process has been rewarded by substantial cost savings which are likely to increase in the future. There is also the added protection from the potential cost of litigation, which could arise as a result of non-compliance with regulations. These cannot be ignored.'

CASE STUDY 2: LOUDWATER (UK COMPETENT BODY FOR EMAS, 1996)

Loudwater is a printer based in Watford. Its core business is printing greeting cards and it sells more that a million cards a year. The company became certified to BS 7750 in 1995 and became registered under EMAS in 1996 – the first small company (ie less than 50 employees) in the UK to do so. Loudwater started on the EMS path out of a desire to achieve targeted efficiencies and commercial success. It was also a way of dealing with supply chain pressures. As managing partner Marc Cox says, 'The large retailers, and also the publishers, were asking more and more questions about environmental aspects of our business and we had to be prepared and ready with answers'.

Loudwater has achieved substantial cost savings as a result of implementing its environmental management system and its improved reputation has resulted in a substantial amount of new business. In fact, Loudwater's turnover has almost doubled to nearly £5 million since achieving EMAS registration. As Marc Cox says, 'We have saved in excess of £20,000 by reducing our waste, cutting down on our energy consumption and by recycling or selling our unavoidable waste. We are winning new business all the time, particularly from blue-chip companies which previously would not have considered us. The fact that we can prove our green credentials through EMAS and demonstrate our ability to work within the framework of environmental legislation in a wider Europe gives us that competitive edge'.

Table 4.5 EMAS registrations and ISO 14001 certifications within the EU

EU Country	EMAS Registration	ISO 14001 Certification
Germany	1,227	about 500
Austria	115	80
Sweden	95	191
UK	50	about 650
Denmark	54	42
Norway	38	20
Netherlands	20	about 230
France	16	91
Spain	12	61
Finland	11	90
Belgium	7	10
Ireland	4	35
Italy	3	51
Luxembourg	1	1
Portugal	0	2
Greece	0	1

Table 4.6 Non-EU certifications of ISO 14001

Country	ISO 14001 Certification	Country	ISO 14001 Certification
Japan	861	Turkey	11
Korea	200	Poland	8
Taiwan	195	Czech Republic	8
Switzerland	194	New Zealand	6
US	121	Philippines	4
Australia	80	Egypt	4
Thailand	46	Slovakia	4
Canada	45	Israel	3
China/Hong Kong	25/16	Pakistan	2
Singapore	28	Chile	2
Brazil	27	Slovenia	2
Indonesia	26	United Arab Emirates	2
South Africa	20	Croatia	1
Argentina	16	Columbia	1
Malaysia	15	Peru	1
Mexico	15	Costa Rica	1
Hungary	14	Morocco	1
India	11	Iran	1

Improved Public Image and Increased Market Opportunities

Not only do ISO 14001 and EMAS enable a firm to meet its environmental policy commitments and its objectives and targets, they also enable the firm to demonstrate sound environmental management to stakeholders. There may be considerable public relations benefits and increased market opportunities for a firm that can demonstrate to the outside world that it has a sound system of environmental management.

Viewed More Favourably by the Regulator and the Financial Sector

Having a management system can mean less supervision from environmental regulators and preferential treatment from banks and insurers. And the fact that an EMS demonstrates sound environmental management may well improve a firm's ability to attract investment.

A number of these benefits are illustrated in the above case studies of two firms, one large and one an SME, who have established an EMS.

ISO 14001 CERTIFICATIONS AND EMAS REGISTRATIONS

The number of registrations to EMAS and the number of certifications to ISO 14001 as of April 1998 is shown in Table 4.5, and the number of certifications to ISO 14001 in non-EU countries is shown in Table 4.6 (German Federal Environment Agency, 1998).

As yet, the number of ISO 14001 certifications and EMAS registrations is relatively low. However, large companies are beginning to push ISO 14001 down the supply chain. For example Rover (ENDS, 1998a) has asked all of its 700 first-tier suppliers to make a commitment to become certified to ISO 14001 or registered under EMAS and would like to see the majority certified/registered by the year 2000. In addition, Rover has obtained European funding to enable 30–40 of these suppliers to hold workshops at which each of these suppliers will invite around 100 of its own suppliers to set up an environmental management system. Other companies such as Jaguar and Shell Expro (ENDS, 1998b) are also encouraging suppliers to adopt an EMS and if this becomes a widespread trend, and having an environmental management system (like ISO 9000) becomes a prerequisite for doing business, then the number of ISO certifications and EMAS registrations can be expected to rise substantially.

REFERENCES

British Standards Institution (1997) 'BS 0 A standard for standards' British Standards Institution, London

British Standards Institution (1998) 'Facilitating Business: Case studies – Vauxhall Motors' http://www.bsi.org.uk/bsi/environ/casestud.htm, British Standards Institution, London

CEN – European Committee for Standardization (1997) 'Use of EN ISO 14001, ISO 14010, ISO 14011 and 14012 for EMAS related purposes' *CEN Report* CR 12969, European Committee for Standardization, Brussels

Commission of the European Communities (1993) 'Council Regulation (EEC) No. 1836/93 of 29 June 1993 allowing participation by companies in the industrial sector in a Community eco-management and audit scheme' *Official Journal of the European Communities*, L168/1-18, July 10 1993

Commission of the European Communities (1997a) 'Commission Decision of 16 April 1997 on the recognition of certification procedures in accordance with Article 12 of Council Regulation (EEC) No. 1836/93 of 29 June 1993 allowing participation by companies in the industrial sector in a Community eco-management and audit scheme' *Official Journal of the European Communities*, L 104/35-36, April 22 1997

Commission of the European Communities (1997b) 'Commission Decision of 16 April 1997 on the recognition of the international standard ISO 14001:1996 and the European standard EN ISO 14001:1996, establishing specification for environmental management systems in accordance with Article 12 of Council Regulation (EEC) No. 1836/93 of 29 June 1993 allowing participation by companies in the industrial sector in a Community eco-management and audit scheme' *Official Journal of the European Communities*, L 104/35-36, April 22 1997

DNV (1997) 'Environmental management systems: An independent guide' DNV Quality Assurance Guide, London

European Accreditation of Certification (EAC) (1996) 'Guidelines for the accreditation of certification bodies for environmental management systems' European Accreditation of Certification

ENDS (1998a) 'Rover and Jaguar raise the stakes in greening of corporate supply chains' *The ENDS Report* No 279, April 1998, London

ENDS (1998b) 'Boost for green procurement as Shell Expro goes for ISO 14001' *The ENDS Report* No 279, April 1998, London

European Community (1980) *European Community Treaties* Sweet & Maxwell, London

German Federal Environment Agency (1998) personal communication

Hillary, R (1993) *The Eco-management and Audit Scheme: A Practical Guide* Technical Communications (Publishing) Ltd, Letchworth

International Organization for Standardization (1996a) *ISO 14001 Environmental Management Systems – Specification with Guidance for Use* International Organization for Standardization, Geneva

International Organization for Standardization (1996b) *ISO 14004 Environmental Management Systems – General Guidelines on Principles, Systems and Supporting Techniques* International Organization for Standardization, Geneva

International Organization for Standardization (1998) *ISO 9000 News 2/1998* International Organization for Standardization, Geneva

International Organization for Standardization/European Committee for Standardization (1991) *Agreement on Technical Cooperation Between ISO and CEN (Vienna Agreement)* International Organization for Standardization, Geneva/Brussels

International Organization for Standardization/International Electrotechnical Commission (1996) *ISO/IEC Guide 2:1996* International Organization for Standardization/International Electrotechnical Commission, Geneva

Starkey, R (ed) (forthcoming) *Environmental Management Tools for SMEs: A Handbook* European Environment Agency, Copenhagen

UK Competent Body for EMAS (1996) *Case Study One* Department of the Environment, HMSO, London

United Kingdom Accreditation Service (1996) *UKAS Supplement to EAC Guidelines for Accreditation of Certification Bodies for Environmental Management Systems (EAC/G5)* United Kingdom Accreditation Service, London

Chapter 5

Environmental Policies

Michael Brophy

THE ESSENTIAL CHARACTERISTICS OF AN ENVIRONMENTAL POLICY

An environmental policy is the very foundation upon which an organization should base all of its interactions, decision-making and future policies, regarding environmental concerns. It has been defined as 'the overall environmental intentions and directions of an organization as regards the environment...' (Canadian Standards Association 1994). An organization's environmental policy forms the backbone and skeletal framework from which all other environmental components are hung (including environmental management systems, audits, assessments and reports); if the policy is flawed then all environmental systems could be weakened and prevented from functioning effectively. The importance of an organization's environmental policy therefore cannot be overstated.

Developing an environmental policy is the first step for any organization committed to improving its environmental performance, and wishing to demonstrate to others that it is intending to take environmental matters seriously. It is not, however, something that can be rapidly or easily 'clicked on' to existing policies for the purpose of some quick public relation points. If an environmental policy is thrown together without adequate thought being given to the commitment, the time and the resources it will require, then the policy may well create greater problems than those it was intended to solve. A public environmental policy will allow an organization to be externally assessed and examined on environmental issues. If a shallow policy is put together with bland statements, designed solely to score public relation points, then such a policy will invariably fail to withstand external scrutiny, and will provide no lasting benefit for the organization itself. Designing and implementing an environmental policy is not a process that can be approached half-heartedly.

An environmental policy serves a dual purpose in any organization. First, there is the purely functional role that the policy needs to fulfil, and secondly there is a more informative aspect that it can achieve. From the functional perspective the policy acts as a guide for future action. It establishes the overall sense of direction of an organization in environmental matters, and sets the parameters and boundaries within which action is to be taken. Specific targets and objectives are defined which the organization will work towards. The opportunity also exists for prioritizing issues, so that an organization can concentrate on those areas it deems to be of greatest importance.

In an informative role, the aim of an environmental policy is to communicate to a wide and varied audience the level of commitment an organization has towards the environment. The audience is invariably composed of the various stakeholders of an organization. The actual role of the policy will differ slightly depending on the stakeholders concerned. In general terms, an environmental policy should:

- assure bankers, insurers and shareholders that the organization is at the very least in compliance with all environmental regulations and legislation;
- seek to reassure employees that the company has adopted a responsible approach, and inform them of their own responsibilities;
- try to attract investment from ethical investment concerns; and
- allay the fears and concerns of local communities and environmental campaigners. Ultimately the end goal of any environmental policy will be to instil confidence in each stakeholder that the organization has adopted a responsible approach to environmental affairs.

There is no standard universal environmental policy that can be applied, ready made, to all business sectors. The unique activities, priorities and concerns of individual organizations demand their own policies if they are to be transformed into practical realities. There are, however, several key features which have come to be recognized as essential for any environmental policy if it is to be both effective and credible. Thus an environmental policy must ensure that:

- it is relevant to the activities, products and services and the environmental effects of the organization concerned;
- it is communicated, implemented and maintained at all levels in the organization;
- it is publicly available;
- it includes a commitment to continual improvement of environmental performance;
- it provides for the setting and publication of environmental objectives;
- it states clearly and precisely how each objective will be achieved; and
- it indicates how environmental objectives will be made publicly available.

The commitment of top management is fundamental to the success of an environmental policy. An individual at the highest level, be they on the Board of Directors or the Chief Executive, must take on the responsibilities and be ultimately accountable for the organization's environmental policy. There are various managerial advantages from such a move, including motivational and leadership benefits, but perhaps more importantly it provides the quickest and easiest 'acid test' with which to judge an organization's environmental commitment. If organizations are assessed externally, and it is observed that no member of senior management is publicly prepared to take on the responsibilities of an environmental policy, then such a stance would almost certainly be viewed as having a negative impact upon the policy's long-term effectiveness.

In order to demonstrate the commitment of top management, organizations have a choice of two strategies: they can allow policies to be developed in detail at the operating level, and then ratified by top management; or alternatively they can be outlined in broad principle by top management and passed down to be worked into detailed guidelines by operational managers. Whether they retain or delegate policy-making, top management has a responsibility to ensure that such policy is reinforced with a management structure that integrates environmental principles into the corporate culture of the organization.

It is also a prerequisite of any credible environmental policy that it be fully integrated into all aspects of an organization's functioning. An environmental policy is not a separate entity and it cannot stand alone; for such a policy to become a reality it must be incorporated at all levels, and be understood by all involved. Environmental issues cannot remain 'the new plaything of a managing director or quality manager' (Roll 1993). Until environmental considerations are applied to every aspect of an organization's functioning, and every employee is aware of their responsibilities, an environmental policy can exist in name only.

The targets and objectives set out within an environmental policy are, in essence, the bones on which that policy is formed. It is impossible to envisage a credible environmental policy where no targets or objectives of any kind have been clearly defined. There is a fine line in setting environmental targets that are practical and challenging, as opposed to those which err on the side of caution. When targets and objectives are defined within an environmental policy statement they must be both quantifiable and measurable. It is pointless for an organization to make bland statements of intent which are impossible to substantiate or assess at a later date. If an organization is to demonstrate that it goes beyond mere lip-service, then targets and objectives must be both specific and measurable.

DEVELOPING AN ENVIRONMENTAL POLICY

For an environmental manager or director suddenly faced with the prospect of designing an environmental policy from scratch, the problem of where to start can often appear overwhelming. The Canadian Standards Authority (CSA) have suggested that any environmental policy should be developed from five main strands:

I.   The organization's mission;
II. The organization's vision;
III. Core values and beliefs;

IV. Stakeholder requirements; and
V. Guiding principles.

Mission (I) is the reason the organization exists, the societal need it fulfils, and the business focus it will have acquired. **Vision** (II) is the state to which the organization aspires. Both I & II are intended to provide long-term guidance for the organization and they should be specifically stated within the policy.

An organization's **Core values and beliefs** (III) are part of the cultural and ethical position it will have adopted. **Stakeholder requirements** (IV), as have already been referred to, include the expectations of shareholders, bankers, insurers, employees and local communities; while **Guiding principles** (V) serve to focus the actions of the organization and can provide an ethical stance in areas of importance to stakeholders.

In theory, if these five conceptual strands are identified and woven together, a tightly knit environmental policy can be produced. In reality, however, few individuals would have the time, the commitment or the ability to adequately identify and then define any of these issues. More often than not an individual charged with developing an environmental policy will cannibalize an existing statement from another organization, and remould it to meet their own needs. This may not be the ideal approach to designing an environmental policy, but unfortunately it has become the reality.

When developing an environmental policy organizations have a number of choices in the tone they wish that policy to take. At the 'lowest' level organizations can put together a shallow 'publicity' statement which may serve immediate needs, but is unlikely to provide any medium- to long-term benefits. Alternatively organizations may develop an environmental policy for 'compliance' purposes, ie a policy which demonstrates to stakeholders and authorities that the organization intends to meet all legal requirements. Such policies have become the minimum that would be expected from any responsible organization. If an organization's environmental policy is to receive credit, then it must demonstrate to all stakeholders that the organization is proactive and intends to go beyond mere minimum compliance. In order to be proactive there are a number of general principles which any environmental policy statement will need to include. The policy will need to:

- adopt and aim to apply the principles of 'sustainable development' which meet the needs of the present, without compromising the abilities of future generations to meet their own needs;
- strive to adopt the highest available environmental standards in all site locations and in all countries, and meet or exceed all applicable legislation;
- adopt a total 'cradle to grave' environmental assessment and accept responsibility for all products and services, the raw materials used and the disposal of products after use;
- aim to minimize or eliminate the use of non-renewable materials, supplies and energy, and wherever possible use renewable or recyclable materials and compounds;
- expect high environmental standards from all parties involved in the

business including suppliers, contractors and vendors, and put pressure on such groups to improve their environmental performance in line with that of the organization; and

• accept strict liability for environmental damage.

DISTINGUISHING BETWEEN ENVIRONMENTAL POLICY AND ENVIRONMENTAL POLICY STATEMENTS

The issue of an 'environmental policy' has already been defined in this chapter. It should be viewed as an all-inclusive concept that covers 'the overall environmental intentions and activities of an organization' (Canadian Standards Association 1994). An 'environmental policy statement', by comparison, is merely a technical term for the attempt to document this policy. In an ideal world the statement would truthfully and accurately reflect all aspects of an organization's environmental policy.

Many texts and authors fail to draw a distinction between the two terms, and refer to both the policy and the statement as if they were one and the same. This may not always be the case and it is important to disentangle the two concepts in order to avoid confusion and prevent possible problems from arising. It is important to recognise the distinction since an environmental statement may not always include all aspects of an environmental policy. There are a number of reasons why this apparent anomaly may arise. It may, for example, be an intentional decision on the part of the organization. There are numerous cases where an organization may not want to disclose specific environmental information, either for competitive advantage or to avoid bad publicity. In order to protect itself an organization will naturally not wish to make such a decision public, and will therefore omit it from the environmental statement.

Alternatively such omissions may be entirely unintentional. For example, decisions or policies may be implemented in other sectors of the organization, such as the legal or personnel departments, which would have significant environmental implications. Yet if their environmental implications are not recognized, then they will be omitted from the environmental statement.

The significance of such omissions will vary, depending on the organization and the issues concerned. However such examples do serve to demonstrate a key point, it should always be borne in mind when examining an environmental policy statement, that the statement itself may not necessarily reflect all aspects of an organization's environmental policy.

Environmental Policy Statements

An environmental policy statement should accurately reflect all aspects of an organization's environmental policy, including targets and objectives relating to environmental matters. As such, environmental policy statements will clearly vary, and will be specific to the requirements of each organization. Having said that, there are a number of key points that have come to be recognized as essential in any environmental statement.

A succession of authors have established a 'checklist' for environmental policy statements (Gilbert 1993, Welford & Gouldson 1993). Such lists, while not exclusive, do provide the first steps for guiding anyone trying to ensure that an environmental statement includes all areas of an organization's environmental policy. The benefits of such checklists lie in the fact that they should be uniformly applicable to any organization attempting to develop an environmental policy. Such lists also allow independent observers a degree of comparability when examining different environmental policy statements. A typical checklist would try to ensure that an environmental statement made specific reference to an organization's policy on the following issues:

- methods of minimizing impacts upon the natural environment;
- legislative compliance;
- waste management;
- energy efficiency;
- working with suppliers to minimize impacts;
- review and reporting of environmental policies and practices;
- environmental training;
- public disclosure;
- liability; and
- transport strategies.

Environmental policy statements can be an extremely difficult documents to construct. Not only should the statement ensure that all aspects of the environmental policy are covered, but also that issues are clearly communicated to the audience concerned. Since the audience for such a document normally consists of the various stakeholders, this can often include a range of conflicting groupings, each with their own agendas and requirements. Thus the document must be detailed enough to adequately portray the policies, objectives and targets concerned, yet be in a format that is easily understood by all stakeholders involved. To try and overcome such problems some organizations have elected to define and state their environmental targets within the environmental statement, but to give the details and technical terms in a separate document that is readily available if required.

Possibly the greatest failure of many environmental statements, is that they may not give a balanced picture of the organization's environmental policy. All too often such statements only relay the 'positive' aspects of an environmental policy, that is they tend only to refer to areas in which environmental action is actually undertaken. Examples of such 'positive' actions would include references to environmental management systems, environmental audits, or individual environmental initiatives, such as waste minimization or energy conservation programmes. Such references tend to form the bulk of many environmental policy statements.

There is nothing inherently wrong in referring to the positive environmental actions of an organization; quite the contrary, they form an essential part of any environmental statement. Problems, however, arise when they become the *only* issues referred to in an environmental statement. The result is a rather biased view of an organization's environmental policy. If a more balanced account is to be given, then there needs to be some reference in the environmental statement to areas of environmental inaction, or negative policies, by the organization. Environmental inaction would include deliberate policy decisions taken by the organization to, for example, *not* produce an environmental report, or *not* to undertake an annual audit.

Producing environmental statements which contain examples of inaction should never be viewed as a negative process, especially if the company takes the opportunity to publicly back up and justify its decisions. The result is a solid, well reasoned, and honest environmental statement. Yet unfortunately this approach is all too uncommon.

When attempting to externally define the overall environmental policies of an organization, it is just as important to learn of decisions of environmental inaction as it is to be informed of current environmental plans and objectives. If environmental policy statements are to truly reflect all aspects of an environmental policy and become credible in the process, they must begin to include all environmental policy decisions, be they positive or negative.

REVIEW OF ENVIRONMENTAL POLICIES

It has already been stated that environmental policies are necessarily specific to the activities of individual organizations. Thus, rather than provide detailed case studies of a limited number of corporate environmental policies, which may have little significance for wider organizations, this chapter will instead review some of the larger scale surveys that have been undertaken, and are thus applicable to all organizations. This review will draw primarily upon the findings of four of the more wide ranging surveys: the Institute of Directors' (IoD) Business Opinion Survey – 'The Environment' (1994); the Lloyds Register Environmental Assurance – 'Developing Environmental Principles' (1995); *Developing an Environmental Policy – Can Accounting Help?* (Gibbon and Holland 1994); and the Centre for Corporate Environmental Management's 'Environmental Policy Review' (CCEM 1995). A review of these four surveys provides a comprehensive understanding of the current position of corporate environmental policies within the UK. The IoD's Business Opinion Survey, for example, drew upon the findings of over 300 of its members, while Gibbon and Holland's survey examined the responses of 120 SMEs in the UK. The Centre for Corporate Environmental Management's (CCEM) review was perhaps the most extensive of the surveys having examined only those organizations already known to have implemented environmental policies. Thus CCEM analysed environmental policies from over 90 organizations, ranging from SMEs to multinational corporations, all of whom were either members of the ICC Charter on Sustainable Development, The Confederation of British Industry (CBI)'s Environmental Business Forum, or had subscribed to the 1994 Corporate Environmental Register.

A review of environmental policies in the UK paints on the whole a rather bleak picture. Despite being the preliminary step for almost any type of environmental activity, relatively few organizations have yet adopted formal environmental policies. The IoD found that only 26 per cent of its members had any stated environmental policy, and Gibbon and Holland gave a figure of 38 per cent for SMEs. Perhaps somewhat more worrying was the discovery by the IoD that 37 per cent of their members had never even discussed environmental issues at board level. Even among those organizations who had supposedly taken up environmental issues a certain apathy can still be observed. CCEM identified a number of organizations who had still not produced an environmental policy some two years after becoming signatories to the ICC Charter, or the CBI's Environmental Business Forum.

When examining the actual content of environmental policies in the UK, it can be found that most organizations tend to place an emphasis on environmental activities which may result in direct financial gains for the organization concerned (see Figure 5.1). Thus 73 per cent of the environmental policies reviewed recognize the need for waste reduction and minimization within their organizations, and 63 per cent have policies on energy reduction and conservation. Legislative compliance is also a prominent issue in UK environmental policies. Sixty-six per cent of policies specifically stated that their organizations would strive to meet current environmental

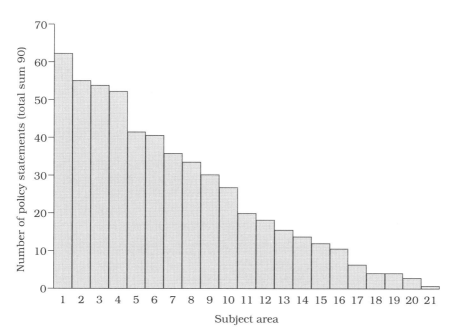

1 Waste minimization
2 Legislative compliance
3 Assessment of environmental performance
4 Energy efficiency
5 Shared responsibility
6 Minimize impacts upon the environment
7 Environmental training
8 Targets and objectives set
9 Liaison with local community
10 Public disclosure
11 Transport

12 Beyond minimum compliance
13 Sustainable development
14 Habitat conservation
15 Research and development
16 LCA
17 BS7750 and EMAS
18 World-wide standard
19 Compensation for environmental damage
20 Reduce consumption of non-renewable resources
21 Liability on environmental issues

Figure 5.1 Content of Environmental Policy Statements by subject

legislative requirements. This finding is supported by the IoD's survey and Gibbon and Holland (1994), both of whom found that environmental legislation was the single most important factor in persuading organizations to undertake environmental actions. 'The requirement to comply with regulations is the main factor affecting directors' thinking about environmental issues..., and the reason for substantial proportions of their environmental investment.' (IoD 1994).

CCEM observed that there were a number of further issues frequently cited in UK environmental policies. These included the need for environmental performance to be assessed and monitored; and the introduction of 'shared responsibility' – ie the need to work environmental policies into the supply chains of organizations. Even though the assessment of environmental performance was one of the more commonly cited issues in UK environmental policies (65 per cent), it is still somewhat surprising to realize that 35 per cent of organizations who develop environmental policies see no need to evaluate the performance of that policy. Similar results were obtained by Gibbon and Holland who found that of the SMEs who had developed environmental policies, only 61 per cent had undertaken any form of environmental audit or evaluation. Of the remaining 39 per cent the authors commented, 'It is questionable how effective a policy can be if it is not being checked' (Gibbon & Holland 1994). The IoD survey observed even lower rates of performance evaluation, noting that only 14 per cent of the members they surveyed had conducted an environmental audit.

As might have been expected, all four surveys recognized that generally, there were similarities among the environmental policies of organizations within the same industrial sector. For example, CCEM noted that UK electricity companies tended to emphasize their policies on energy conservation and renewable energy resources, while food retailers by comparison tended to prioritize waste minimization and transport concerns.

Perhaps the most significant findings from a review of UK environmental policies do not come from what the policies actually state, but rather what they fail to state on many occasions. CCEM, for example, observed that not one of the environmental policies they reviewed mentioned the subject of environmental liability. Similarly less than 6 per cent of UK environmental policies made any reference to the issue of compensation for environmental damage caused as a result of the organization's activities. It is difficult to accept that organizations would not even have considered issues as important as environmental liability or compensation, when developing their environmental policies. Yet normally no reference to such issues is ever made. Taking this into account, it might therefore be suggested that organizations would prefer not to publicly state their policies on issues as delicate as environmental liability or compensation. If this is true, then it may be no coincidence that two-thirds of the environmental policies reviewed by CCEM, also failed to give any indication of their position on disclosing environmental information to the general public.

A number of the surveys examined the subject of environmental management systems standards. Gibbon and Holland were able to demonstrate that the majority of organizations they surveyed (on average 61 per cent) were 'aware' of environmental standards. It is therefore surprising to realise how few organizations have actually implemented them. The IoD found that only 6 per cent of its members had actually registered for the standard, and a further 5 per cent were undertaking registration. CCEM's results closely resemble those of the IoD, observing very little reference to environmental standards among environmental policy statements. These results would tend to indicate that although there is a general awareness in the UK of environmental management standards, there appears to be a certain hesitancy among organizations to their adoption at this point in time.

It is widely accepted that for an environmental policy to be effective, it must be endorsed by senior management. The IoD and CCEM therefore sought to establish who was ultimately responsible for the implementation of environmental policy within UK organizations. Both surveys concluded that responsibility normally rested with either the Managing Director, the Chief Executive or other senior members of the board. The IoD, however, noted that almost a quarter of their organizations gave no one person specific responsibility for environmental policy. When examining the actual policies themselves CCEM observed that almost 40 per cent lacked any sign of formal endorsement from senior management, and no indication was given of who was responsible for their implementation. Without signs of serious commitment from top management, it is questionable how effective or long-term such environmental policies can be.

The problems highlighted in this review demonstrate that there is now an urgent demand for a standardized approach to developing environmental policies. This call has been echoed by the Lloyds Register: 'In developing a modern dynamic policy, it is important to [show that]... a consistent method of analysis has been applied which permits independent external influence' (Lloyds Register 1995). A standardized methodical approach to developing an environmental policy would ensure that comprehensive statements are produced, and that all environmental initiatives undertaken by an organization receive recognition. The current inadequacy of environmental policies has been demonstrated by CCEM's review. Of the 21 basic environmental issues identified in Figure 5.1, no organization's environmental policy referred to more than 14 of these issues. Even if organizations are not currently active in all areas at once, if a comprehensive statement is to be produced, they must at least identify their policies for each of the basic environmental issues.

A standardized approach to environmental policies would also greatly increase the ability to undertake meaningful comparative studies between different organizations. At present, it is extremely difficult to compare the environmental policies of organizations even within the same industrial sector. Without a defined format, as CCEM noted, environmental policies may range from half a page of A4 size paper, to 90 page booklets. Even where organizations identify the same issues, for example energy conservation, comparisons are often hampered by the use of different measurement techniques and classification systems.

The present absence of 'a consistent method of analysis' among environmental policy statements was one of the key factors which promoted the Lloyds Register to conclude: 'the majority of environmental policy statements do not adequately demonstrate to stakeholders that the company has considered its present and future impacts on the whole environment' (Lloyds Register 1995).

CONCLUSIONS

The current position of environmental policies is far from satisfactory. As the IoD demonstrated, only a quarter of organizations have taken the preliminary steps towards environmental action, by introducing environmental policies. The fact that a far greater number of organizations have never even discussed environmental issues at board level, is an indication of the work that needs to be done.

Where environmental policies have been developed, the end products still contain a number of intrinsic faults. Environmental statements rarely reflect all aspects of an organization's environmental policy. Statements tend to concentrate on the positive actions of an organization, with little or no reference to areas of inaction. The result is frequently an unbalanced view of an organization's environmental policy.

When organizations define the content of their environmental policies within their statements, many tend to prioritize areas that will provide direct financial benefits for the organization. The one notable exception here is legislative compliance, which is given precedence by the majority of organizations, and is widely seen as the single most important factor driving environmental action.

A number of important issues, including environmental liability, are frequently omitted from environmental statements. One third of organizations who produce environmental policies, never assess or evaluate the performance of those policies. Forty per cent of policies lack any formal sign of endorsement from senior management, and give no indication of who is responsible for their implementation. While many organizations are apparently aware of environmental management standards, it would appear that only a minority are, as yet, prepared to adopt them.

This catalogue of problems is testimony to the fact that a new approach needs to be taken when developing environmental policies. There is now a demand for standardization among environmental policies, to ensure comprehensive statements are produced, and references are made to the basic issues of any environmental policy. These changes must be coupled with a willingness on the part of organizations to disclose *all* of their environmental decisions. It is only when these processes are undertaken that environmental statements can truthfully and accurately reflect an organization's environmental policy. Until these changes are brought about many environmental policy statements, and by implication environmental policies themselves, will continue to lack credibility.

REFERENCES

Canadian Standards Association (1994) A Voluntary Environmental Management System: Z750-94, CSA, Ontario, Canada

Centre for Corporate Environmental Management (1995) Environmental Policy Review – 1995 Report No 1/95, Michael Brophy, University of Huddersfield

Gibbon, J & Holland, L (1994) *Developing an Environmental Policy – Can Accounting Help?* University of Northumbria and De Montfort University

Gilbert, M J (1993) *Achieving Environmental Management Standards* Pitman, London

Institute of Directors (IoD) (1994) Business Opinion Survey, The Environment, Institute of Directors, London

Lloyd's Register Advisory Services (1995) Quality Safety & Environment – Developing Environmental Principles, Case Report, Lloyds Register, Croydon

Roll, R (1993) *Corporate Environmental Policy in Perspective: Corporate Environmental Register* The Environment Press, London

Welford, R & Gouldson, A (1993) *Environmental Management and Business Strategy* Pitman, London

Chapter 6

Environmental Guidelines and Charters

Michael Brophy

INTRODUCTION

Environmental guidelines and charters (hereafter referred to as environmental charters) are usually documents produced by non-governmental organizations, with the general aim of helping businesses manage and improve their environmental performance. Environmental charters are intended to be statements of 'good faith' on the part of businesses, and they rarely contain legally binding commitments. The target audience of charters can fall into one of two categories: the documents can be intended to apply to all organizations, be it on a national (CBI Forum) or international scale (ICC Charter), or alternatively charters may be developed to target a specific industrial sector, as with the European Petroleum Industry Association's 'Environmental Guiding Principles'.

Organizations which produce environmental charters also tend to fall into one of two categories. There are those organizations who come from 'within' business or industry, and represent their views (CBI, ICC and the Chemical Industry Association – CIA), and there are those organizations 'independent' of business and industry, and have their own individual agendas – for example the Coalition of Environmentally Responsible Economies (CERES). Among organizations producing environmental charters, the former category is by far the more numerous.

Environmental charters, regardless of their origin and target audience, tend to share a number of common objectives. All environmental charters would ultimately aim to:

- help business move forward. An environmental charter should provide the first steps for any organization that decides to undertake environmental action. Environmental charters should assist organizations in setting their environmental policies, and enable them to develop positive programmes designed to prevent environmental degradation;
- assist businesses who have already implemented environmental programmes. Environmental charters may allow businesses to keep up

to date with new trends, to identify and discuss good practice and to be part of a network of peers committed to environmental action. Environmental charters should help corporations working together to increase dialogue and understanding between themselves, government and environmentalists. In so doing organizations will be pooling ideas and experiences, helping to achieve progress with a minimum of wasted effort;

• increase public confidence in industry's commitment to good business and environmental protection. By implementing environmental charters companies can demonstrate to government and to every shareholder that industry is concerned about environmental issues, and is taking voluntary action beyond compliance. In this manner business hopes to allow voluntary and market forces to set the agenda, rather than be subjected to increasing legislation.

Public charters hold a number of significant advantages over 'home grown' environmental policies. Since they are external to organizations, they are likely to be free of internal bias, providing clearer and sharper objectives for an organization to work towards. Since the charters are standard and applicable to more than one organization they will make it easier to externally assess and compare both environmental policies and environmental performance in differing organizations. As all charters are public documents they should, in theory, allow subscribers to be publicized, and for non-signatories to be easily identified.

Grand all-embracing charters, however, are not without their own problems. Clearly guidelines and documents intended to be applicable to all organizations can cause difficulties in interpretation and implementation when exercised at an individual level. Furthermore any form of external charter needs to have adequate monitoring and follow-up procedures if it is to prevent declarations being used solely for PR benefits.

This chapter will examine and comment on three of the main environmental charters currently in circulation. All three are designed for use at a national or international level, and are applicable to any organization considering environmental policies.

THE CERES PRINCIPLES

The CERES Principles were developed in the wake of the *Exxon Valdez* disaster in April 1989. The Principles were developed to help prevent such a disaster happening again. The model for their design was based loosely around the 'Sullivan Principles', a code of conduct for US companies operating in South Africa during the 1980s.

The CERES Principles brought together key US environmental groups and members of the social investment community, with the aim of drafting a corporate code of conduct on the environment. The code provides a set of goals which companies are expected to strive towards. The CERES Principles are by far the most progressive and demanding of the public charters currently available.

The Charter was designed to help investors make informed decisions based on environmental criteria. The principles were tailored for organizations committed to sustainable development – in their introduction CERES clearly state that 'corporations must not compromise the ability of future generations to sustain themselves' (CERES 1995). The Principles are targeted at companies who are prepared to implement environmental management systems, and remain ahead of legislative developments. The intention is 'to create a voluntary mechanism of corporate self-governance that will maintain business practises consistent with the goals of sustaining [the] environment for future generations' (CERES 1995).

At the time of going to print, 81 companies had become signatories to the CERES Principles, the vast majority of whom are US based organizations. CERES companies represent an enormous range of activities, sizes and geographical locations, and include members of the 'Fortune 500 List'. Major organizations who endorse the Principles include Sun Company Inc., H B Fuller, Polaroid, and General Motors. The benefits such companies have gained from signing up to the CERES Principles have been defined as:

- proactive relationships of trust with the investor, environmental, labour and public interest groups that compose CERES, on a wide range of environmental issues;
- improvement in companies' environmental performance through collaboration with other endorsers, and by annual completion of the comprehensive and interactive CERES Report, the annual environmental performance report for endorsing companies;
- important leadership positions in their industries by being among the first to help establish standardized and voluntary public access of environmental performance information;
- recognition in the media, from social investors, and in the confidence of environmentally discriminating consumers.

CERES have stated that companies undertaking their Principles have found environmental proactivity can be accomplished while saving money, and improving the overall efficiency of the operation. In addition, 'Anticipating governmental regulations and voluntarily going beyond current regulatory requirements has proven a cost effective strategy in avoiding expensive legal liabilities' (CERES 1995).

To demonstrate that the Principles have real practical implications CERES can point to the achievements of Sun and General Motors. Sun has succeeded in reducing energy consumption at its refineries by a rate of 1 per cent a year, it has reduced the release of toxic compounds from £3 million to £2.1 million over a six year period, and the company has also reduced the 483 spills from its pipelines and underground storage tanks by 30 per cent in a one year period. In a similar manner, by use of the CERES Principles in 1992 General Motors implemented a pollution prevention programme which eliminated or reduced emissions and wastes going to the environment by 318,000 tons. With such successes CERES may be justified in claiming 'Many corporations are rightly starting to equate environmental responsibility with improved profitability and a new long-term competitive advantage'. Commenting on their endorsement of the Principles, J Robert Banks, Vice

Table 6.1 The CERES Principle

1. Protection of the Biosphere
We will reduce and make continual progress towards eliminating the release of any substances that may cause environmental damage to air, water, or the earth or its inhabitants. We will safeguard all habitats affected by our operations and will protect open spaces and wilderness, while preserving biodiversity.

2. Sustainable Use of Natural Resources
We will make sustainable use of renewable natural resources, such as water, soils and forest. We will conserve non-renewable natural resources through efficient use and careful planning.

3. Reduction and Disposal of Waste
We will reduce and where possible eliminate waste through source reduction and recycling. All waste will be handled and disposed of through safe and responsible methods.

4. Energy Conservation
We will conserve energy and improve the energy efficiency of our internal operations and of the goods and services we sell. We will make every effort to use environmentally safe and sustainable energy sources.

5. Risk Reduction
We will strive to minimize the environmental, health and safety risks to our employees and the communities in which we operate through safe technologies, facilities and operating procedures, and by being prepared for emergencies.

6. Safe Products and Services
We will reduce and where possible eliminate the use, manufacture or sale of products and services that cause environmental damage or health or safety hazards. We will inform our customers of the environmental impacts of our products or services and try to correct unsafe use.

7. Environmental Restoration
We will promptly and responsibly correct conditions that we have caused that endanger health, safety or the environment. To the extent feasible, we will redress injuries we have caused to persons or damage we have caused to the environment and will restore the environment.

8. Informing the Public
We will inform in a timely manner anyone who may be affected by conditions caused by our company that might endanger health, safety or the environment. We will regularly seek advice and counsel through dialogue with persons in communities near our facilities. We will not take any action against employees for reporting dangerous incidents or conditions to management or to appropriate authorities.

9. Management Commitment
We will implement these basic Principles and sustain a process that ensures that the Boards of Directors and Chief Executive Officer are fully informed about pertinent environmental issues and are fully responsible for environmental policy. In selecting our Board of Directors, we will consider demonstrated environmental commitment as a factor.

10. Audits and Reports
We will conduct an annual self-evaluation of our progress in implementing these Principles. We will support the timely creation of generally accepted environmental audit procedures. We will annually complete the CERES Report, which will be made available to the public.

President of Sun Company, commented 'after a years worth of being in partnership with [CERES], we couldn't be happier. It has produced a tremendous amount of value-added to our corporation' (GreenBusiness Letter 1994).

CERES have emphasized that the Principles are to be a long-term commitment by organizations; they are not intended to be adopted and implement overnight. Coupled with this belief is the view that the Charter is not an end product in itself, it is not a static entity – companies are to revise their pledge continuously, and will take on board any future advances.

In examining the ten Principles it can be seen that the first six are designed to form a comprehensive environmental policy. The last four are compliance principles, developed to ensure that the first six are enforced and continually validated. Herein lies one of the great strengths of the CERES Principles. Not only will the Charter ensure that a progressive environmental policy is constructed, but it provides the mechanism to ensure such a process is effectively monitored. Signatories to the Charter are required to conduct an annual self-evaluation of their environmental progress, and complete a CERES report annually, which is made available to the public.

The CERES Principles do not create any legally binding obligations. Many of its ten Principles do not ask companies to commit to anything more than what responsible companies are already doing. When the Principles are examined individually it can be seen that they are not radically new, but rather provide a comprehensive declaration of current beliefs. Principles 1 and 2 are undeniably stringent, but it would be difficult to envisage any organization arguing against the concepts of progress towards the elimination of substances causing environmental damage, or the sustainable use of renewable natural resources and the conservation of non-renewable natural resources.

Principle 3, entitled 'Reduction and Disposal of Wastes', calls for endorsing companies to pledge: 'We will reduce and where possible eliminate waste through source reduction and recycling. All waste will be handled and disposed of through safe and responsible methods'. For a company not to endorse such a commonsense principle would be tantamount to economic suicide. Principles 4–6 merely state the requirements of any efficient environmental audit. Principles 7 and 8 confirm what the public would expect from any responsible organization, while numbers 9 and 10 ensure regular and consistent environmental monitoring and reporting.

The terminology used in the CERES Principles is noteworthy. Each Principle is a direct commitment by signatories to a specific action or undertaking. Thus organizations declare that they '*will* conduct an annual self-evaluation'(Principle 10) or that they '*will* conserve energy and improve energy efficiency...' (Principle 4). These are specific commitments by organizations to undertake direct action and reduce the scope for misinterpretation.

The CERES Principles have not gone without criticism. The Charter has been rejected by some organizations as being far too demanding and unrealistic in its expectations, and there is a general fear, especially among industrial companies, of the financial implications involved in implementing such principles. Organizations are hesitant to sign up to a declaration that may effectively require a 'blank cheque' to be written for environmental concerns. Some of these worries can be allayed by examining the track record of over 80 organizations who have already signed up to the Charter, including General Motors – 'the World's largest company'. Their experiences have effectively shown many of the financial worries to be inflated and pessimistic. J Robert Banks, for example, Vice President of Sun stated that 'compiling the report turned out not to be overwhelming' and estimated that the time required to complete the report to be just over 'about a quarter of a person-year'. In fact Sun discovered that much of the data required to compile the report 'already existed somewhere in the company' (GreenBusiness Letter 1994).

The fact remains however, that there has been a distinct lack of enthusiasm for the CERES Principles particularly among industrial organizations. The trend has been for most industries to opt for other less demanding and less stringent Charters. It is perhaps no coincidence that in the US where legislative controls are tight, especially under Superfund, over 80 organizations have chosen to endorse the CERES Principles. In the UK, under a less stringent legislative regime, and where voluntary action still forms the basis of environmental management, only one company has been prepared to sign up to the declaration.

THE BUSINESS CHARTER FOR SUSTAINABLE DEVELOPMENT

First developed by the International Chamber, the Business Charter for Sustainable Development is the most widely supported Charter, with over 1500 signatories worldwide. The Charter was officially launched at the Second World Industry Conference on Environmental Management, in Rotterdam in April 1991 and is now managed by the World Business Council for Sustainable Development (WBCSD). The Charter (Table 6.2) has three specific aims:

1. to provide common guidance on environmental management to all types of business and enterprise around the world, and to aid them in developing their own policies and programmes;
2. to stimulate companies to commit themselves to continued improvement in their environmental performance; and
3. to demonstrate to governments and the electorates that business is taking its environmental responsibilities seriously, thereby helping to reduce the pressure on governments to over-legislate and strengthening the business voice in debate on public policy.

(Source: ICC 1991)

The ICC/WBCSD Charter is seen by many as a 'code of conduct' for industry in response to governmental and activist pressures.

Technically there is no established mechanism for monitoring or controlling an organization's compliance with the Charter. The WBCSD has specifically stated that it will not monitor compliance. Instead the Charter is viewed as a public commitment to a good faith process, and as such it is envisaged that public interest will be the monitoring mechanism.

Table 6.2 ICC/WBCSD Business Charter for Sustainable Development

1. Corporate Priority
To recognize environmental management as among the highest corporate priorities and as a key determinant to sustainable development; to establish policies, programmes and practices for conducting operations in an environmentally sound manner.

2. Integrated Management
To integrate these policies, programmes and practices fully into each business as an essential element of management in all its functions.

3. Process of Improvement
To continue to improve policies, programmes and environmental performance, taking into account technical developments, scientific understanding, consumer needs and community expectations, with legal regulations as a starting point; and to apply the same environmental criteria internationally.

4. Employee Education
To educate, train and motivate employees to conduct their activities in an environmentally responsible manner.

5. Prior Assessment
To assess environmental impacts before starting any new new activity or project and before decommissioning a facility or leaving a site.

6. Products and Services
To develop and provide products or services that have no undue environmental impact and are safe in their intended use, that are efficient in their consumption of energy and natural resources, and can be recycled, reused or disposed of safely.

7. Customer Advice
To advise, and where relevant educate, customers, distributors, and the public in the safe use, transport, storage and disposal of products provided; and to apply similar considerations to the provisions of services.

8. Facilities and Operations
To develop, design and operate facilities and conduct activities taking into consideration the efficient use of energy and materials, the sustainable use of renewable resources, the minimization of adverse environmental impact and waste generation, and the safe and responsible disposal of residual wastes.

9. Research
To conduct or support research on the environmental impacts of raw materials, products, processes, emissions and wastes associated with the enterprise and on the means of minimizing such adverse impacts.

10. Precautionary Approach
To modify the manufacture, marketing or use of products or services or the conduct of activities, consistent with scientific and technical understanding, to prevent serious or irreversible environmental degradation.

11. Contractors and Suppliers
To promote the adoption of these principles by contractors acting on behalf of the enterprise, encouraging and, where appropriate, requiring improvements in their practices to make them consistent with those of the enterprise; and to encourage the wider adoption of these principles by suppliers.

Table 6.2 *continued*

12. Emergency Preparedness
To develop and maintain, where significant hazards exist, emergency preparedness plans in conjunction with the emergency services, relevant authorities and the local community, recognizing potential transboundary impacts.

13. Transfer of Technology
To contribute to the transfer of environmentally sound technology and management methods throughout the industrial and public sectors.

14. Contributing to the Common Effect
To contribute to the development of public policy and to business, governmental and intergovernmental programmes and education initiatives that will enhance environmental awareness and protection.

15. Openness to Concerns
To foster openness and dialogue with employees and the public, anticipating and resonding to the concerns about potential hazards and impacts of operations, products, wastes or services, including those of transboundary or global significance.

16. Compliance and Auditing
To measure environmental performance; to conduct regular environmental audits and assessments of compliance with company requirements, legal requirements and these principles; and periodically provide appropriate information to the Board of Directors, shareholders, employees, the suthorities and the public.

Over 400 organizations in the world have signed up to the ICC/WBCSD Charter, and they include many leading companies: Shell, BOC, British Airways, BAT Industries, ICI, National Power, British Gas, Samsung, General Motors and Ford.

Many of the organizations who are signatories to the ICC/WBCSD Charter have implemented the Charter by accommodating its recommendations within existing environmental policy initiatives or management systems. British Airways, for example, noted that as a result of its ongoing environmental management system and the ICC/WBCSD Charter, a number of tangible benefits had been observed, including for instance greater fuel efficiency. British Airways also reported that both staff and other stakeholders had responded positively to the ICC/WBCSD Charter and its own EMS (ICC 1994).

Northumbrian Water Group ran a pilot scheme to implement an EMS and in doing so was able to meet many of the recommendations of the Charter. Northumbrian Water observed that its EMS initiative: 'Above all... [it] has helped to promote ownership of environmental responsibilities by the workforce, who are proud of it and the national recognition it has brought' (ICC 1994). The company also noted that by undertaking the EMS initiative they had met the recommendations of Principle 4 in the Charter, which advises signatories 'to educate, train and motivate employees to conduct their activities in an environmentally responsible manner'.

Similarly National Power plc is required by UK Health and Safety legislation (CIMAH – Control of Industrial Major Accidents and Hazards) to establish emergency plans to minimize the frequency of accidents and reduce impacts if and when they do occur. In undertaking such action National Power has observed that it also meets the recommendations of the Charter's twelfth Principle on Emergency Preparedness. The benefits of Principle 12 have been defined by National Power as providing:

- a means of minimizing the risks of damaging accidents;
- a means of testing the adequate understanding of staff about the environmental profile of their workplace; and
- a signal to staff and external interested parties that site managers take their environmental responsibilities seriously.

The ICC/WBCSD document declares that it is a charter for sustainable development, yet despite a brief reference to the key role of environmental management (Principle 1) and the suggestion that organizations should consider the sustainable use of renewable resources, there is no further attempt to demonstrate that the document is in any way compatible with sustainability. Although the Charter's title is the *Business Charter for Sustainable Development*, its subtitle is 'Principles for Environmental Management', and the Charter is almost entirely preoccupied with the latter, making little attempt to justify the former.

As a framework for implementing environmental policy, the ICC/WBCSD Charter does contain many of the essential components. Yet the Charter consistently falls short of demanding any solid action or specific requirements from its signatories. There is a marked difference in language between the CERES Principles and those put forward by the WBCSD. Nowhere in the ICC/WBCSD document is there a declaration that signatories 'will' undertake any specific actions. Instead of absolutes the Charter takes a softer approach, stating general undertakings which are open to wide interpretation. For example, organizations are advised to provide products and services 'that have no undue environmental impact' (Principle 6). The term *undue* could be interpreted in almost any manner, and no two organizations are likely to develop the same definition.

One of the key issues of the ICC/WBCSD Charter is that there is no established mechanism for monitoring or ensuring compliance. Public interest is intended to serve this function. Yet at the same time the ICC/WBCSD Charter provides no guarantee that public information will be forthcoming. While Principle 16 asks organizations to measure environmental performance and conduct regular audits, it later qualifies this request by stating that organizations need only to periodically provide appropriate information to the public. Further details are given in the 'Background Notes' where the term environmental auditing is defined as 'an internal tool the results of which are for company use' (ICC 1991). The Charter does recognize the need for a strong programme of public information; however, it is hard to envisage any form of compliance or monitoring functioning effectively when the organization concerned can choose to release information selectively and on an infrequent basis, with no requirement for it to be consistent or comparable.

There is a general feeling when examining the ICC/WBCSD Charter that the document was originally far stronger, with specific requirements and statements built into it. The Charter does include the major components of an environmental policy. It would appear, however that the document has become watered down and specific demands or requirements have been dropped in order to gain wider acceptance among industry. The question has to be asked why, for example, the Charter felt unable to require organizations to produce environmental reports or audits on a defined periodic basis. Even if this information is produced the Charter fails to insist that it be made public, or even submitted to the WBCSD or any other independent body.

Perhaps the most striking aspect of the ICC/WBCSD Charter is the fact that one of its principle intentions is to demonstrate to government and the electorate that business is taking its environmental responsibilities seriously. The 16 Principles are intended to form a code of conduct by which industry will judge itself, and thus remove the need to legislate. In this respect the Charter is an indication of the furthest that business is prepared to go on a voluntary basis to meeting its environmental commitments. Bearing this in mind, it is perhaps only natural to contemplate legislative alternatives to voluntary action, when implementing environmental policies.

THE ENVIRONMENT BUSINESS FORUM (CBI)

The Environment Business Forum is an initiative of the Confederation of British Industry, and with 175 members it is the most widely supported Charter in the UK. The guidelines are seen to serve a dual purpose:

• to help businesses improve their environmental performance;
• to allow businesses to demonstrate the actions they are taking.

The criteria for organizations gaining membership to the Forum is based on implementing the CBI's 'Agenda For Voluntary Action'. Its requirements are set out in Table 6.3.

Organizations are requested initially to submit an Action Plan to the CBI outlining how the organization will address the points set out in the Agenda for Voluntary Action. Within the first twelve months of membership signatories will be required to produce a Corporate Environmental Policy Statement as part of their overall action programme. Thereafter organizations will be asked to assess their environmental performance and to report on their progress in a public document on an annual basis.

The CBI hold an Environment Business Forum Convention every year which signatories are invited to attend. The intention of the Convention is to update members on progress, and to provide attendees with examples of experiences that members have had in meeting the Agenda for Voluntary Action. Organizations as diverse as Pfizer Ltd, Nuclear Electric and Wessex Water have all made presentations to the Convention outlining the means by which they have implemented environmental policies, and the benefits they have received from the Business Forum. The annual Convention has also been used by British Ministers for the Environment as a platform for

Table 6.3 The Agenda for Voluntary Action

- Designating a board level director with responsibility for the environment. If there is no board then the most senior representative should be nominated
- Publishing a corporate environmental statement
- Setting clear targets and publishing objectives for achieving the policy
- Measuring current performance against targets
- Implementing improvement plans
- Communicating company environmental policy and objects to employees, seeking their contribution to improvement and providing appropriate training
- Reporting publicly on progress in achieving the objectives

---

reiterating Government support for the Environmental Business Forum as a credible voluntary initiative on the environment.

The CBI's Agenda for Voluntary Action is a genuine attempt to try and ensure environmental policies are incorporated into the workings of an organization. The seven principles cover the core issues of any environmental management system: there is a recognition of the key role environmental policy must play; there is commitment to continual environmental improvement; and perhaps most importantly there is the principle that organizations must annually assess and report their environmental performance. In this respect the CBI document has already surpassed the ICC Charter, as it ensures environmental information is available on a continual basis for public scrutiny. In fact the CBI notes that a failure to undertake regular environmental reporting would result in the guidelines being tagged as mere 'window dressing'.

The great strength of the CBI document lies in its commitment to annual environmental performance reports, which are open to independent external assessment. The document could be criticized for allowing organizations to determine their own standards and the 'reasonable levels' they wish to work towards. However, by calling for continual improvement coupled with annual environmental performance reports, it can be argued that the CBI document will inevitably lead to an overall improvement in environmental standards. Even in a worst-case scenario where an organization may initially set low standards and only seek limited improvement, such a system will, over time, lead eventually to environmental improvement.

It remains to be seen if the CBI Environment Business Forum is capable of delivering significant environmental improvement within an acceptable time period. There is always the danger that when faced with challenging standards on a voluntary basis, organizations may elect to switch to other less demanding charters. In addition, it may be dubious that meaningful environmental improvement can occur when organizations are free to voluntarily decide the rate of their own environmental improvement.

OTHER ENVIRONMENTAL CHARTERS

Table 6.4 provides a brief outline of a further six environmental charters, and gives a general breakdown of their contents. The Business Council on National Issues, the NRTEE and the Keidanren Charters are intended to be applicable to all organizations. The first two are Canadian based charters, while the latter is primarily concerned with Japanese companies. EUROPIA, CCPA, and CIA are all industrial associations, EUROPIA being the European Petroleum association, while both CCPA and CPA represent the chemical sector.

It should be noted that Table 6.4 merely indicates the presence or absence of subject areas within the relevant charters, it provides no indication of the wording or the degree of commitment attached to each principle. Thus for example, the ICC/WBCSD, CERES and CBI Charters all request that audits or assessments are undertaken by signatories; the ICC/WBCSD Charter does not specify a specific time frame for this activity, and states that auditing is an 'internal tool the results of which are for company use'; the CERES and CBI Charters in comparison require signatories to conduct annual audits and assessment reports, the results of which are to be made public.

Table 6.4 does, however, demonstrate a number of general points which are common to many environmental charters; and guidelines. Charters targeted at specific industrial sectors tend to be oriented around issues of legal compliance and cost-cutting measures, such as energy conservation and waste reduction. The only other issues commonly referred to involve raising employee and supplier awareness. Those charters aimed at a general audience, however, tend to be more proactive in their recommendations. Both the Keidanren and Business Council Charters for example, request signatories to undertake environmental impact assessment studies, and to implement the principles of sustainable development into their operations. The Business Council on National Issues also requests organizations to conduct life cycle assessment, while Keidanren requires companies to conduct world-wide operations to the highest standard. Both charters also state that organizations should set environmental targets and objectives, Keidanren requires that activities be audited, while the Business Council suggests that performance reports should be regularly published. Such issues are notably absent from any of the industry association charters.

CONCLUSIONS

When examining environmental charters and guidelines it is relatively easy to become pessimistic. The degree of support given by industries to proactive charters, as opposed to those which are mere 'window dressing', is on the whole disheartening.

The more demanding environmental charters tend to originate from independent organizations, and are aimed at a general audience. Those charters that have been developed by industrial associations, for specific industrial sectors, generally concentrate on issues of legal compliance and cost-cutting exercises.

Table 6.4 Analysis of environmental charters and guidelines

Charter/guideline Principle	Business Council	EUROPIA	NRTEE	CCPA	Keidanren	CIA	CERES Principles	ICC/WBCSD Charter	CBI
Meet or exceed legal requirements	•				•		•	•	
Set targets and objectives	•				•		•	•	•
Internal/external audits or assessments					•	•	•	•	•
Publish performance	•				•		•	•	•
Integrate environmental management		•					•	•	•
Reduce/conserve energy use		•	•		•	•	•	•	•
Minimize/conserve use of non-renewable resources			•						
Increase recycling			•						
Minimize/reduce waste production		•	•		•		•	•	•
Waste disposal with minimal impact		•		•	•	•	•	•	•
Educate general public									
Support local communities		•		•					
Raise employee awareness				•		•	•	•	
Raise supplier awareness						•		•	
Life Cycle Assessment				•					
Word wide standard									•
Environmental Impact Assessment		•			•		•	•	
Continuous improvement					•		•	•	•
Environmental restoration							•	•	
Sustainable development		•	•		•		•		

Business Council Business Council on National Issues *Business Principles for a Sustainable and Competitive Future*

EUROPIA European Petroleum Industry Association *Environmental Guiding Principles*

NRTEE National Round Table on the Environment and the Economy *Objectives for Sustainable Development*

CCPA Canadian Chemical Producers' Association *Responsible Care*

Keidanren Japan Federation of Economic Organizations *Keidanren Global Environment Charter*

CIA Chemical Industry Association *Responsible Care*

The CERES Principles which are truly proactive, and request signatories to pledge specific commitments to undertake direct environmental action, have received a less than enthusiastic response from industry. The CBI's Environment Business Forum is a serious attempt to promote environmental responsibility among its members. The fact remains however that endorsing companies are free to set their own targets and objectives, and define their own rates of environmental improvement. Thus the theoretical absurdity of a company 'progressing' from appallingly bad to very bad over a twenty year period, and still maintaining membership of the Environmental Forum, is a reality under the Agenda for Voluntary Action. In addition it is questionable whether signatories may not switch to other less stringent charters should future demands become too challenging. The ICC/WBCSD Charter by comparison avoids any absolutes, and asks only that organizations support general undertakings, open to wide interpretation.

It can be no coincidence that the ICC/WBCSD is the most widely supported Charter. It is also notable that one of the principle intentions of the Charter, as defined by the ICC/WBCSD, is to demonstrate to government and the public, that industry is taking its environmental responsibilities seriously, and thus reduce the pressure to legislate. As a result the ICC/WBCSD Charter is an indication of how far industry is prepared to go on a voluntary basis to meeting its environmental responsibilities. Bearing such considerations in mind it is tempting to consider the alternatives offered by stricter legislation, especially when charters truly trying to create a credible voluntary mechanism of corporate self-governance are largely ignored.

REFERENCES

CERES (1995) *Guide to the CERES Principles* Coalition for Environmentally Responsible Economies, Boston, United States

The GreenBusiness Letter, March (1994) 'Into The Fast Lane – G M Could Help Make CERES the Reporting Vehicle of Choice' Tilden Press, United States

Green Alliance (1989) 'The Valdez Principles – A Background Note' Green Alliance Press Release, London

International Chamber of Commerce (1994) *Principles for Environmental Management – Summary Report of a Seminar Organized by ICC United Kingdom* London

International Chamber of Commerce Working Party on Sustainable Development (1991) *Background Note on the ICC 'Business Charter For Sustainable Development'* Doc 210/364 Rev, ICC, Paris

Chapter 7

Environmental Auditing

Richard Welford

INTRODUCTION

The importance of environmental audits has increased immensely during the last few years, with the launch of the eco-management and audit scheme (EMAS) in 1993 and the publication of ISO14001 in 1996. More and more companies are finding it valuable to undertake and audit their environmental impacts. This commonly leads to the identification of risks as well as pinpointing cost saving opportunities. However, owing to the undue emphasis being laid on complying with current legislation, too many companies are using environmental audits only in order to evaluate and verify compliance. This is a very narrow approach and misses the many more positive reasons for undertaking the audit. Seen as part of a process of continuous improvement and building on the systems based approach identified in earlier discussions, this chapter therefore seeks to identify ways in which a company can use environmental audits for gaining a competitive edge over its competitors, and ultimately for moving towards a sustainable future.

Moreover, in the spirit of the environmental management systems standards it is argued here that environmental audits are an important tool for any company taking a proactive stance towards environmental issues. While a passive or reactive stance towards the environment focuses on doing the minimum that is required by law, a proactive stance aims at moving beyond compliance. The chapter discusses how a proactive strategy enables a company to use environmental audits not merely for complying with the existing legislation, but also for identifying problems, measuring and comparing one's environmental performance, becoming eco-efficient, providing a database for taking corrective steps and future action, for developing one's environmental strategy and for identifying environmentally based opportunities for gaining an edge over one's competitors.

Environmental auditing is not a particularly new discipline; however its popularity as a means to assessing environmental performance has recently increased substantially. Indeed, the first environmental audits can be traced back to the US, where corporations adopted this methodology during the

1970s in response to their domestic liability laws. During the 1980s these audits were extended beyond simply adhering to legislation and regulations. In general, environmental auditing is a series of activities initiated, by management, to evaluate environmental performance, to check compliance with environmental legislation and to assess whether the systems in place to manage environmental improvement are effective. Audits are undertaken at regular intervals to assess the environmental performance of the company in relation to the company's stated objectives and environmental policy. The environmental audit is therefore an integral part of the environmental management system discussed in Chapter 3.

The definition of an environmental audit provided by the International Chamber of Commerce (ICC, 1989) is:

> *A management tool comprising a systematic, documented, periodic and objective evaluation of how well environmental organization, management and equipment are performing with the aim of helping to safeguard the environment by: (i) facilitating management and control of environmental practices; and (ii) assessing compliance with company policies, which include meeting regulatory requirements.*

While this definition is rather 'management' oriented and the full role for everyone in the organization should be recognized, it gives an idea of its basic approach. Much stress should be laid on the words *systematic, documented, periodic* and *objective*. In other words, the audit must be an ongoing and thorough assessment of environmental performance which is documented and at the very least verified by an objective third party. This definition of the environmental audit has become standard but the definitions given by the Confederation of British Industry and the eco-management and audit scheme are often seen as being more robust.

The Confederation of British Industry defines an environmental audit as:

> *The systematic examination of the interactions between any business operation and its surroundings. This includes all emissions to air, land and water; legal constraints; the effects on the neighbouring community, landscape and ecology; and the public's perception of the operating company in the local area.... Environmental auditing does not stop at compliance with legislation. Nor is it a 'green-washing' public relations exercise. Rather, it is a total strategic approach to the organization's activities.*

The definition of the environmental audit given within the eco-management and audit scheme, which is again based on the ICC definition, is:

> *A management tool comprising a systematic, documented, periodic and objective evaluation of the performance of the organization, management system and processes designed to protect the environment with the aim of: (i) facilitating management control of*

practices which may have impact on the environment; (ii) assessing compliance with company environmental policies.

ENVIRONMENTAL MANAGEMENT SYSTEMS AND THE ENVIRONMENTAL AUDIT

We know that the auditing process is central to the effective implementation of an environmental management system and the EMS standards put much emphasis on the role of the audit to monitor continuous improvement processes. The ICC's (1991) model sees the environmental audit as the control function of the environmental management system (see Figure 7.1) where planning, organizing, implementing and controlling the audit need to be seen within their own cycle of activity. However, as has been emphasized by the definition given by the CBI, the environmental audit is not merely a control function, but is at the very core of the EMS. Elkington and Hailes (1991) see the environmental audit as part of a circular wheel of the environmental or green management system (see Figure 7.2) where the audit process is directly linked to corporate strategy and communications.

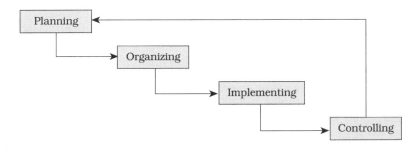

Source: ICC Guide to Effective Environmental Auditing, 1991

Figure 7.1 Elements of a sound environmental management system

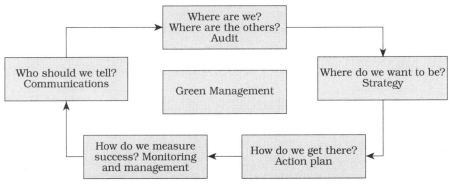

Source: Elkington & Hailes, 1991

Figure 7.2 The green management wheel

Whatever starting point we take, it is therefore important to recognize that an environmental audit is central to a company committed to the implementation of an environmental management system. Indeed, it would be wrong for the environmental audit to be seen in isolation – it is one very important component of a comprehensive approach to environmental management and is recognized as such in standards such as ISO14001. As with much of environmental management the role of senior management in the audit process is crucial. Without top management support an internal environmental audit programme will not succeed. Moreover, management needs to be fully committed to environmental compliance and to correcting any deficiencies uncovered by the audit programme. The ICC position paper on Environmental Auditing (ICC, 1989) includes the following statement on full management commitment:

> *It is important that management from the highest levels overtly supports a purposeful and systematic environmental auditing programme. Such commitment is demonstrated by, for example, personal interest and concern, the adoption of high standards, the allocation of appropriate manpower and resources, and the active follow-up of recommendations.*

An environmental audit is more than a simple inspection or assessment which offers an opinion based primarily on professional judgement. It has to be a methodological examination of a facility's procedures which will include analyses and testing in order to verify that legal requirements and internal policies are being met. In this context, auditors will base their judgements of compliance on evidence gathered during the audit. An audit can look at particular issues facing the company or it can be a wide-ranging audit which includes a full assessment of the effectiveness of an environmental management system as well as compliance, safety and quality control. The ICC approach clearly promotes the latter.

Neither is the audit a one-off activity. It needs to be seen as an on-going programme where the audit is not only repeated periodically but also developed in terms of scope and sophistication over time. Seeing a single audit as a panacea would not only be wrong but is likely to lead to more problems than it solves. Central to the audit programme therefore, is a commitment to see the process as continuous and part of a company's wide range of assessment activities. In effect, an auditing system helps the firm anticipate environmental damage and therefore prevent it from happening. However, before a company is even in a position to audit, it needs firstly to establish its baseline performance which is achieved via the environmental review and secondly, to begin to implement an action plan through a clearly structured environmental management system.

AIMS AND OBJECTIVES OF THE ENVIRONMENTAL AUDIT

Once the environmental review has been completed and the management system is in place there will be a need to regularly assess that system, and to further measure the environmental performance of the firm. There will also be a need to verify that any actions being implemented as the result of any previous report are effective. This is the role of the regular environmental audit. The overall aim of environmental auditing is therefore to provide an on-going status check which will enable environmental improvement within the organization to continue, and in so doing will help to safeguard the environment and minimize the risks to human health. Although auditing alone cannot achieve environmental improvement, it is a powerful managerial tool. The key objectives of the environmental audit are:

1. **Verifying compliance** – one of the primary purposes of an audit is to verify compliance with local, national and international standards or best available techniques, as well as the company's own internal standards, as stated in its environmental policy.
2. **Identifying problems** – the aim of an audit is to detect any leakage, spills or other such problems with the operations and processes at an early stage, thus reducing the risk of a future problem. Deficiencies which may emerge over time can also be traced.
3. **Formulating environmental policy** – normally, formulation of an environmental policy should precede the audit. However, if such a policy does not already exist, then an environmental audit can be used for formulating the organization's environmental policy. Similarly, the results of an audit can also be used for modifying and updating an existing policy.
4. **Measuring environmental impact** – an environmental audit should measure the environmental impact of each and every process and operation on the air, water, soil, worker health and safety and society at large.
5. **Measuring performance** – an environmental audit gives one a measure of the organization's environmental performance which can then be compared with best practices in environmental auditing, thus enabling management to know where their organization stands with regard to its environmental performance.
6. **Confirming environmental management system effectiveness** – being the very core of an environmental management system, an environmental audit gives an indication of the effectiveness of the system and how it can be improved.
7. **Providing a database for corrective action and future plans** – an environmental audit identifies areas where steps have to be taken or can be taken to reduce wastes, raw material and energy consumption and adverse impacts on the environment, and improve the environmental performance of the company.
8. **Developing the company's environmental strategy** – the results of an audit should enable management to develop its environmental strategy

for moving towards a greener corporate culture.

9. **Communication** – by reporting the results of its environmental audit, a company can effectively communicate its environmental performance to the stakeholders, which goes a long way in enhancing the image of the company.

There are a number of benefits to firms in having an environmental audit undertaken. These include assurances that legislation is being adhered to and the consequent prevention of fines and litigation, an improved public image which can be built into a public relations campaign, a reduction in costs (particularly in the area of energy usage and waste minimization), an improvement in environmental awareness at all levels of the firm and an improvement in overall quality. Many environmental audit programmes are established on the direct orders of top management for the purpose of identifying the compliance status of individual facilities and thereby providing management with a sense of security that environmental requirements are being met. Increasingly, ignorance will not be tolerated as a excuse when environmental litigation is being pursued.

On the other hand there are some potential disbenefits of the audit. These include the initial costs of the audit and the cost of compliance with it and the temporary disruption of plant operations. It is also vital that management sees that the recommendations of the environmental auditor are adhered to, otherwise an audit report could be incriminating in a court case or insurance claim. An audit report is a 'discoverable' document and may therefore be used in any legal proceedings which may follow. Before an audit is undertaken therefore, management must recognize that the audit may recommend changes which require immediate action because they are either illegal or hazardous to human health. There is a need therefore to establish a contingency budget to cover expenditure which may be required in response to such recommendations.

There is also often a natural reluctance on the part of management and workers to see outsiders entering the organization and assessing their own performance. In particular, management can become unhappy about its line of responsibility being invaded. The legitimacy of any auditing team, which may not have the same level of knowledge of an industry as do personnel, will often be challenged. In these respects therefore it is vital that senior management are seen to be supportive of both the audit team and the process.

As has already been made clear the primary benefits of environmental auditing are to indicate in good time whether environmental measures are satisfactory and to assist with the subsequent compliance with legislation, company policy and the public's demands. Experience of auditing in a number of companies has however highlighted a range of less tangible benefits. These include for example:

- increasing awareness of environmental policies and responsibilities among the whole workforce;
- providing an opportunity for management to give credit for good environmental performance;

- identifying new working practices which can significantly aid waste minimization and energy usage;
- providing an up-to-date environmental database which can be drawn on when making decisions on plant modifications or for use in emergencies; and
- evaluating training programmes and providing information for the training of staff.

AUDIT PRINCIPLES

An increasing number of consultancies have been established during the late 1980s and the 1990s which aim to undertake environmental audits. Some of these have grown out of quality assurance operations and others out of the expertise developed through environmental impact assessment. However, environmental auditing requires skills and attributes which go beyond both of these frameworks and entails a much more interdisciplinary approach.

Increasingly some degree of external help and consultancy will be needed by business for four reasons:

1. All but the largest of firms are unlikely to have the necessary expertise to cover the legal, scientific and technical and management related requirements of the audit process.
2. Increasingly companies are looking for third party verification of their audit results. This is required, for example, by the EU eco-management and audit scheme. External consultants can bring a degree of objectivity to the process and introduce fresh ideas.
3. Traditionally many audits have been strictly site specific and have not sought to assess linkages along the supply chain and external environmental effects of operations. There is, however, a clear trend towards an assessment of external environmental effects such as pollution and disamenities where expertise and measurement beyond a single plant or operation are required.
4. The findings of audits were traditionally for internal company consumption but there is now a move by some companies, reacting to demands from pressure groups and encouragement from industry itself, government and the EU, to publish the results more widely and to consider the provision of public information. Thus the information resulting from the audit needs to be comprehensible to the public and believed by them. This can be achieved with external impartial advice and third party verification.

However, in using external advice organizations need to assure themselves that they will be getting value for money and a quality service. It is possible to identify ten key elements necessary for the conduct of effective and reliable environmental audits. Unless these can be adhered to by auditors, companies cannot be assured of the quality and objectivity of the auditing procedure and will need to take their business elsewhere.

1. Clear and explicit objectives need to be formulated before the commencement of the environmental audit. In addition there needs to be a clearly defined benchmark in terms of environmental legislation, standards and the best practice of other companies in order that the audit results can be assessed.
2. The audit team needs to be proficient and expert with appropriate knowledge of the issues under consideration and an appropriate environmental understanding with respect to scientific, technical, legislative and management issues. Each audit member needs to be able to demonstrate his/her particular expertise.
3. Auditors need to be independent and to work in a confidential manner and due professional care should be exercised at all times.
4. Firms specializing in environmental auditing and individual consultants should be able to demonstrate their own adherence to general principles of environmental improvement.
5. The on-site audit should be planned, managed and supervised so as to ensure minimum disbenefit to the company and appropriate security and safety to the individual auditor.
6. Environmental audits should include the proper study of management systems in operation and an assessment of the reliability of internal environmental controls. Tests should be devised so as to ensure the effectiveness of management structures.
7. Sufficient, reliable evidence should be gathered through enquiry, observation and tests to ensure that the audit findings are objective.
8. Audit reports should be clear concise and confidential. They should ensure full and formal communication of audit findings and recommendations.
9. Auditors should ensure that strategies for the implementation of the recommendations of the audit are practicable and possible and should contribute to the implementation of corrections.
10. Auditors should clearly indicate to companies the consequences of not correcting deficiencies particularly where they may result in litigation being taken against the firm. If this is not done then auditors should accept their own negligence.

INCENTIVES TO UNDERTAKE THE AUDIT

Over the last decade, as public attitudes towards environmental degradation have changed, as insurance markets have become more aware of the potential risks associated with pollution and as more national and transnational legislation has come on to the statute book, the incentives to undertake an environmental audit have increased. The particular reasons for undertaking a regular environmental audit are therefore likely to include the following considerations.

Insurance

Costs of remediation following pollution incidents have been increasing dramatically and consequently premiums have increased and the number of exclusions from policies has extended. While it is still possible to find insurance cover for pollution which is sudden, accidental and unforseen, there are very few insurance companies which will cover general pollution risks unless regular environmental audits are carried out.

Market Forces and Competition

One of the consequences of public interest is that consumers are increasingly willing to switch to products which are in some way more environmentally friendly than their normal purchase. Companies need therefore to demonstrate that their product and their processes cause minimum harm to the environment. In the past the marketing of 'green' products has often been misleading and sometimes dishonest and many firms have had their 'green' products exposed as not being environmentally friendly at all. With the growing strength of pressure groups, dishonesty will be exposed and it is therefore necessary for firms who wish to tell their consumers about their environmental improvements to undertake independent and regular environmental audits of their processes. With the introduction of an eco-label for some products across Europe, which will assess not only the product but the production process before an award is made, the role of the audit becomes crucial.

Acquisitions

Major organizations are becoming increasingly aware of the massive potential risks involved in acquiring land which has already been contaminated or acquiring a business which has poor environmental performance. Costs associated with ground remediation, the capital cost associated with introducing or upgrading pollution control plant and the cost of potential compensation claims for past mistakes can easily outweigh any financial advantage of an acquisition. It is increasingly standard practice, therefore, for purchasers to commission a pre-acquisition environmental assessment or want to examine the reports from an organization's environmental audits.

Legislation

The Environmental Protection Act (1990) in the UK requires organizations to reduce emissions to the atmosphere and discharges to rivers and sewers using methods which present the Best Practicable Environmental Option (BPEO) and the Best Available Techniques Not Exceeding Excessive Cost (BATNEEC). Specific industries involved in the processing of toxic materials have, in addition, to apply to Her Majesty's Inspectorate of Pollution (HMIP) for an authorization to operate. For smaller units there is commonly a need to gain an Authorization to Operate from the Local Authority Air Pollution Control. Applications for such authorization, which are likely to be expanded in the future, require the completion of a complex questionnaire and this is often not possible without the information which results from an environmental audit. In addition there are mounting European directives and legislation to be considered so that part of the audit needs not only to verify compliance but also to look forward to future legislative and regulatory demands.

PARTIAL ENVIRONMENTAL AUDITS

The environmental audit has to be systematic and comprehensive. However, some firms have carried out specific narrower assessments of part of their activities for particular purposes. In effect these are partial audits and although their general methodology may be similar they do not adhere to the main task of the audit which is to assess the environmental management system and to measure environmental performance. A partial environmental audit will be specific to a particular task or process or issue. These narrower types of audit continue to exist and for that reason are briefly reviewed here.

Compliance Audit

Compliance auditing has, until recently, been the most common form of environmental auditing. The audit regularly checks the extent to which an organization is complying with existing environmental laws and company policies. A more progressive compliance audit will examine areas not yet covered by legislation and other standards in an attempt to be more proactive in its environmental strategy.

Process Safety Audit

A periodic process safety audit will seek to identify the hazards and quantify the risks arising from the production process. It will look closely at procedures for accidents and emergencies and may be combined with a compliance audit to cover health and safety legislation. Accident reporting and investigation systems will be checked along with emergency response preparedness and the appropriateness of training in the areas of health and safety, accident prevention and accident response.

Occupational Health Audit

Occupational health auditing examines the exposure of the workforce to pollution and physical disamenities (eg noise and temperature) and is measured and recorded periodically. The availability, quality and usage of protective equipment and clothing, training and information will be assessed.

Product Audit

At companies such as The Body Shop an analysis which they have called a product audit has been carried out. The Body Shop's approach is to analyze a particular product line examining most aspects of sourcing production, packaging and waste disposal. In effect this sort of approach is equivalent to a life-cycle analysis of the product.

Product Quality Audit

Quality auditing is increasingly being linked to quality standards such as ISO 9000. Here auditing is focused on product or operational quality systems. Existing safety and product control systems would be analyzed, quality assurance programmes assessed, consumer information appraised and labelling, packaging and safety data examined.

Issues Audits

At British Petroleum (BP) audits have been conducted which are neither site, organization or product specific. They have introduced the concept of an issue audit which focuses on how the whole group is dealing with specific environmental issues of key concern such as the loss of tropical rainforest habitat. This audit involves an evaluation of policy, guidelines, operating procedures and actual practice within all businesses.

Pre-Acquisition Audits

This sort of audit or review (more strictly speaking what it is more likely to be) is associated with merger or acquisition activities. We have already seen that it is risky not to have some sort of environmental assessment in such situations. Such investigations concern the assessment of significant environmental liabilities (past, present and future) associated with an installation or organization about to be acquired. These liabilities may be associated with contaminated land or groundwater, existing or potential litigation and the need to install new pollution control technologies. Pre-acquisition audits are sometimes referred to as due diligence investigations.

While the general principles for conducting any type of audit are usually similar, for the remainder of this chapter we assume that we are dealing with a comprehensive audit of a site or organization after an environmental review has been conducted.

IMPLEMENTING THE AUDIT

All environmental audits involve gathering information, analyzing that information, making objective judgements based on evidence and a knowledge of the industry and of relevant environmental legislation and standards. There is also the need to report the results of the audit to senior management with recommendations and possible strategies for the implementation of the findings. This all needs considerable preparatory work as well as follow-up time in order that the findings are accurate and comprehensive. Ideally, therefore, there needs to be three clear stages to an audit (see Figure 7.3).

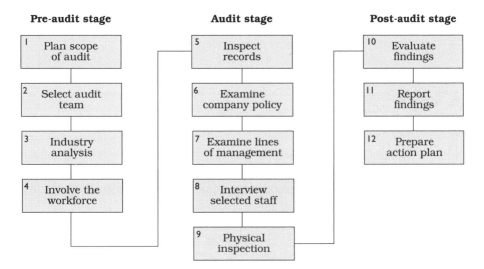

Figure 7.3 Stages of an environmental audit

The first stage, the pre-audit activities, will aim to minimize the time spent at the site and to maximize the audit team's productivity, and will involve the following:

1. Planning the nature and scope of the audit and providing a framework for setting goals and objectives, developing strategies for their achievement and specifying accountability for accomplishing the work and scheduling the audit process. Information must be gathered from secondary sources like previous audit reports, previous audit reviews and other corporate reports. Sites and facilities must be prioritized according to risks involved with regard to hazardous wastes, air pollution, water pollution, soil contamination, inventory, non-compliance with legislation and worker health and safety. Then a framework for an environmental audit programme with clearly defined procedures must be developed.
2. Selecting members of the audit team and allocating resources to the strategies and policies determined in (1). The audit team will consist of people chosen for their expertise not only in environmental matters but also having knowledge of the industry in which a company operates. An assignment of audit responsibilities should be made according to the competencies and experience of the team.

3. Getting to know the industry and company to be audited. A useful strategy here is to use pre-survey questionnaires submitted to management in order for the audit team to familiarize themselves with the type of instalment, the site and the location. It will also focus the minds of management on what will be required of them during the audit. In addition, the geographic area, as well as the areas within the field of health, safety and environment, that have to be covered by the audit should also be clearly defined, as also should the total time allocated for conducting the audit.
4. Questionnaires may also be sent to a representative sample of the workforce (to be filled out in confidence) asking about key issues such as communications, planning, health and safety and working conditions.

The second stage is the on-site audit itself. This will include:

5. An inspection of records kept by the company, certificates of compliance, discharge consents, waste licenses etc.
6. The examination of inspection and maintenance programmes and the company's own policy on what to do in the event of spills and other accidents. Auditors will have to assess the soundness of the facility's internal controls and assess the risks associated with the failure of those controls. Such controls will include management procedures and the equipment and engineering controls that affect environmental performance.
7. Examining lines of management and responsibility, competence of personnel and systems of authorization. There needs to be a working understanding of the facility's internal management system and of its effectiveness.
8. A confidential interview of selected staff at all levels of operation with a view to collecting information, particularly in the area of the effectiveness of systems and waste management.
9. A physical inspection of the plant, working practices, office management systems and surrounding areas including a check on safety equipment, verifying the company's own sampling and monitoring procedures, investigating energy management systems and where necessary taking samples of waste, liquids, soil, air and noise.

The final stage of the audit will involve:

10. Confirming that there is sufficient evidence on which to base and justify a set of findings and evaluating the audit information and observations. Such evaluation will involve the audit team meeting to discuss all facets of the environmental audit.
11. Reporting the audit findings in written form and in discussion with the management of the audited company. This entails a formal review of the audit findings to avoid misinterpretation and discussion about how to improve the environmental performance of the firm based on the audit report. Management is thus provided with information about compliance status and recommendations regarding action which should be taken.

12. This will often result in the development of an action plan to address deficiencies. This will include assigning responsibilities for corrective action, determining potential solutions and establishing timetables. Recommendations for the next audit may also be made.

The environmental audit is more likely to be successful if the general ethos of the firm is supportive to the success of the programme and the welfare of the company. To this extent it is useful to consider some key characteristics which will provide the foundation for a successful programme. These factors will include:

- comprehensive support for the programme throughout management and particularly by senior management;
- acceptance that an auditing programme is for the benefit of management rather than a tool of individual performance assessment and is a function which, in time, will improve management effectiveness;
- the recognition that useful information will come out of the audit programme and that that information needs to be shared and acted upon;
- the commitment to considering the comments and suggestions at each level of the organization's management and workforce and encouraging responsible participation;
- a commitment to establishing systems for managing and following up on results;
- clearly defined roles and responsibilities and clear operational systems;
- the recognition of an integrated approach where the auditing system is linked to a wider environmental management system which in turn is linked to all the other systems in use in the company.

Much stress needs to be placed on the idea that audits should be seen by management as a positive help rather than a threatening or hostile exercise. The company must create a culture led by its main board directors which recognizes the positive benefits of the audit and sees it as good day to day management practice. Management must feel that they own the audit and even though some external expertise may be used it is an activity which is promoted and driven internally rather than externally.

SUCCESS FACTORS

An effective environmental audit is one that is conducted within a structured management system, is integrated with the overall management activity and considers all aspects that are essential for good environmental performance. Some factors that are of extreme importance for an environmental audit to be effective are listed below.

Top Management Commitment

Although top management support is regarded as the most crucial factor for the success of an environmental audit, lack of it is also the biggest hindrance encountered in the implementation of an environmental audit programme. To gain top management support, the management must be made to realize that environmental management is no longer a passing fad and is here to stay. Standards are becoming higher, regulations stricter and penalties harsher.

Involvement and Participation

Staff involvement and participation is important for the success of an audit because the cause of any problems or deficiencies in a particular facility or operation can best be understood by the persons working there. Worker participation becomes especially important since a small slip by a single worker can result in a fatal accident, which could have catastrophic results for the entire company. A single accident is sufficient to wipe out a company's goodwill and whatever good it may have done in the past, as has been witnessed in the case of Union Carbide (Welford, 1994). It must however be emphasized here that a positive approach has to be taken by the auditors in order to prevent the staff from being defensive, thus obstructing rather than helping with the audit.

Recognition of an Integrated Approach to Environmental Auditing

An environmental audit must not be considered in isolation, but as an integral part of an environmental management system, which in turn should be integrated with the other systems in the organization. Such an integrated holistic approach is in keeping with the arguments laid out earlier in this book.

Third Party Verification

An external consultant or auditor not only provides the necessary skill and expertise required for conducting an audit, which might otherwise be missing, but also provides an impartial third party verification of the audit results. This becomes especially important when the results of the audit are communicated to the stakeholders as it gives them an additional authenticity.

Well-qualified Audit Team

An audit team generally comprises of 3–5 persons. While some smaller companies may be audited by just one person, it is usually more beneficial to have more than one person on the audit team. Two minds are always better than one as anything overlooked by one may draw the attention of the other. Using the same audit team for different sites also proves to be useful as it becomes easier to understand and find solutions to similar problems at different sites.

Established Audit Frequency

Environmental audits should be conducted at regular intervals. While an audit should not take place infrequently, neither should it be carried out so often that no time is left for the action plan developed during the previous audit to be implemented. Then having the same audit frequency for all operations and sites may not always work. Sites/operations that are more risky should be audited more often than others.

THE SCOPE OF THE AUDIT

It is clear that the environmental audit must be defined with some boundaries. If possible, the audit should use the same boundaries as the environmental management system since one of its key tasks is to assess the performance of this. However, in large companies with integrated environmental management systems the scope and coverage of them may be just too wide and unwieldy to assess using one single audit. In addition the measurement of environmental performance needs to be done within manageable parameters. It is often therefore necessary to break down the assessment of the system and environmental performance into parts based on the following sorts of considerations.

Geographical Scope

Most audits are considered as site-specific, but even if we take that as a norm the geographical scope of the actual environmental assessment and measurement needs to be clearly defined. Ultimately any organization will have an impact upon the global environmental situation but while reference to these factors is valid, measurement is clearly impossible. Equally, most organizations will in some way pollute the community around them but again the definition of the community is difficult and measurement equally problematic.

It is most appropriate to keep the geographical scope small and to begin with familiar territory and then expand that scope as the programme matures. Within a multi-plant firm for example, one site may be chosen initially. If the geographical coverage is to be expanded over time then a plan for this expansion needs to be drawn up and communicated.

Cultural differences and language barriers will make auditing in unfamiliar settings more difficult and this will have a clear impact on the planning stage. It may mean that extra personnel are taken on by the auditing team to cover such problems, but there are benefits in using the same core auditing team so that consistency and comparability in assessing the overall picture can be achieved.

Subject Scope

The precise scope of the subjects to be audited will depend on the particular company or facility under consideration. It is vital, however, to recognize the interdependence between environmental issues and other key elements of a company's activities. Environmental audits often include some assessment of the following broader areas:

- Occupational health
- Safety in the workplace
- Product safety
- Security
- Employment practices
- Transportation safety
- Transportation to and from the workplace
- Inventory control
- Production methodology
- Corporate culture
- Industrial relations
- Participatory arrangements
- Animal testing

Since environmental considerations need to be integrated at least some comment on these areas might be expected. However, the extent to which they are properly assessed will have an impact on the cost and length of the audit and therefore some boundaries are clearly necessary.

Scope Within the Organization

In large companies senior management will have to decide which operations and business units are to be covered by the audit programme and there will need to be a step-by-step or gradualist approach. The environmental impact and significance of different business units will be quite disparate. Once again though, there is a need to identify priorities and in many companies, at least initially, there is a need to target segments of company activity which are perceived as being the most likely to cause environmental damage. Top of the list here tends to be central production processes and research laboratories. More extensive audits will include warehouses, administration systems, and empty premises. In time, the scope of the audit should be expanded to include joint ventures, suppliers, contractors, vendors and distributors. There are already some large companies committed to the environmental auditing process who are expressing a preference for buying from companies which have an auditing system in place themselves.

The Scope and Development of the Audit Over Time

As corporate audit programmes mature, they will be conducted against an evolving set of criteria. The environmental review will have concentrated on investigating the broad environmental context in which the firm operates, identifying problems so that they can be corrected, and putting stress on verifying compliance status. At first audits will replicate this procedure and will include an assessment of the impact of any chemicals used and the measurement of polluting emissions and deposits. In time however, more sophisticated audits will have to assess the effectiveness of the environmental management control systems and will be expected to gradually extend their scope. The more sophisticated the audit, the more it will help the company control its overall environmental performance and provide assurance that environmental functions are operating satisfactorily and eliminating the gaps or 'blind spots' that may exist. Over time the audit should help to develop a uniform approach to managing environmental activities and further develop the integrated environmental management system.

Environmental management effectiveness should be so defined as to be measurable over time. Basic measures which are quantitatively measurable will include an improved compliance record, reduced number and size of fines, improved accident and incident statistics and a reduced volume or potentiality of environmental hazards. There will be other measures more difficult to quantify but nevertheless important. These include improved reputation, favourable publicity and being cited as an example of good practice.

THE NEED FOR OBJECTIVITY AND INDEPENDENCE IN THE AUDIT PROCEDURE

Environmental auditing, like financial auditing, requires independence and objectivity if the results of the activity are to be credible. In time, just as with financial auditing, such independence will not only be desirable but will become mandatory. Auditors need to be able to carry out their work freely and objectively, so that they are in a position to provide management with an honest, impartial and unbiased view of the environmental status of the subject under assessment. No auditor of any value will take on a contract unless independence can be guaranteed since interference will lead to competing objectives, compromise and incomplete conclusions. The auditing system requires that any assessment should be based on facts and that those facts should be documented.

Post-audit there may be a need to weigh up the audit findings against other objectives and imperatives but this is beyond the scope of the auditor and is a task which clearly returns to senior management and policy-makers. The auditor should not be influenced by outside factors such as the impact on profitability, market share or production schedules. Optimum strategies to assure objectivity and independence include the following requirements:

- At least part of the audit team should not be employed by the company in any other capacity than as an external consultant, neither should they have a vested interest in the ownership of the company.
- In the first instance the audit report should be presented to senior

management and where necessary only to those who do not have day to day responsibility for the business units being audited.

- The audit team itself should be brought together from a range of backgrounds and disciplines and put into a situation where there is little potential for bias. Companies wishing to undergo an environmental audit should be wary of using consultancy firms which claim that they can offer a complete package without the use of any external personnel brought in for specific reasons. In this way bias may often be introduced by the wish to gain repeat business.

There are however cost implications to bear in mind here. Using only external consultants will not be cheap and may seem to be wasteful of considerable expertise within the organization. Many large organizations may wish to develop their own internal auditing unit but at the very least some form of third party independent verification should be seen as essential.

USING QUESTIONNAIRES FOR ENVIRONMENTAL AUDITS

One very efficient and relatively cost-effective way of collecting data on a company's environmental performance is by the use of questionnaires. A well designed questionnaire will save auditors time both in data collection and in subsequent analysis. Questionnaires may either be sent to key personnel to be completed by them or administered by an interviewer.

When a pre-audit questionnaire is used there are three major objectives which should be taken into consideration. First, it should prepare management for the type and detail of the information which will be required for the audit, helping them to put the audit requirements into perspective. Secondly, the questionnaire should collect basic information, such as plans and records, to be gathered and forwarded to the audit team in advance of the site visit thus saving on on-site time. Thirdly, a key role of the questionnaire will be to help in the identification of the key individuals at the facility responsible for managing key areas of the facility's activities and who will be required for interview at the time of the site visit. This information will ensure that the audit team are familiar with operations on site prior to visiting.

To be effective, however, questionnaires have to be systematic and provide for a full coverage of environmental issues. The following common principles should therefore be adopted in the design of questionnaires:

- They should be easy to understand and unambiguous.
- They should be as simple and brief as possible without losing any of the information required.
- Questionnaires should be designed with measurement and analysis in mind and most responses should be quantifiable in some way.
- They should minimize the potential for errors during completion.

These four principles together mean that a commonly used and successful approach is to design the questionnaire with as many tick boxes as possible and encourage a graded response where appropriate. It is useful to invite whoever is completing the form to use rating scales and ranking procedures. This structured approach using closed questions will be easy to analyze. However, such a structured approach will require a detailed knowledge of the organization's activities in order to prepare, and it may sometimes limit the respondent's replies.

Therefore there will also be a need for some more open questions on the questionnaire, where an unconstrained response is encouraged. If attitudes or opinions about issues or policies are being sought, space should be provided for respondents to express themselves more freely and an introductory letter with the questionnaire should make it clear that any criticism of the company will not be seen as disloyalty but as a constructive attempt at aiding the company's environmental improvement programme.

The way in which specific questions are worded will also be an important factor in determining the quality of information obtained. Questions should only ask for one piece of information at a time and complicated questions should be broken down into parts. Ambiguous questions and ambiguous terminology should be avoided. For example the word 'efficient', although important in determining the environmental performance of the firm, should be avoided in questionnaires because it may mean different things to different people. In circumstances like these the question must be precise in asking for information.

Where a questionnaire is to be given to a respondent to complete, the presentation and layout of the questionnaire is important. A professional-looking document which explains the purpose of the study is likely to be treated with more respect, and consequently answers should be of a higher quality.

The questionnaire should contain an introductory page which outlines:

- the purpose of the questionnaire;
- the likely benefits of the survey to the organization and the respondent;
- the confidentiality of the respondent's answers where opinions are being sought;
- the fact that the questionnaire and information gathering process has the support of senior management;
- a contact name and contact point, should further information or clarification be required.

The questionnaire is not easy to compile and will often contain hundreds rather than tens of questions. Consultants usually guard their questionnaires with much care since they are valuable resources which will have taken a long time to compile if they are comprehensive. It is nevertheless possible to provide the broad headings under which detailed questions will be asked. They are:

1. General information about the company, its ownership, activities, products, production processes, markets and suppliers.
2. A site history including the length of time the process has been operated, modifications of the site, earlier uses of the site, drainage and

water sources and whether there have been any accidents or spillages on the site.

3. External factors such as local amenities, information about the local geography and infrastructure and other industries in the area.
4. The environmental management system and environmental policy of the organization, contacts and relationships with local authorities, accident and emergency procedures and statutory regulations applying to the site.
5. Legal compliance, the discharge of gases and effluent, air emissions, waste management and noise nuisance.
6. Storage of raw materials, semi-finished and finished products, the storage of hazardous materials and construction details.
7. Transport and transport policies including the number and type of vehicles operated from the site.
8. Special substances.
9. Relationships with the local community, local authority, regulatory bodies and pressure groups.
10. Accident and emergency procedures and communications with emergency services.
11. Other issues which may be relevant to the environmental performance of the organization and/or site.

Questionnaires may also be used to identify the environmental performance of suppliers, contractors and vendors. Increasingly there is a need to integrate their performance into your own assessment and this is particularly the case where organizations are committed to cradle to the grave responsibility of their products. Confidentiality is at the heart of such questionnaires although they are likely to be more general and less extensive than pre-audit questionnaires. They will enquire about environmental policies, environmental management systems and the results of environmental reviews and audits carried out. Although they will be somewhat different in their scope and coverage, the general principles relating to questionnaire design and delivery outlined here remain the same.

CONCLUSIONS

In the early 1990s when we experienced a rapid growth in environmental awareness in industry, it was the environmental audit which was seen as the first great step towards improving environmental performance and many companies boasted about the fact that they had had an environmental audit. Because of developments such as the introduction of ISO 14001, businesses are coming to realize that it is the environmental management system which should be at the centre of the organization and that environmental auditing is an integral part of that system, which checks not only compliance and measures environmental improvements, but also checks the effectiveness of the system itself. What we mean by an environmental audit and how it is implemented is also becoming clearer and the key difference between a review and an audit needs to be clearly recognized.

However, there are still too many firms who, having undertaken a single environmental audit, subsequently claim to be an environmentally conscious firm. Conscious they might be but effective they are not. As with so much of environmental management, the audit has to be an ongoing process which never ends. The key role of the audit must be to check and assess all the other activities of the firm in relation to environmental improvement. EU moves to standardize the auditing process and an encouragement to publish audit reports is to be welcomed. But auditing is a technique which is still in its infancy and there is much scope for experimentation. This is particularly so in the area of measuring environmental performance.

REFERENCES

Elkington, J and Hailes, J (1991) *The Green Business Guide*, Victor Gollancz, London

ICC (1989) 'Environmental Auditing' International Chamber of Commerce, Paris

ICC (1991) 'ICC Guide to Effective Environmental Auditing', International Chamber of Commerce, Paris

Welford, R J (1994) *Cases in Environmental Management and Business Strategy* Pitman Publishing, London

Chapter 8

Life Cycle Assessment

Richard Welford

INTRODUCTION

Up until now we have stressed the internal workings and organization of the firm as the focus for corporate environmental management. However, we must recognize that the products and services which a company provides will also have their own environmental impacts. Life cycle assessment allows us to track the environmental impact of these products services throughout their life (from cradle to grave) and identify areas of environmental damage. In so doing we are then able to redesign products and production and distribution methods which will reduce environmental damage. This methodology therefore represents a very powerful tool in the strategies available to businesses to improve their environmental performance.

The principals of life cycle assessment are not new. In the 1970s, fuel cycle studies were common amongst very high energy users who wanted to minimize energy consumption. Life cycle costing techniques have also been used by some management accountants in trying to build up a clearer picture of overhead cost allocation. Only in the past few years, however, has life cycle assessment really spread to become a tool which identifies the activities that are involved in the whole life of a product. This profile can then be used in the assessment of environmental burdens.

Life cycle assessment (LCA) is about taking a cradle to grave approach. In other words it is an analysis covering every stage and every significant environmental impact of a product from the extraction and use of raw materials through to the eventual disposal of the components of the product and their decomposition back to the elements. However, in trying to stress the complete life cycle of the product we might consider using the terms from conception to resurrection and for practical purposes of business strategy we should stress that it is about design to recycling. We will see that it is at the design stage where much can be done to improve a product's overall environmental performance.

LCA has sometimes been seen as a controversial field of study. Fundamentally it is a tool to be used to shed light on the product's environmental impact at every stage from extraction to disposal. The detailed LCA research study may, for example, include mining, forestry techniques, energy and water use, air and water pollution, solid and hazardous waste production, damage occurring during the use of the product (including an assessment of possible misuse) and the repair, re-use, recyclability and disposal of a product. LCA can be used to compare the environmental impacts of similar products. For example, it might be used to assess the environmental impact of a polystyrene cup versus a paper cup versus a conventional pottery cup. Starting from the acquisition of the raw material and the effects of the manufacturing processes, and working throughout the product life cycle from manufacture to disposal (including an evaluation of the energy and water used in washing the pottery alternative), the sum of net effects can be evaluated, compared and a decision taken about the option which causes least damage.

The LCA process is necessarily quite complex and detailed. It requires the active cooperation of suppliers and collaboration is a prerequisite for progress. However, since LCA has been taken seriously by businesses, there is increasing concern that it may become a non-ecological activity. For example, it is clearly in the interest of suppliers of bulk commodities to draw the boundaries of LCA quite tightly in order to focus attention on those factors which are most easily controlled: wastes, polluting emissions and energy consumption. However, a full ecological consideration of product life cycles also has to take into account the impact of raw material procurement on biodiversity, endangered habitats, human and animal rights and non-renewable resources. Ignoring these issues may be convenient (especially to the agrochemical, petrochemical, chemical and mining industries), but it is not tolerable from an ecological perspective (Wheeler, 1993).

THE ADVANTAGES OF LIFE CYCLE ASSESSMENT

Life cycle assessment brings with it a number of advantages often overlooked by traditional environmental auditing methodologies. The concentration on the product, rather than the system, facilitates direct measurement of environmental impact. Being directly linked to products also means that environmental strategy can be linked into the marketing system and therefore marketing and environmental strategy become intertwined. LCA also widens the environmental analysis beyond management systems and site-specific production attributes which can so easily hide environmental damage up or down the supply chain. The product specific approach also aids environmental communication because of the clear link between LCA and eco-labelling.

A concentration on products also allows us to track the inputs into the production process, to track the sources of those inputs and, therefore, to say something about possible impacts on developing countries and the concepts of equity and futurity. It is therefore a tool which can more directly measure progress towards sustainable development. Moreover, tracking the life cycle of the product forward enables us to say much more about environmental damage then we can in a traditional assessment of processes. It fundamentally places the concept of futurity (which is a key issue for sustainable development) within our overall measurement of performance.

The process of LCA puts more emphasis on the role of design and re-design. It is often accepted that 80–90 per cent of the total life cycle costs associated with a product are committed by the final design of the product before production or construction actually begins (Fabrycky and Blanchard 1991, Gatenby and Foo 1990). Similarly, waste resulting from the product creation, use and disposal are largely determined by original design. To date, this has not been the central focus of the design phase, nor have designers commonly thought about futurity and equity implications of the products which they are developing. However, the LCA approach begins to raise these issues (outlined in chapter 1) and pushes them to the forefront of the design task. Traditional auditing methodologies cannot perform such a function.

The main application of LCA should therefore be as an internal management tool to assist in the minimization of product environmental impact. LCA provides an analytical framework through which this can be achieved. As such it should be incorporated into all environmental strategies and the management systems which seek to improve environmental performance.

To date, LCA is, however, a very underdeveloped area in terms of research and the development of methodologies. For this reason it has not been taken up by that many organizations. It is useful at this stage to highlight one of the key problems with the LCA approach which has dogged its inception. The problem concerns how impractical LCA can be if it is unbounded. In a far reaching life cycle assessment absolutely everything connected with a particular product would have to be measured and all measurements and impacts would have to be assessed according to an unlimited time horizon. While this is perhaps desirable in measures associated with sustainability, it is nonetheless impossible. Unless bounds are placed on the assessment, the inventory of impacts grows exponentially. There is therefore a fundamental need to put boundaries in place and this will involve fundamental decisions being made. Such decisions are not easy when our ultimate aim is measurement with respect to the environment, to equity and to futurity. This is therefore an area where we need some fundamental research and debate.

LCA aims to assess and therefore help producers to minimize the environmental impact of a product at all stages in its life. As an internal management tool for the company, the application of LCA is a way of clearly establishing the impact of a product throughout its life and hence a way of identifying key areas for attention. Within the firm, whether this is carried out in an exact, objective or quantitative way is not of fundamental importance. The benefits of LCA accrue through the focusing of managerial minds on all aspects of the product's environmental profile. The undertaking of this process will automatically aid future decision making to better incorporate the environmental dimension and therefore to lessen impact.

The EU eco-labelling scheme is based on the application of LCA. It aims to assess and recognize best practice in minimizing overall product impact and to communicate these achievements to potential customers. It is therefore necessary to compare and rank the environmental impact of a number of different products and to award the label to the best environmental performers. Once the label becomes widely adopted it could provide the necessary information on product environmental impact to all those who are interested and negate the need for supplier questionnaires. To do this effectively, the process of LCA must be developed to provide an objective and widely accepted framework through which the environmental impact of similar products can be measured and compared. However, the process of LCA is as yet far from being an exact and objective science.

THE LCA PROCESS

The aim of LCA is to highlight those particular areas in the environmental profile of a product where producers or vendors should focus their response in order to minimize their environmental impact. In many cases such a response will be through the redesign of the product. Should the major area of environmental impact be during use, for example, with the case of washing machines, then efforts to reduce the impact of the good should centre on providing the consumer with better knowledge and advice on how to use the product, and redesigning the product so that its environmental impact during use is reduced. Alternatively, if the major area of environmental impact occurs as a result of the use of non-renewable resources then alternative sources should be sought and again, the product might well undergo some redesign to reduce or eliminate the dependence on scarce resources. In all cases, those aspects of the product which generate significant environmental impact should be revised.

In practical terms, LCA provides a systematic framework through which the constituents of the product and their environmental impacts which are selected for study can be analyzed and the potential for impact reduction assessed. In effect, life cycle assessment is an information gathering exercise. It is fundamental to new product development and should be a regular tool of analysis whenever a product is redesigned. LCA attempts to provide information on all facets of a product's environmental performance and the results of the assessment must be incorporated into the overall environmental management strategy of the firm. As process and product design are inextricably linked, the importance of an integrated approach which aims to minimize the overall environmental impact of a company cannot be overemphasized.

The LCA itself involves a number of stages. These are:

1. The identification of areas of environmental impact in order to enable further assessment.
2. The quantification of energy and material inputs, emissions and waste outputs and any other potential area of environmental damage within the areas identified in 1.
3. An assessment of the environmental impact and impact mechanisms of the areas identified in 2.
4. The establishment of options and strategies for improving each stage of the life cycle of the product.

The strength of the LCA lies in the systematic collection and collation of quantitative data which should establish the extent of any environmental impact and its scope for improvement. Simply going through the LCA process will focus attention on issues which can so easily be ignored and not considered. The process will confirm or challenge any assumptions and preconceptions made and it will facilitate a greater understanding of the ecological impacts involved.

There are of course difficulties in the LCA process. One controversy relating to LCA arises when it attempts to quantify and rank a range of different environmental impacts. For example, LCAs undertaken for washing machines have established that without any doubt the most considerable environmental impacts for all washing machines are in their consumption of energy and water during their use (Hemming, 1992). Should one particular washing machine use less water and energy than a competitor, it is clear that its environmental impact is the lower of the two. However, should one be more energy efficient and thus make a lower contribution to global warming while a second uses less water and detergent and thus has a lower impact on water consumption and pollution, then establishing objectively which has the lower impact becomes very difficult. With a product significantly more complex than a washing machine (eg a car) many argue that the LCA process and any comparisons between products using this process would be impractical. Quite simply, the extraordinary range of raw materials and components used in modern products and the infinite range of interactions with different ecosystems which will occur when emissions are released into the environment, means that quantitatively assessing and ranking the environmental impact of many products with many different impacts becomes virtually impossible.

The potential scope of an LCA is enormous if we were to consider absolutely every environmental impact of the product and all the knock-on effects caused by direct impact on the environment. Aspects which have little or no impact on the environment have to be ignored and there must be some limit to the examination of knock-on effects. It is clear therefore that before beginning the process of LCA, it is important to decide upon the scope and objectives of the exercise and to consider what constitutes a significant environmental impact. It is necessary to set the boundaries of the LCA to manageable limits. Current LCA methodology selects those facets of the process which are likely to provide the most relevant information, for instance in highlighting any inputs which are especially damaging or any stages of procurement, distribution, processing, use or disposal which can be readily improved. For internal use, the scope of LCA may be very selective or partial depending on the objectives to be achieved. However, for external use where comparative measures of total environmental impact are needed, the LCA must be much more detailed and comprehensive.

There are four generally accepted stages in the LCA methodology:

1. **Inventory** – The definition of the inventory involves gathering quantifiable data relating to the material and energy inputs into a product
across its whole life cycle and any associated emissions, discharges and
wastes. This should relate to all stages of the product life cycle from
extraction and cultivation, procurement, processing, manufacture,
packaging, distribution, use, disposal and decomposition. Resources

used and emissions generated should be measured per unit of output produced. Although this stage may demand extensive research, particularly for companies which use a large number of inputs or who operate along lengthy supply chains, it is relatively straightforward.

2. **Impact analysis** – Impact analysis considers how the inventory may affect the environment and it is therefore much less straightforward than the definition of the inventory. It involves establishing the environmental impact of each of the areas documented under the inventory. This may be extremely complicated because, in many cases, the impact of an emission will depend upon the nature of the emission, the environment into which it is emitted and the interaction of a number of characteristics. The analysis should cover ecological damage, human and animal health, habitat modification and lifestyle changes as a minimum. The boundaries of this stage of LCA will therefore be defined by the depth of analysis which is deemed appropriate, necessary and possible.

3. **Impact assessment** – Once the scope and level of environmental impact has been established, some assessment or measurement of this impact is needed. Impact assessment is often broken down into three distinct phases:

    Classification – This involves grouping the data in an inventory table into a number of impact categories (eg human health, natural resources, ecological impact etc)

    Characterization – This phase involves the quantification, aggregation and analysis of impact data within the agreed impact categories. This leads to a number of impact profiles consisting of impact descriptions and associated measures.

    Valuation – This phase involves the weighting of the different impact categories so that they can be compared. Impacts can be established both quantitatively and qualitatively. Quantitative impact assessment develops a list of the amounts of emissions and some measurement of their impact. In many cases, this is as much factual assessment as is possible in the absence of an element of subjectivity. However, an LCA to this point can provide an internal benchmark against which to compare future performance and is therefore of considerable use.

4. **Improvement** – The final stage of LCA represents feedback for improving the environmental profile of the product. In effect, the improvement stage demonstrates where the environmental profile of the product ought to be altered through redesign of the product and its manufacturing process. A formal and systematic appraisal of the product's environmental impact will often reveal areas where relatively simple fine tuning will reduce environmental impact. The improvement stage will assess the technically and economically feasible options available at all stages of the product's life to improve the environmental impact of the good.

The LCA process is therefore quite intricate and requires considerable analytical skills. There is, of course, a real resource cost to the LCA process itself. In many cases, however, the scope of the study may not necessitate such a comprehensive LCA and the process of LCA might be simplified in a number of ways. Different components of the study can be collated in relation to separate impacts, for instance all those areas where solid waste is generated, energy is consumed and so on. This will reduce the number of variants and simplify the process considerably. For some commonly used inputs such as energy and some raw materials, databases of environmental impacts are being established in order to provide common LCA measures. These databases can offer standardized impact assessments for a range of energy and material inputs.

As experience of LCA progresses skills can be built up and levels of subjectivity will be reduced. As LCA becomes more widely applied, the availability of widely accepted data will increase and hence the process will be simplified. The external application of LCA, although considerably more complex, is therefore set to increase as environmental credentials need to become more transparent.

PROBLEMS WITH LCA

We have already identified the fact that LCA can be difficult and that outcomes will be very dependent on the scope and depth of analysis to be applied to the situation. On top of this we must be aware that when used as a tool of assessment this methodology will introduce other problems because of the judgement and subjectivity which is introduced into an otherwise objective exercise. Let us consider some of these problems in more depth.

Problem 1: Parameters

A fundamental problem occurs at the outset of the environmental inventory which is related to deciding how far reaching the assessment should be. If we consider paper production for example, should we consider the type of saw used for tree felling? An even deeper assessment might consider where the petrol comes from to drive a chain saw, who is the most efficient petrol producer, where the nuts and bolts came from for the saw and what emissions are generated during its use. There is therefore a need to define appropriate levels of investigation and this can be defined in terms of primary, secondary and tertiary levels of analysis. These boundaries set the cut-off points for analysis and must be agreed before any inventory is finally compiled.

In our example we might consider the sources of wood used in paper production to be at the primary level along with issues of distribution, processing, use and disposal. The environmental impact of the chain saw itself might be considered at the secondary level and the production of the chain saw itself as a tertiary level issue. The decision then relates to how much of the impact at the secondary and tertiary levels is considered in the life cycle assessment.

Problem 2: Comparison of Data

Data for energy can be expressed in joules, mass of physical waste can be measured in kilogrammes and air pollution in terms of parts per million. A problem arises when the environmental impact of these different measures are to be compared in terms of their impact on the environment. For example, is one extra part per million of an air pollutant more or less damaging than an extra kilogramme of a waterborne waste, given the same toxic level? Any such comparison would seem to depend on a significant degree of subjectivity because it is impossible to combine all the inventory data into a single number that gives a weighting to all the possible unknowns.

The same sorts of issues are relevant to the comparison of end products. For example, to what extent is it really possible to compare two different technologies which perform the same task? Consider the electric kettle versus a gas kettle. Where would we begin to make the sorts of comparisons necessary to begin to form some sort of judgement?

Problem 3: Combination of Issues

Problem 2 introduced the idea that disposal to ground may or may not be more damaging than disposal to air or sea but we cannot really tell without a thorough investigation of the impacts on ecosystems in the short and long term. Moreover, our one kilogramme of waste may not cause much damage alone but when combined with other wastes and discharges it may react to cause a significant problem into the future. Thus any comparison of wastes must consider timescales, the combined impact of other polluters' activities and must, in turn, value different kinds of ecosystems in different ways. Thus any comparison of different effects must consider the direct and indirect impacts of a pollutant and might involve some scenario planning and analysis.

Problem 4: Disposal and Decomposition

A major problem in our modern consumerist age is that when some products have been used up it is economically and (arguably) environmentally more efficient to throw them away rather than to use up the energy and other resources which might be needed in recycling them. However, what is rarely considered in this sort of analysis is the damage done to the environment in the longer term. If products are sent to landfill sites then we evaluate the disposal in terms of the cost of landfill and the loss of resources. We rarely consider the impact of decomposition, of landfill leakage which will in part be caused by our product and the effect of land use change. Extending our analysis beyond disposal to include decomposition effects is extremely difficult of course.

Problem 5: Assignable Cause

The whole process of LCA and the quantification of environmental damage assumes that impact occurring as a result of the product belongs to that product and should be assessed and costed accordingly. This assumes that there are clearly identifiable and assignable property rights. However, since property rights do not exist for much of the environment, then exact quantification of environmental damage is subjective and quantitative assessment must be based on judgements. Moreover where pollution is caused by a combination of impacts from two or more different products, which should be assigned that damage? It might be that one product's impact is negligible until mixed with the other. Both owners of the product are likely to want to assign the damage to the other in those cases.

These five problems need to be addressed at the planning stage of any LCA. They will sometimes be difficult to reconcile but that does not make the LCA process ineffective or useless. In many cases a change in attitude or business practices towards ecological management holds the answer to the problem. In terms of the problem over assignable cause, the acceptance of strict liability would seem to provide an answer here. In terms of disposability, if we imposed the true cost of disposal and decomposition into the price of the goods less may be bought. Moreover, if we put more emphasis on designing products which were worth repairing and reusing then the issue of disposal is reduced. This, in turn, is about producing goods which are of high quality.

WIDENING THE INVENTORY AND IMPACT ANALYSIS

Because LCA puts the emphasis on the product it is much more feasible to track ecological impacts (widely defined) along the whole life of the product. If we are ever to reach the aims of sustainable development, therefore, we will have to widen our definition of environmental or ecological impacts. When we conduct an LCA our inventory must include wider issues associated with sustainability. Although this makes the process more complex we ought, for example, to include in our inventory issues such as animal testing, an appropriate respect for all living things and their habitats, biodiversity and species preservation, human health, the rights of indigenous populations to lead traditional lives if they so wish, workers' rights and industrial democracy, the rights of women and minority groups and impacts on developig countries. LCA provides us with a tool to take a wider holistic approach and it should be central to our strategies for ecological management and sustainability (see Chapter 14).

CONCLUSION

LCA is an underused, under-researched and underrated tool of analysis. By forcing us to track a particular product (or service) from cradle to grave it forces us to widen our environmental dimensions. Central to the outcomes of the LCA is the improvement analysis which enables us to redesign products to improve their environmental characteristics at all stages of the life cycle. Although we have identified many problems in reaching this stage, further research in LCA techniques and the construction of databases detailing the environmental impacts of common processes, components and substances will begin to make fuller life cycle assessments more feasible. There will always be problems with assigning the cause of environmental problems to particular products and particular producers because of the range of processes and impacts which have diverse knock-on effects. However, a more responsible attitude to the environment based on the precautionary principle will begin to mitigate this problem as well. As with most management tools LCA must be used effectively, there must be commitment to correcting the deficiencies which the analysis turns up and there must be a continuous process of improvement. Such an approach will need to be ethical and take an ever wider view of the definition of the environment and sustainability.

REFERENCES

Fabrycky, W J and Blanchard, B S (1991) *Life cycle cost and economic analysis* Prentice Hall, New York

Gatenby, D A and Foo, G (1990) 'Design for X: the key to competitive and profitable markets' *AT&T Technical Journal*, 69, 2

Hemming, C (1992) 'Eco-labelling of Washing Machines: A UK Pilot Survey' *Integrated Environmental Management*, 1, 2

Wheeler (1993) 'Auditing for Sustainability: Philosophy and Practice of The Body Shop International' *Eco-management and Auditing*, 1, 1

Chapter 9

Measuring Environmental Performance

C William Young

INTRODUCTION

This chapter is concerned with the issue of measuring environmental performance at a company level. It will examine what can be measured and review the different techniques of measuring environmental performance in business. These include:

- quantitative and qualitative measures;
- contributor measures; and
- external relations measures.

'An evaluation of measures currently applied in business' (p 162) will then examine some practical examples of the above techniques currently used in industry. The next section examines theoretical methods, frameworks and models . Broadening the measures of environmental performance, the issues associated with measuring sustainability will then be discussed, followed by concluding remarks.

The business community is continually monitoring its performance so it can satisfy the market's needs, such as customer demands, while still achieving its internal goals. One of the most notable features of the environment debate in the late 1980s and early 1990s was the way in which the seemingly irreconcilable objectives of enhanced environmental performance and improved business performance moved closer together (Roberts, 1994). Environmental concerns now figure alongside a number of other key business objectives, and many organizations now contribute through in-house projects and area-based schemes to the improvement of local environmental conditions. Environmental management systems have been one of these routes followed by many organizations in the United States and Europe.

Previous chapters have described the workings of environmental management systems (EMS) and associated standards, where 'continuous improvement' of the organization's effect on the environment is a requirement.

Current EMS standards measure the organization's environmental performance by auditing the workings of the EMS and the self-determined objectives and targets. Some individual companies do use crude environmental measurements for their own ends, for example, number of skips of waste removed from the company and number of miles travelled on business. There is, nevertheless, a gap between auditing the workings of EMS and measuring the organization's environmental performance; 'Environmental performance indicators are measures of company proficiency in protecting the environment' (European Green Table, 1993). Hence carbon dioxide and methane emissions, for example, could be indicators of an organization's effect on global climate change.

James (1994) points out that the rising costs of controlling present pollution, cleaning up past pollution and dealing with communities, environmental groups and other stakeholders has made the environment a significant 'bottom line' issue for many companies. Senior managers in large firms may be aware of the ecological risks to society and the environmental risks to their companies, for example contaminated land, but what they desperately lack is the knowledge of how to operationalize systems to manage that risk (Gabel & Sinclair-Desgagne, 1992).

A possible solution is to develop a system for measuring the environmental performance and sustainability of organizations. Measuring performance is not alien to organizations, as the financial area of operations has been measured in terms of costs, revenues and profit. Using financial measures as indicators of a company's environmental performance without other forms of measurement would, however, be impossible. Measuring emissions would be based on current regulatory fines which would vary and only be valid if the emissions are above permitted levels. To measure company environmental policies through financial means would be impossible without other types of measures such as qualitative measures. On this note Jacobs (1991) argues that as far as indicators of environmental performance are concerned, withdrawing the requirement that the environment should be measured in monetary terms is extremely helpful.

Organizations may be aware that their operations affect the environment, but the question which will arise is 'why measure?' Increasingly organizations are under pressure to quantify their environmental performance and, in Figure 9.1, some principle motivations are suggested by James (1994), Ashford & Meima (1993) and Fiksel (1994).

The general groups of principle drivers are:

- financial stakeholders including investors;
- non-financial stakeholders such as regulators and local communities;
- company systems including costs – adverse and beneficial; and
- standards.

James suggested that the biosphere is a driver of environmental performance because activities such as pollution imply that pollution and other activities were starting to affect business. Perhaps this is happening in the form of the other groups of principal drivers, such as regulatory pressures.

Figure 9.1 Principle drivers of environmental performance (adapted from James, 1994; Ashford & Meima, 1993 and Fiksel, 1994)

From an economic policy viewpoint, environmental performance measurement can provide the tools to study the effectiveness of environmental regulation, taxes and various other kinds of economic instruments as means to improve the quality of the environment. The information derived from environmental performance measurement can provide policy makers with meaningful guidelines in order to implement relevant economic and/or regulatory instruments (Tyteca, 1994a).

Ashford & Meima (1993) explain that the environmental performance of the firm is the extent and effectiveness of actions which the firm takes to mitigate its environmental consequences. Four key environmental performance areas in organizations are identified by Welford & Gouldson (1993), in Figure 9.2. These areas are the company and its products, direct environmental impacts, infrastructure and external relations. These areas are split into further sub-sections, giving a spectrum coverage of the company:

- 'The company and its product(s), processes, procedures and operations' covers areas such as the involvement and integration of the company in the supply chain and the product(s)' use and disposal;
- 'Direct environmental impact' areas includes energy use and the impacts of the company on nature and ecosystems;
- 'Infrastructure' environmental performance areas include buildings and management systems;
- 'External relations', environmental performance area include education and environmental initiatives.

It is important that the environmental performance areas in Figure 9.2 are

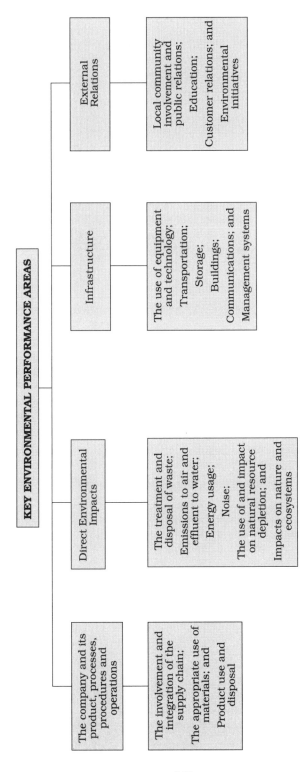

Figure 9.2 Key environmental performance areas in organizations (adapted from Welford & Gouldson, 1993)

151

used as the basis of any measures of an organization's environmental performance. These areas will provide a broad range of measures which will reflect the organization's environmental performance to a fuller extent.

WHAT CAN BE MEASURED?

Welford & Gouldson (1993) suggest that environmental performance needs to be integrated with other aspects of business performance; for example, shareholders may not be impressed with environmental improvements which reduce their dividends significantly. This may imply that each industrial sector or even each company needs to decide on individual measurement areas and priorities based on the formal EMS review. Information gained from the measures will lead to the formation of priorities which will deal, primarily, with the worst environmental performance areas in the company. These priorities may well coincide with or be led by national and international legislation or agreements on the reduction of use of certain substances and processes.

There are no absolute rules concerning what to measure, but some basic principles for choosing appropriate measures are:

- the areas identified must be capable of being measured;
- measures need to be consistent with environmental policy objectives;
- too many measures might confuse issues and be costly to implement;
- the measures need to be appropriate and understandable to those who have to act upon them;
- measures must be transparent and not reflect a hidden agenda; they should be clear to all involved and encourage participation and commitment; and
- measures must be appropriate over time so that significant improvements or deterioration can be mapped out and results can be communicated to stakeholders (Welford & Gouldson, 1993).

This is expanded on by James & Bennett (1994), who put forward the Principles of Successful Environment-Related Performance Measures, which are listed below:

- **Cascade:** Broad measures must be derived from strategic business objectives and then broken down into sub-measures appropriate to different levels and activities.
- **Commitment:** Environmental improvement depends upon the commitment of all employees. Involvement in the design and implementation of measures is the best means both of achieving 'buy-in' and of ensuring that they are workable.
- **Comparison:** Comparison is needed to place results in perspective and to provide benchmarks to drive continuous improvement.
- **Comprehensible:** Measures work best when they are simple and easily understood.
- **Comprehensive:** No one measure can encompass all environment-related concerns. A 'balanced scorecard' of multiple measures is needed.

- **Continuous improvement:** Measurement is a means to an end – that of improving environmental performance. Measures need to focus on areas where improvement is both necessary and feasible.
- **Controllable:** Measurement is demotivating and unproductive if there is not a clear relationship between a measure and actions for improvement.
- **Cost:** Corporate environmental management has to balance business and environmental considerations. Simple calculations of financial costs and benefits from environmental activities can help define priorities and identify 'win-win' options.
- **Credibility:** Measures have to be credible with key stakeholders, especially employees and environmental groups. On the one hand, they must be seen as fair and feasible, but on the other, focused on key areas and not just the easiest to deal with.
- **Customer focus:** It is vital that every measure has clearly defined customers, whose needs are taken into account in design and implementation.

Fiksel (1994) has identified some areas of environmental performance which could be measured, placing them under the headings of source and impact. Source measures address the presumed root causes or origins of environmental consequences associated with an organization's activities, for example emissions from a company. One advantage of source measures is they are both readily observable and controllable. Conversely, a disadvantage is that they are an indirect indicator of potential impacts and generally ignore differences in the fate, transport, exposure and effect pathways of substances among different organizations.

Impact performance measures directly address the impacts of concern, for example the quality of a river. However the technical and statistical uncertainties involved in assessing impacts and attributing them to specific sources can be problematic. In practice, company-specific and source-oriented indicators cover a broader range of categories of environmental impacts. The use of source measures also allows companies and regulatory agencies to establish clear targets for improvement (Fiksel, 1994).

Setting priorities and targets is important in order that objectives can be translated into workable programmes and those programmes become manageable. It is important when setting performance targets that they should be realistic and attainable but still sufficiently challenging. Objectives and targets should be quantified wherever practical to ensure that real attainment is recorded against the targets (Gilbert, 1993).

A method of recording the success or failure of a company's environmental programme is to produce a scorecard of differing weighted categories, (see Table 9.1). Rice (1993) produced a scorecard with a simple weighting scale for various categories of environmental performance areas of *very important, important, slightly important* and *not important*. The scorecard for US major companies includes categories such as toxic chemical releases and the comprehensiveness of the company's environmental programme. This produces a ranking of companies through the use of values that ranged from zero (worst) to ten (best) for performance in 20 key environmental areas.

Weighting schemes may be a method for monitoring a company's progress towards targets. Fiksel (1994) puts forward an argument for weighting schemes that may be adopted to reflect a variety of different considerations, including:

- values of different stakeholder groups (eg customer versus community);
- relative importance of environmental impacts (eg human health importance as opposed to ecology as a whole); and
- internal business priorities (eg strategic advantage).

An example of the method of calculating weightings in the form of an index of emissions is shown in Table 9.1. The weighting factor is subjective and will ultimately change over time due to the priorities of the decision maker. The actual discharge of components X, Y and Z is multiplied by the relevant weighting factor, resulting in a weighted discharge value for each component. To produce an overall figure for the company's current discharges the individual weighted discharges are added giving, in this case, 10540 units. This value is compared to the previous year's discharge value to produce the current year's emissions index, in this example 0.901. A value less than 1 means the company's environmental performance is improving as the emissions have reduced; a value of 1 means the company has neither increased or decreased its effect on the environment from the previous year, and a value greater than 1 means that the company's environmental performance has deteriorated.

Table 9.1 An example of a composite index of emissions*

	Weighting Factor	Actual Discharge	Weighted Discharge
Discharge of component X	1	300	300
Discharge of component Y	2	5000	10,000
Discharge of component Z	0.2	1200	240
			Total = 10540

$$\text{Current year's emissions index} = \frac{\text{Current year's discharge}}{\text{Previous year's discharge}} \quad \frac{10540}{11700} = 0.901$$

* adapted from *Business in the Environment* and KPMG Peat Marwick, 1992

While the aggregation of measures may be desirable for purposes of simplifying decision making, Fiksel does point out a number of problematic aspects of weighting schemes for environmental measures. Firstly, and maybe most importantly, there are usually implicit policies and value judgements embedded in the weighting system which are not apparent, yet may skew the results in unintended ways. For example, a company in a smog laden city may put more emphasis on reducing emissions to air than a similar company located out of the city.

Another disadvantage is that performance measures are much more meaningful when considered separately, whereas the significance of improvement in an aggregated score is unclear. For example, an organization's successful efforts to reduce solid waste disposal may be offset by the increased production of goods and hence increased emissions. Finally, aggregated measures invite comparisons among dissimilar products or facilities while concealing important differences between organizations, such as differing sizes and manufacturing processes.

It is possible to avoid the disadvantages of aggregated measures by, for example, a measurement system that captures the sources and rationales for all aggregated scores and will allow later exploration and decomposition of the results. Generally it is accepted that there is no universal weighting scheme that will suit the needs of diverse organizations and each industry and/or company should develop a scheme that suits its business characteristics (Fiksel, 1994).

In this field of environmental performance some authors are using the term environmental performance indicators (EPIs), which Tyteca (1994b) defines as tools that allow the analysis of the improvement (or deterioration) of a given firm's environmental performance. The environmental performance can be compared over time, or between various plants within a firm, or between various firms in an industry, or between the industrial sectors.

Another term used is 'envirometrics', described by James & Bennett (1994) as being the measurement of environmental phenomena. Ashford & Meima (1993) describe three categories of envirometrics:

1. Consequence envirometrics, which aim to measure the impacts of firms on the ecosystem.
2. Performance envirometrics seek to measure the relationship between environmental consequences and business practices and performance.
3. Sustainable envirometrics (measures of sustainability), where the information contained in consequence envirometrics must be considered in relation to what the ecosystem can sustainably bear, and link sustainable consequences to the business and technological practices which cause them.

In Table 9.2, James (1993) classifies envirometrics by the nature of the measure and stages of the product life cycle. The left hand column of Table 9.2 indicates the increasing complexity of the measures; from simple and uni-dimensional through normalized measures (relating data in two different dimensions), to more complex aggregate measures (which summarizes two or more individual measures). The top row of Table 9.2 indicates the life cycle stages and moves, in simple terms, from inputs through internal business processes to outputs of pollution and products.

Table 9.2 A typology of business envirometrics (adapted from James, 1993)

Increasing Complexity of Measurement	Stages of Life Cycle			
	Resources	*Business processes*	*(Pollution) outputs*	*Products*
Simple	Quantities Sourcing Recycled materials	Management Systems Training	Quantities Compliance Effects Financial	Durability Reconsumption Market share Produ
liability			costs/liabilities	
	Perceptions Conversion efficiency (energy/materials/quality)			
Normalized	Emissions/turnover Value added/emissions			
Aggregate	Financial (externalities/aggregate financial costs/liabilities) Scientific (Critical Volume) Scoring (eco-points, indices)			

Most of the simple/objective measures mentioned in Table 9.2 fall into six basic categories:

1. physical measures of mass and volume;
2. efficiency measures;
3. measures of environmental impact;
4. financial measures;
5. implementation measures; and
6. customer measures.

Many of these areas are measured to some extent in organizations at present. Some problems arise when they are not normalized or made relevant to business activities. For example, if a company's emissions fall, good environmental performance may be inferred from this, but in fact production may have decreased, causing the reduction in emissions. Another problem may arise when comparisons are made between organizations of differing sizes. A larger organization may be seen as a heavy polluter compared to the smaller company. If emissions are related to production then a better comparison can be made.

Aggregated measures are being developed to reduce complex information to a single number so that comparisons can be made between organizations. James (1993) has identified three methods; financial, scientific and scoring, though only scoring has been developed with any success, for example by Volvo. Aggregated measures are complex, often using involved equations and large databases, and subjective due to the use of biased value judgements about differing environmental factors, and hence they are difficult to develop.

QUANTITATIVE AND QUALITATIVE MEASURES

All organizations face the same challenge: how to identify measures that track and quantify change in an effective and useful way. In evaluating the different environmental performances of companies, Wehrmeyer (1993) suggests that three elements should be considered:

1. The attempt to provide an 'objective' assessment in the sense that the value judgements and assumptions taken are made prior to the data analyses. This focus restricts the evaluation of the physical dimensions (energy consumption, solid waste production) and does not consider 'social' or 'judgmental' issues, such as animal welfare, intellectual property rights of indigenous people and the like.
2. The problem of impact substitution. The difficulty of how to compare different environmental effects; for example, what is better: 10 mg of cadmium in the water medium or 15 $mg.m^3$ of SO_2 in the atmosphere?
3. The problem of what to do with local impacts. Most existing systems either treat all firms universally and hence do not adequately consider local impacts, or are very local in design and hence make corporate comparisons cumbersome.

It is clear that quantitative measures are obviously the easiest to deal with. These measures will relate to physical things where objective measures are possible. Davis (1994) states that quantity measures give weight and usefulness to qualitative information such as environmental policies, but only as long as the qualitative message is clear. A problem may arise in that current measures may, over time, become obsolete. This may be overcome by a regular audit of currently used measurements.

Fiksel (1994) describes quantitative measures as relying on empirical data and deriving numerical results in physical, financial or other meaningful terms. Thus these measurements are objective, meaningful and verifiable, but the data may be burdensome to gather or simply unavailable. Fiksel also identifies:

- *absolute or simple measures* – those that are defined with respect to a fixed measurement scale; and
- *relative or normalized measures* – those that are defined with respect to another metric or variable. A common approach is to use relative metrics over a given time period.

As previously suggested a general fault with the use of absolute or simple measures is that it could lead to inappropriate comparisons of performance between two or more organizations, but on the other hand, relative or normalized measures are generally less biased by differences in organizational characteristics. This potential for abuse of information has rightly made many companies wary of reporting their environmental performance results (Fiksel, 1994).

Taking a closer examination of qualitative measurements, Fiksel explains that these rely on semantic distinctions based on observation and judgement. Again it is possible to assign numerical values (or scores) to qualitative measures. An advantage of qualitative measurements is that they impose a relatively small data collection burden and are easy to implement. However, a disadvantage is that they implicitly incorporate subjective information and therefore are difficult to validate. Thus a combination of qualitative and quantitative measures would give a broad range of indicators of environmental performance.

CONTRIBUTOR MEASURES

Contributor measures as defined by Welford & Gouldson (1993), or process improvement indicators as described by Wolfe & Howes (1993), measure the internal workings of the organization, such as work systems and management systems. The following are some examples given by Wolfe & Howes of process improvement indicators:

- *environmental investment* – money invested in technology change;
- *training* – number of sites with employees trained in environmental health and safety;
- *management commitment* – number of times a year plant managers address environmental issues with staff;
- *employee awareness* – percentage of employees aware of environmental issues, tracked by survey; and
- *systems* – existence of a management plan for each underground storage site.

Caution must be taken when using the above process improvement indicators; for example measuring the money spent on research and development or measuring the number of employees trained does not indicate the effectiveness of how the money is spent, or the effectiveness of the people being trained. Expenditure is just one indicator and as such will only tell one part of the story.

In Table 9.3 Welford & Gouldson (1993) provide some examples of contributor performance measures. The examples may already be included in an EMS or LCA.

Life cycle assessment, (see Figure 9.3), or cradle to grave assessment, is a form of environmental audit for product assessment (Gilbert, 1993). The life cycle model shown in Figure 9.3 analyses the different stages of a particular product, eg washing powder, from when it is produced until it is destroyed or disposed of.

The life cycle model includes inputs of raw materials into the product, the product in use and the disposal of the product into the natural environment.

Table 9.3 Examples of contributor performance measures (Welford & Gouldson, 1993)

Performance area	Examples of measure
Technology	Level of investment in new technology; substitution of clean technology; and effectiveness of new systems
Materials	Utilization of process materials; and use of renewable resources
Products	Implementation of design changes; level of investment to meet higher environmental standards; and level of rejects and direct waste
Suppliers	Achievement of supplier survey; implementation of supplier awareness initiatives; and new procurement procedures
Management systems	Level of implementation of system; effectiveness of new procedures; performance against audit; level of organizational commitment and participation; and existence of training programmes

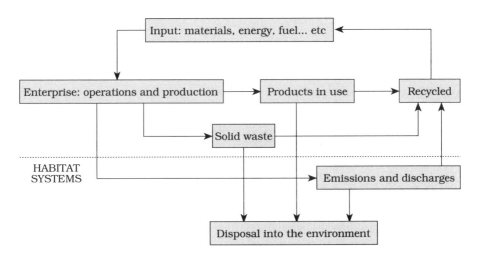

Figure 9.3 Life cycle model (Ledgerwood, Street & Therivel, 1992)

Currently LCA may be most useful within a company context (ie, within an intra-organizational network), and best integrated into a broader environmental management system.

Contributor measures of performance include the appropriate use of technology and materials, product and supplier performance; and the effectiveness of environmental management systems. Some of these measures could go further, for example the existence of training programmes could include the effectiveness of the training of personnel. The achievement of a supplier survey could be extended to what action the customer company takes on the strength of the results, for example by not buying from certain less environmentally friendly companies. However these measures may be beyond the scope of many companies because of lack of commitment, finance and appropriate expertise.

EXTERNAL RELATIONS MEASURES

James & Bennett (1994) use the term environment-related performance measurement which includes not only environmental performance measurement but also measures of the impact of environmental action or inaction on customer perceptions and profitability. Wells et al (1992) also identify customer satisfaction as an important measure of effective environmental measurement systems. The environmental performance measure looks from three linked perspectives:

1. process improvements;
2. environmental results; and
3. customer satisfaction.

Wells et al explain that process measures evaluate (generally through management audits) how effectively EMSs are working. They may produce environmental results showing whether, in fact, they affect environmental and bottom-line performance. Customer satisfaction measures determine whether customers respond, by changing purchasing behaviour, to improvements in company performance. Only implementing all three measurements will give a complete picture of the success of environmental programmes. Ultimately the success of the environmental programmes will be measured by whether the programme's customers are satisfied.

Customer satisfaction measures, continue Wells et al, are critical because they provide a single independent and comprehensive measure of success. It is suggested that, over the long term, the best indicator of success for the corporate environmental programme is the satisfaction of multiple customer groups. In the past and currently, some organizations have seen and continue to see corporate environmental programmes as a matter of regulatory compliance. By recognizing that environmental programmes support customer-oriented business objectives, the use of customer satisfaction measures can promote the integration of environmental programmes into corporate strategy. Information about customer values can be a powerful tool for gaining the attention of the stakeholders in organizations whose support may be needed to take action. Such stakeholders include process managers, engineers and others on which it is depended on for implementation of programmes. Additionally, a variety of intermediate stakeholders such as regulators, legislators, community groups and others who may have a strong influence on the allocation of the company's environmental management resources. Useful measures of customer satisfaction can be made qualitatively as a result of contact with customers, eg surveys (Wells et al, 1992).

Identifying audiences beyond the customer is a good first step, suggest Wolfe & Howes (1993). Different measures are important to people at different levels in the organization, as well as to those outside. The following are relevant when preparing to communicate with external stakeholders:

1. Identify the audiences (regulators, shareholders, community groups and so on).
2. Identify key influencers within these groups to help you uncover their agenda.
3. Determine what they want to know and why.
4. Test communications with key influencers in target groups before public release.
5. Report on what has been done, and have the data to back it up. (Typically, external stakeholders are more interested in environmental results and customer satisfaction than in process measures).
6. Provide a mix of 'good' and 'bad' news.
7. Tell the truth, and keep communications clear and consistent with the work; consumer tolerance for hype is at an all-time low.
8. Put money into good work, rather than into a good report about mediocre work.
9. Use information as an opportunity to get feedback.
10. Create a dialogue, which can help build trust and credibility.

In Table 9.4 Welford & Gouldson (1993) give examples of measures of external relations performance which are split into three areas; impact measures, positive measures and risk measures. Impact measures such as the number of prosecutions and levels of complaints may already be recorded as part of management policy or environmental legislation. Dealings with the public and media may also be recorded by the marketing department of the company, as good or adverse exposure will directly affect sales.

Positive measures include public awareness programmes which must be credible and from which transparent or adverse results may occur. It is likely that this information will be readily available if the company has sound health and safety procedures and environmental management systems and associated standards in place, with regular audits of these areas.

External relation measures need to be used in conjunction with contributor, qualitative and quantitative measures for a true overall picture of a particular company's environmental performance. These measures have been put into practice to a certain extent by companies, trade organizations and others with a mixture of success.

Table 9.4 Examples of external relations performance measures (Welford & Gouldson, 1993)

Area	Examples of measures
Impact measures	Number of prosecutions; levels of complaints; positive and negative exposure from pressure groups; number of complimentary or adverse media reports; and falls or increases in sales related to environmental impact
Positive measures	Level of public disclosure; availability of environmental impact information; level of consultation with outside agencies; public awareness programmes; and level of support for external environmental programmes
Risk measures	Measures of the probability of accidents; existence and understanding of emergency plans; speed and effectiveness of emergency plan; communication with emergency services; and public disclosure of likely impact of accidents

AN EVALUATION OF MEASURES CURRENTLY APPLIED IN BUSINESS

Welford & Gouldson (1993) suggest that much information needed in the analysis of performance may already be available in, for example, accounts, but may need converting into a format for monitoring and control. Other information will have to be sought and hence monitoring equipment may have to be installed. A problem may arise in trying to verify some information – this could be resolved, in part, by adherence to environmental standards. However not all information gained from certain measures will be included in environmental standards. Hence external independent verifiers will be needed to accredit the information from the measures.

Wolfe & Howes (1993) suggest methods of verification to determine if organizations have measures that work:

1. Ask who in the organization is looking at the information and why, as the usefulness of a specific measure depends on the vision or environmental goals of the organization. (As in TQM, the information–goal connection is explicit, and progress is tracked continuously).
2. Make measures reliable and consistent. The data should be based on actual performance and be accessible and understandable.
3. The benefits of obtaining the information should outweigh the costs of collection.

4. Be careful when assuming that historical information is sufficient; it may not truly satisfy the criteria for quality data.
5. Reflect stakeholder priorities while keeping in mind organizational goals.
6. Measure what is in the company's control: global warming is too big, but carbon monoxide/dioxide emissions can be measured and controlled.
7. Measures should be easily understood and few in number.

The environmental performance areas that organizations are currently measuring are generally waste discharges, emissions and energy usage. Performance areas such as product and process design, raw materials usage and linkage along the supply chain also need to be measured.

Thus, at present, there are a few organizations who are using a range of environmental performance measures. Currently these are company-specific and hence there is little scope for comparison between organizations. An example of an industry's response to this situation is the Responsible Care Programme which is unique to the chemical industry and originated in Canada in 1984 (Welford 1995). The scheme was launched in 1989 in the UK by the Chemical Industries Association. The guiding principles require companies to:

- conform to statutory regulations;
- operate to the best practices of the industry;
- assess the actual and potential health, safety and environmental impacts of their activities and products;
- work closely with the authorities and the community in achieving the required levels of performance; and
- be open about activities and give relevant information to interested parties.

However the CIA's published data for 1992 revealed that only 57 per cent of the sites operated by its members supplied data; this increased to 76 per cent in 1993 (ENDS Report, 1994). This may suggest that voluntary disclosure of information on environmental performance is not enough for industry wide disclosure but legislation may be the answer.

Wolfe & Howes (1993) use Ontario Hydro as an example of a company which currently has a range of environmental indicators. These are as follows:

1. Environmental expenditures.
2. Material and waste management: recycling, low-level PCB decontamination, PCB inventories, coal ash production and utilization, inventories of radioactive liquid waste, solid radioactive liquid waste, solid radioactive waste generated and spills.
3. Water management: fish impingement, radioactive effluents and water level adjustments.
4. Air management: coal sulphur content, acid gas emissions, carbon dioxide emissions (fossil plants), visible emissions performance and radioactive emissions.
5. Land management; herbicide use, secondary land use and reforestation and tree replacement.

6. Energy management (load saved and shifted).
7. Non-utility generation (load and energy provided).

The Norwegian aluminium industry has produced a summary report of a project which studied the effects of industrial emissions from primary aluminium plants in Norway (Ongstad et al, 1994). Various impact measures of environment performance were used, these being:

- vegetation, soil and freshwater;
- wildlife and livestock;
- the marine environment; and
- human health.

For example, in the area of the marine environment polycyclic aromatic hydrocarbons (PAHs) were used as an impact measure. PAHs can be detected in mussels and snails at relatively large distances from the aluminium plants, whereas they only become concentrated in fish and other shellfish to a lesser degree. No signs of harm which can be linked to PAHs have been found in fish, shellfish or hard-bottom organisms in the fjords by the seven smelters. As a result of emission reductions, the PAH levels in mussels and snails have now been substantially reduced in most places (Ongstad et al).

In 1993 the Journal *Fortune* selected environmental performance measures and applied them to a range of US companies. Among the categories given the most importance were:

- the amount of a company's toxic chemical releases, adjusted for sales, and its percentage reduction of those releases;
- the comprehensiveness of a company's environmental programme; for example, whether it has a written policy and goals or offers employee incentives;
- violations of environmental laws that carry large fines and penalties;
- ratings by credible environmental groups.

Other important categories, carrying slightly less weight, include:

- whether a company is potentially responsible for cleaning up an inordinately large number of US Superfund sites;
- whether it reuses and recycles hazardous and solid waste;
- whether it participates in EPA's voluntary programs, such as 33–50 (so called because it aims to reduce releases of 17 targeted chemicals by 33 per cent and 50 per cent by 1995 from a 1988 baseline) (Rice, 1993).

The results from this approach were used to compare companies, producing a list of the ten leaders, the ten most improved and the ten least improved. This was a bold attempt to portray a general view of environmental performance in large organizations using a limited number of measures. A wide range of categories were covered by the environmental performance measures but each category had few measures – such as the comprehensiveness of the company's environmental programme while not including the measurement of environmental management systems or environmental standards. The measures used may not be comprehensive enough for a comparison to be applicable to all industries, for instance the service industries, but the approach was useful for a general comparison of large companies. However there may be too little information for each company to analyze its own environmental performance in all areas.

British Airways have gone some way in formulating specific measures of corporate environmental management. Table 9.5 gives some examples of these measures, including the main contributors to the measures and where the responsibility for these measures lie. For example the measure of congestion would be the amount of fuel burnt by aircraft during delays, the contributors would be the weather and runway capacity and responsibility would be with Eurocontrol and so on. A value would be assigned to the performance measure for annual comparisons, but what form this would take is not known. Identifying who is responsible for different performance areas is important for not only the measurements themselves but also improvement of the environmental performance.

The approaches described in this section which are currently adopted by industry may not reach far enough in measuring environmental performance in organizations. These measurements are still short-term oriented and need to encompass sustainability if they are to be effective in protecting the environment. This means that measures of inter-generational equity are needed – for example the extent to which long-term decisions are made with environmental concern.

PROPOSED METHODS AND FRAMEWORKS FOR MEASURING ENVIRONMENTAL PERFORMANCE

The previous section gave some practical examples of measures currently used in industry. This section will go a step further by reviewing some theoretical methods and frameworks of measures of environmental performance in companies. There are various models used by commentators to express environmental performance measurements in organizations.

Wehrmeyer (1993) uses the notion of local (geographically) and general performance measurements, thus formulating a way of dividing the overall score into two components:

Environmental Performance = $\sqrt{(\text{(Local components)}^2 + \text{(General component)}^2)}$

The general component is based on the ratio between ambient concentration of a substance and the legal limit, thus giving a guide to the overall stress the substance is causing the environment, while the local component is the ratio between the actual discharge made by the firm and the legal limit applicable to that firm. This approach is complicated and cumbersome and is only based around emissions, and hence fails to give an overall view of the organization's environmental performance.

A small number of other approaches exist, but the basic idea of providing 'common level denominators', as scores with which the various physical

Table 9.5 Examples of measures of corporate environmental performance by British Airways (adapted from Business in the Environment & KPMG Peat Marwick, 1992)

	Value 1993/4	Value 1994/5	Performance Measure	Contributors	Responsibility
Noise			% fleet that conforms to regulations.	• fleet replacement, plans, ie retirement of older, noisier aircraft and new aircraft purchase	• corporate strategy of the main British Airways board
Emissions & Fuel Efficiency			fuel use per ATK (Available Tonne Kilometre)	• world-wide operations; fleet composition (% of new fuel efficient aircraft); • flight crew procedures; fleet scheduling; and weather	• marketing and operations of the main British Airways board; and flight crew
Waste, Materials, Energy & Water			electricity consumption at London Heathrow & London Gatwick per ATK	• number of personnel • use of PCs and computers • installation of energy monitoring systems • weather	• all staff • energy management team property
Congestion			fuel burned as a result of delays on arrival & departure at London Heathrow & London Gatwick per ATK	• Air Traffic Control operation • terminal & runway capacity • weather	• Eurocontrol • BAA • British Airways • fuel planning
Tourism & Conservation			shipments of fauna & equipment as actual numbers of movements	• budget for BAANC programme • available cargo space • requests from partnership organizations	• British Airways Assisting Nature Conservation Coordinator, Environment Branch
Staff & Community			total sponsorship & donations, including non-environmental charitable donations (£)	• budget available • requests from organizations & charities	• charities • Administrator, Environment Branch
Overall					

substances can be weighted and subsequently summarized, forms the basis of all these approaches. However it is conceded that the lack of scientific knowledge about many ecological processes; means that most 'scientific' approaches are as yet reliant on general assumptions made about the process.

Tyteca (1994a) outlines some methodologies being used in the measurement of environmental performance in firms. The Data Envelopment Analysis (DEA) approach takes into account three categories of factors: inputs, desirable outputs and undesirable outputs. Data Envelopment Analysis is used to define standardized, aggregate performance indicators; that is, quantities comprising between 0 (bad performance) and 1 (good performance). The analysis can be applied to a set of plants in a company or to a set of companies in an industry, called sets of decision making units (DMU). The performance of each DMU is considered with respect to a 'best practice' frontier, which consists of the DMUs showing the best environmental behaviour. Hence a standardized global indicator can be defined as:

$$\varepsilon \xi [\, 0\, ,\, 1\,]$$

where the closed intervals refer to the worst and best observed practices. The lower bound would correspond to firms that show no consideration for the environment, while the upper bound would indicate that a firm has adopted the best available technology (BAT) for the industrial sector. This is, of course, a relative concept and the upper bound would have to be adapted each time a new, more environmentally friendly technology is invented.

Frontiers obtained from applying DEA models, reflect best-practice among the observed set of firms or plants, (see Figure 9.4). This is influenced by the state of technology at the time of data gathering. Five types of technology are identified by Tyteca:

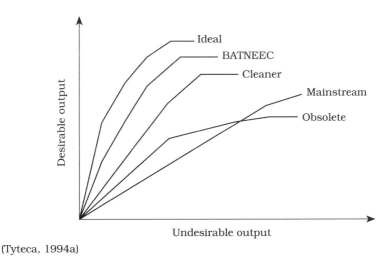

(Tyteca, 1994a)

Figure 9.4 Temporal succession of frontiers and technologies

1. ideal;
2. best available technology not entailing excessive cost (BATNEEC);
3. cleaner;
4. mainstream; and
5. obsolete.

Each of these technologies is likely to correspond to a different frontier depending on the inputs, desirable outputs and undesirable outputs. Figure 9.4 gives a possible outline of frontiers in a two dimensional representation of desirable and undesirable outputs.

Azzone & Noci (1995) suggest that the performance measurement system should be considered in three major categories:

1. Indices pointing out the company's environmental efficiency in the use of resources;
2. measures representing the amount of waste resulting both from the firm's plants and usage of sold products; and
3. indicators aimed at defining product durability. (More precisely, measures pointing out how long the product can be used must be analyzed taking into account, for example, the lifespan of different components making up a product).

To implement this or similar systems James & Bennett (1994) discuss the following concerning measures of environment-related performance; why measure, what to measure, current approaches; and finally suggest how to measure. In the latter, a model in the form of a continuous loop consisting of eight stages of the development of environment-related performance measures is suggested (see Figure 9.5).

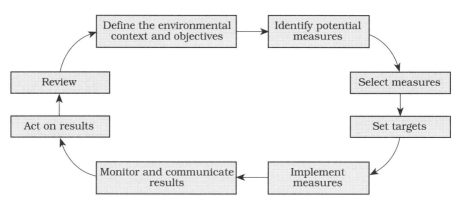

(adapted from James & Bennett, 1994)

Figure 9.5 A continuous loop of stages of environment-related performance measurement

The first stage, which defines the environmental context and objectives, states the organization's impact on the environment. Potential measures, including priority areas, are then identified in the next stage. Step three selects the measures by their appropriateness to their purpose, cost effectiveness, comparability and compatibility with other measures. In step four, the current poster is established, targets are set and the feasibility of achieving this is assessed.

The fifth stage implements the measures through systems which collect and report the information. It is important that the targets are communicated to the relevant staff and stakeholders, and that staff are empowered and resourced to achieve the targets. The results are monitored and communicated in the sixth step. The results will have to be verified internally and externally if they are to have any credibility. The next stage acts on the results, including identifying what changes are needed to improve the measures and results. The final and eighth stage reviews the overall performance measurement system establishing if it works satisfactorily and if there are new areas where measurement is necessary. The process continues through stage one and back to the review advancing the measures of environmental performance.

The European Green Table (1993) developed a reference framework of environmental performance indicators (see Figure 9.6). Within a framework developed by, adopted by and adapted to individual industry sectors, such an environmental performance indicator system, based on self-assessment, can both enhance the business's own decision making and provide the elements for consistent communication with stakeholders. This framework enables company performance to be measured:

- against set targets;
- across sites;
- over time;
- relative to industry peers; and
- against other defined benchmarks.

The reference framework, shown in Figure 9.6, measures a limited range of environmental performance indicators in two areas: environmental management EPIs and facilities and operations EPIs. Environmental management EPIs measure the extent to which the company has in place best practice management systems, procedures and practices for compliance with environmental regulators and the achievement of wider environmental protection objectives defined by the company or by its stakeholders.

On the other hand the facilities and operations EPIs are designed to measure the actual environmental performance of the company in scientific terms. These EPIs are thus by their nature technical and quantified. Among 5–10 EPIs are to be selected together which encapsulate the key environmental impacts of a company about which its management and stakeholders are most concerned (European Green Table, 1993).

The methods and frameworks for measuring environmental performance in organizations described are yet to be fully proved workable in industry. However, the business community will have to accept that these methods are necessary for progress towards better environmental quality.

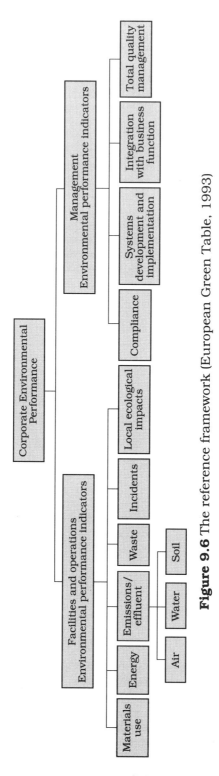

Figure 9.6 The reference framework (European Green Table, 1993)

MEASURING PERFORMANCE CONSISTENT WITH SUSTAINABLE DEVELOPMENT

Through the use of environmental performance measures a positive approach can be taken towards the future evolution of the business and environmental relationship. What is now required is a concerted effort to accelerate the development of the practical measures needed in order for the business community to take the environment seriously and to avoid future problems. This is best achieved through the informed anticipation of future conditions and a knowledge of the requirements of a market which now puts great emphasis upon products, services and production methods which are in harmony with the environment (Roberts, 1994).

Most often, the kind of information using 'business envirometrics' pertains to strict environmental or technical efficiency. It is also important to view company environmental performance in a more global framework, taking into account economic or socio-economic welfare. As such sustainable development measures are needed (Tyteca, 1994b). The United Nations statistical office has put forward proposed indicators of sustainable development as have other international organizations, but on a global scale rather than at an organization level (MacGillivray, 1994).

Ashford & Meima (1993) suggest sustainable envirometrics must possess a binary thresholds function which indicates whether a practice is altogether sustainable. This is obviously a vastly complex matter, and requires a realistic, feasible design and coordination of appropriate sustainability, consequence, and performance envirometrics which firms, industries, regions, nations and other subsets of humanity can use in meeting environmental goals.

In view of the task of designing and implementing a sustainable enterprise, it is necessary to answer such questions as; how is a firm not sustainable, at what rate and in what direction is it moving, and what changes must it make to become sustainable? In answering these, both the environmental consequences of a firm's activities, which include public health and ecological effects, and the environmental performance of the firm, ie the extent and effectiveness of actions the firm takes which mitigate its environmental consequences, must be considered (Ashford & Meima, 1993).

Hence moving towards sustainable development requires a shift in the basis upon which performance is assessed and ultimately, the basis upon which rewards are given or withheld. This requires the use of a more comprehensive framework of indicators, to focus the attention of decision makers and the public on progress towards sustainability. Only with the application of such indicators will it be possible to infuse processes of change with the needed values, practical direction and, where necessary, constraints (MacGillivray, 1994). This issue is further examined in Chapter 14.

CONCLUSIONS

A variety of methods of measuring environmental performance in business have been described in this chapter. These include qualitative, quantitative, contributor and external measures. These measures which cover a broad range of performance areas have to be adapted by individual companies to be compatible with their operations.

Environmental performance measures can be seen as a step up from environmental management systems and associated standards. EMS and standards only prove that an organization is recognizing its environmental impact, not necessarily reducing it significantly. Measures can be used to monitor a company's progress (or lack of it) in reducing its environmental effect. An organization wishes to be seen to improve its performance in the eyes of its stakeholders, such as customers, investors and regulators.

The methods and frameworks currently used in industry and theoretical models described can also be used to assess organizations by third parties. These include ethical investors, customers, regulators and local communities. Here sustainability should be catered for in the environmental performance measures. Current measures should be able to adapt when appropriate measures for sustainability are developed.

Unfortunately most of industry will not measure to the fullest extent unless forced by legislation and for market pressures. The freedom of environmental information has to be increased through legislation. Only when companies are compelled to disclose environmental information to stakeholders will industry respond positively to protecting the environment. This response will be in the form of environmental performance measures, targets and hopefully improvements in environmental effects. Freedom of information legislation will cause customers and investors to be able to select the more environmentally conscious companies. However comparisons will be unfairly made unless a universal measurement system is developed. Governments and international legislators, such as the European Union, will have to provide the facilities, expertise and incentives, as well as sound scientific knowledge, to help companies improve their environmental performance.

REFERENCES

Ashford, N A & Meima, R (1993), 'Designing the Sustainable Enterprise Summary Report', Second International Research Conference, The Greening of Industry Network' Cambridge, Massachusetts

Azzone, G & Manzini, R (1994) 'Measuring Strategic Environmental Performance' *Business Strategy and the Environment*, Spring, 3, 1

Azzone, G & Noci, G (1995), 'How to Design a Performance Measurement System for Supporting Pro-Active Green Strategies' January 12–13, EIASM Workshop on Greening of Management, Brussels

Bennett, M, (1993) 'The Financial Measurement of Environmental Performance' EM & EARN Seminar, Environmental Performance Measurement & Reporting, 25 August, University of Wolverhampton

Business in the Environment and KPMG Peat Marwick (1992) 'A Measure of Commitment – Guidelines for Measuring Environmental Performance' *Business in the Environment* and KPMG Peat Marwick

Davis, J (1994) *Greening Business: Managing for Sustainable Development* Blackwell, Oxford

ENDS Report (1994) 'Uncertain Progress for Responsible Care' 223, June, 16–18

European Green Table (1993) 'Environmental Performance Indicators in Industry – Report 3: Draft Handbook' August, unpublished, Oslo

Fiksel, J (1994) 'Quality Metrics in Design for Environment' *Total Quality Environmental Management,* Winter, 181–192

Gabel, H L & Sinclair-Desgagne, B (1992) 'Managerial Systems and Environmental Performance: A Research Agenda' June, INSTEAD, unpublished, Fontainbleau Cedex

Gilbert, M J (1993), *Achieving Environmental Management Standards* The Institute of Management, Pitman Publishing, London

Jacobs, M (1991) *The Green Economy: Environment, Sustainable Development and the Politics of the Future* Pluto Press, London

Jaggi, B & Freedman, M C (1992) 'An Examination of the Impact of Pollution Performance on Economic and Market Performance: Pulp and Paper Firms' *Journal of Business Finance and Accounting,* 19, 697–713

James, P (1993) 'Environmental Performance Measurement – the State of the Art' EM & EARN Seminar, Environmental Performance Measurement & Reporting, 25 August, University of Wolverhampton

James, P (1994) 'Business Environmental Performance Measurement', *Business Strategy and the Environment,* 3, 2, 59–67

James, P & Bennett, M (1994) 'Environmental-related Performance Measurement in Business; From Emissions to Profit and Sustainability?' unpublished

Ledgerwood, G, Street, E & Therivel, R (1992) *The Environmental Audit and Business Strategy – A Total Quality Approach* Pitman Publishing

MacGillivray, A (ed) (1994) *Environmental Measures – Indicators for the UK Environment* Environment Challenge Group, including The New Economics Foundation, The Royal Society for the Protection of Birds and World Wide Fund for Nature

Nash, J, Nutt, K, Maxwell, J & Ehrenfeld, J (1992) 'Polaroid's Environmental Accounting and Reporting System: Benefits and Limitations of a TQEM Measurement Tool' *Total Quality Environmental Management,* Autumn, 3–15

Ongstad, L, Stoll, C I & Aasland, T (eds) (1994) 'The Norwegian Aluminium Industry and the Local Environment' Hydro Aluminium as, Elkem Aluminium ANS, Sor-Norge Aluminium A/S, Oslo, Norway, unpublished

Rice, F (1993) 'Who Scores Best on the Environment' *Fortune,* July 26, 104–111

Rikhardsson, P M (1994) 'The Measurement and Reporting of Corporate Environmental Performance' The Second Nordic Network Conference on Business and Environment, 1–2 December, Norwegian School of Management, Sandvika

Roberts, P (1994) 'Environmental sustainability and business: Recognising the problem and taking positive action' in Williams, C C & Haughton, G *Perspectives Towards Sustainable Environmental Development* Avebury Studies

Tyteca, D (1994a) 'On the Measurement of Environmental Performance in Firms; Literature Review and Productive Efficiency Approach' unpublished

Tyteca, D (1994b) 'DEA Models for the Measurement of Environmental Performance of Firms – Concepts and Empirical Results' unpublished, Université Catholique de Louvain, Belgium

Wehrmeyer, W (1993) 'The Scientific Measurement of Environmental Performance' EM & EARN Seminar, Environmental Performance Measurement & Reporting, 25 August, University of Wolverhampton

Welford, R & Gouldson, A (1993) *Environmental Management and Business Strategy* Pitman Publishing, London

Welford, R (1995) *Environmental Strategy & Sustainable Development: The Corporate Challenge for the Twenty-first Century* Routledge, London

Wells, R P, Hochman, M N, Hochman, S D & O'Connell P A (1992) 'Measuring Environmental Success' *Total Quality Environmental Management*, Summer, 315–327

Wolfe, A & Howes, H A (1993), 'Measuring Environmental Performance: Theory and Practice, at Ontario Hydro' *Total Quality Environmental Management*, Summer, 355–366

Chapter 10

Environmental Reporting

Michael Brophy and Richard Starkey

This chapter will examine:

- **Environmental reporting:** a catch-all term that describes the various means by which companies disclose information on their environmental activities;
- **Corporate environmental reports (CERs):** Corporate environmental reports are a form of environmental reporting. They are publicly available, stand-alone reports issued voluntarily by companies on their environmental activities.

Corporate environmental reporting first emerged during a period of 'social accounting', which began in the early 1970s and occurred principally in North America.

> *Corporations tried many forms of reporting: within the annual report or within a separate booklet; in financial numbers, in non-financial quantities, in words and pictures; the reports were for employees or management or society-at-large; some were audited, some not; they covered one or more of: plans, polices, interactions with communities, charitable giving, levels of pollution and emissions, energy usage, employment data, health and safety at work, etc... There was virtually no regulatory back-up to these experiments and by the mid- to late-1970s the experiments had all but disappeared and interest in the field had waned to a vestigial level all over the world (Gray, 1994).*

The current wave of environmental reporting began in 1989 when Norsk Hydro, Norway's largest industrial group, published its first report. A spate of bad publicity in 1987, as a result of actions by environmental campaigners, caused the company to closely examine its environmental performance. The results were not good and in 1989, as part of a strategy to restore its reputation, it published a relatively comprehensive report on its Norwegian activities. In 1990 Norsk Hydro published a further report covering all the group's activities worldwide and in the same year Norsk Hydro (UK) became the first of its overseas subsidiaries to follow suit.

Just as Norsk Hydro was the first company to report in Europe, Monsanto was first to tread the reporting path in the US, publishing its *Annual Environmental Report* in 1991. The report included Toxic Release Inventory-style emissions data for Canada, the UK and Belgium as well as the US and set out quantified goals for improvements in environmental performance. As of now, well over 100 companies have produced CERs.

This chapter is divided into 4 sections:

- **Section 1: Disclosure, reporting and CERs – what's the link?** identifies the various forms of environmental disclosure and their relationship to both environmental reporting and CERs.
- **Section 2: Why report?** examines the reasons why companies may or may not choose to voluntarily report on their environmental activities and asks whether the production of CERs should and will become mandatory in the future.
- **Section 3: Who's doing what and how?** examines the content and structure of the environmental reports that have been produced to date and briefly comments on some of the existing environmental reporting guidelines.
- **Section 4: Where do we go from here?** makes suggestions as to the direction in which environmental reporting should move in the future.

1. DISCLOSURE, REPORTING AND CERs – WHAT'S THE LINK?

Coming Clean – Corporate Environmental Reporting (DTTI et al, 1993) identifies three categories of environmental disclosure:

1. **involuntary disclosure** – the disclosure of information about a company's environmental activities without its permission and against its will;
2. **mandatory disclosure** – the disclosure of information about a company's environmental activity that is required by law;
3. **voluntary disclosure** – the disclosure of information on a voluntary basis.

Table 10.1 gives examples from each of these categories.

In this chapter environmental reporting is defined as consisting of both mandatory and voluntary disclosure (see Figure 10.1) ie, it is something that a company does rather than something a company has done to it. Mandatory and voluntary reporting are discussed in more detail below.

Table 10.1 Categories of environmental disclosure

---

1. Involuntary
Environmental campaigns
Press and media exposés
Whistle blowing
Court investigations
'Dirty tricks' campaigns by competitors

2. Mandatory
Annual reports and accounts
Stock exchange requirements
Toxic Release Inventory (US)
Pollution registers (France and UK)
Freedom of access to environmental information (EU)

3. Voluntary
Confidential
Disclosure required by:
1 banks
2 insurers
3 customers
4 joint venture partners
Non-confidential
Social reporting aspects of annual reports
One-off or annual free-standing corporate environmental performance reports
Eco-labelling
Staff newsletters
Press releases and media briefings
Open house days, on-site visitor facilities
Advertized availability of eco-information
Voluntary environmental management schemes with reporting requirements (eg CERES Principles, EMAS etc)

Source: adapted from UNEP, 1994

Mandatory Reporting

Although there is as yet no legal requirement for companies to produce a comprehensive environmental performance report, companies are legally obliged to disclose a certain amount of information about their environmental activities. Below is a brief survey of the information that companies are legally required to disclose in various countries around the world.

The US is the country where mandatory reporting requirements are most stringent. The Toxic Release Inventory (TRI) requirement of the 1986 Emergency Planning and Community Right-to-Know Act (EPCRA), Title III of the Superfund Amendments and Reauthorization Act (SARA), obliges

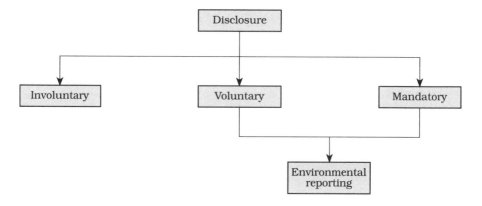

Figure 10.1 Environmental reporting

companies employing over 10 people full-time to provide annual emissions data for 307 toxic chemicals. This information is collected by the US EPA and is made publicly available. (In 1990 over 83 000 TRI reports were filed by US companies.)

In 1980 the Comprehensive Environmental Response Compensation and Liability Act (CERCLA) became law. The Act was designed to force 'responsible parties' to clean up land contaminated by such activities as dumping and waste storage. To enable this to happen in circumstances where the responsible party cannot be found or is unable to fund the cost of remediation, CERCLA established a 'Superfund' to pay for the process. (CERCLA is commonly known as the Superfund programme.) This legislation brought about changes in US company accounting procedures. 'The accounting issues that arise from Superfund...cover the making of provisions for remediation, contingent liabilities and how to account for a fixed asset which suddenly acquires a negative value' (Gray et al, 1993).

In addition, the Securities and Exchange Commission (SEC) requires that corporations make the following environmental disclosures:

- Corporations must disclose material effects that compliance with federal, state and local environmental laws may have on their capital expenditures, earnings and competitive position. Existing estimates of current and future environmental expenditures must also be disclosed.
- Corporations must disclose any environmental, administrative or judicial proceeding, both contemplated and pending, that may have a material effect.
- Management are required to disclose any environmental problems likely to have a material effect and should quantify any liabilities as far as is reasonably practical. Relevant trends, demands, commitments, events or uncertainties should be addressed.

In Canada, the generally accepted accounting principles (GAAP) require that provisions are made for future removal and reclamation costs when accounting for capital assets. The Ontario and Quebec Securities

Commissions require listed companies to include the financial or operational effects of environmental protection requirements on a corporation's capital expenditures, earnings and competitive position.

Only a small number of European countries have legislation requiring environmental disclosure. In Norway, the amended Enterprise Act 1989 requires a company's annual report to state whether it pollutes the environment, and if this is the case to provide information on actions planned or taken to prevent such pollution. However, most companies have merely provided a brief statement confirming that all relevant law has been complied with (DTTI et al, 1993).

In the UK certain information on the environmental activity of companies can be obtained from public registers. Most environmental Acts of Parliament or their derivative regulations provide for public registers of information. The extent and range of the information held on these registers differs from Act to Act but typically a register will be likely to hold the following information:

- applications for consents and possibly details of responses received as a result of consultation;
- consents, licences etc with details of their conditions;
- details of variations, revocations and similar notices;
- records of monitoring data concerning licensed premises and processes;
- information relating to appeals (eg against refusal of consent etc);
- details of convictions for offences under the statute concerned.

There are a total of 15 registers in the UK (Garbutt, 1995). These are shown in Table 10.2. In all cases registers are open to public inspection at reasonable hours free of charge. Public environmental registers also exist in France and Japan.

Table 10.2 Environmental registers in the UK

1. Integrated pollution and local authority pollution control
2. Water: discharge consents
3. Water: resources, abstractions etc
4. Town and country planning
5. Genetically modified organisms
6. Atmospheric pollution
7. Chemical release inventory
8. Alkali etc (Works Regulation Act 1906)
9. Water: trade effluent consents
10. Radioactive Substances Act 1993
11. Local land charges
12. Noise abatement zones
13. Litter control
14. Waste management
15. Waste carriers

Source: Garbutt 1995

European Union legislation on environmental disclosure exists in the form of the 1990 EC Directive on Freedom of Access to Environmental Information (90/313/EEC). Under the Directive, all public authorities with responsibilities for the environment must make environmental information available to any person who requests it. 'Environmental information' is defined widely and includes information on the quality and state of air, water, soil, flora, fauna, natural sites and other land. It also covers activities which adversely affect these areas and the measures which are used to protect them (Ball and Bell, 1994).

Since 1989 companies in Sweden have had to report on their environmental performance in relation to government regulations, and in the Netherlands the government plans to make the publishing of an annual environmental report a legal requirement (UNEP, 1994).

In 1992 India became the first country in the world to require environmental audits by law. The results of these audits must be filed with the state Pollution Control Boards.

Voluntary Disclosure

The production of free-standing environmental reports is a relatively new phenomenon. They are one of a number of internal and external tools which companies have developed to communicate environmental information to stakeholders. Other tools include staff newsletters, press releases and media briefings, open-house days and consultation with the local community (see Table 10.1, p179). The evolution of corporate environmental reporting is discussed below.

2. WHY REPORT?

Why Report? – the Company's Perspective

Companies are not legally obliged to issue CERs – it is a purely voluntary activity. What reasons do companies, have, therefore, for voluntarily disclosing information? Figure 10.2 shows the answers given by companies to this question in the *Coming Clean* (DTTI et al, 1993) survey on corporate environmental reporting. In this survey and in a survey carried out by Gray et al (1993) asking the same question the most common reasons given for reporting were *duty-based* reasons. In the *Coming Clean* survey the most common reason was 'duty to the environment' and in Gray et al's survey it was 'shareholder's and/or the public's right to know'.

In an earlier study on voluntary disclosure Gray, Radebaugh and Roberts (Gray et al, 1990) suggest that any organization considering voluntary disclosure will assess the relative costs and benefits. Here the motivation for disclosure is taken to be one of *self-interest*, with a company choosing to disclose if benefits are adjudged to exceed costs. In reality motivation for reporting is not likely to be based purely on duty or self interest but, to a greater or lesser degree, will contain elements of both.

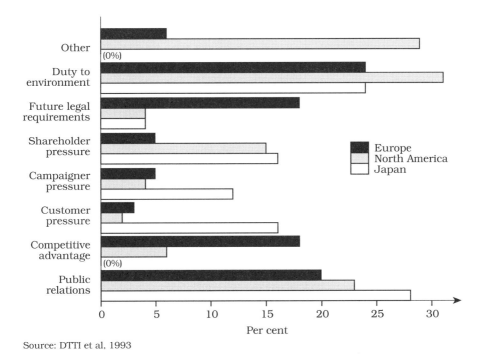

Source: DTTI et al, 1993

Figure 10.2 Reasons for reporting (% of total reasons given)

What benefits can a company derive from environmental reporting? Benefits can be divided into two categories, financial and strategic. If a company can demonstrate good environmental performance and an acceptable level of environmental liability to its stakeholders, it may benefit financially, in that the value of its share price may increase. The various strategic benefits are noted below:

- Environmental reporting may be seen by a company as a way in which it can improve its corporate image. Many of the first companies to issue reports were companies with major image problems who, to some extent, felt they had nothing to lose by reporting. Some (eg Exxon, Union Carbide) had been responsible for major disasters. Others had been under sustained pressure from environmentalists (eg Du Pont, Henkel, ICI, Kemira, Norsk Hydro, Rhône-Poulenc). By producing a report in response to such adverse publicity, a company can put its side of the story and thereby attempt to improve its public standing. By choosing to disclose information it can prevent information on its performance being disclosed by others in a manner that it cannot control.
- In addition to environmentalists, a company may also come under pressure regarding its environmental performance from its shareholders, employees or customers. For instance, *The Guardian's* environment correspondent noted:

Corporate responsibility is on the political agenda as it never was five years ago. Shareholder meetings are increasingly unruly as people demand more from companies than just profit. Mori polls, too, suggest that investors want their money to work for good. Ethical investing... is becoming a powerful force in most countries and is growing in significance here [UK] (Vidal, 1995).

A company may feel that issuing an environmental report would contribute towards building better relations with the relevant stakeholder group.

• A company may feel that corporate environmental reporting will sooner or later become mandatory. By reporting voluntarily it can build up expertise in advance of the expected regulation. This approach can be seen in the following statement by 'a major chemical company' (Gray et al, 1993) which states:

It is increasingly realistic to recognize the need for environmental disclosure. The political climate is changing and it will be impossible to resist it. We also want to take our medicine early and go through the pain barrier early in the process.

• Some companies have decided it would be useful to disseminate the data that they are required to report by law to a wider audience, and are using this data as the basis for a voluntary report. A number of companies in the US have built on their legal requirement to report through the TRI programme and published separate corporate environmental reports. Dow Chemicals uses TRI reporting as the basis for its corporate environmental reports, not only in the US but also in other countries in which it operates. Swedish companies have found that the information that they are required to report to the authorities is not reaching the public and are therefore considering the use of voluntary reporting to get the information across.

• Companies which for internal reasons have begun to collect quantities of environmental data, are using this data as the foundation for public reporting. An investigation by the United Nations Centre for TransNational Corporations InterGovernmental Working Group of Experts on International Standards of Accounting and Reporting (UN CTC ISAR) into the reasons for the high level of environmental disclosure by companies in Switzerland and Germany compared with those in other countries concluded that:

since environmental expenditures were a large and growing share of their total expenditures, they felt they needed to keep track of them. Once having the information, they also claimed that the publication of this information was valuable. They received fewer questions on their environmental performance in shareholders meetings and local governments were more likely to grant approvals for their projects based upon their reputation for being 'open' about information disclosure (UN CTC ISAR, 1991).

- Several environmental management schemes either recommend or require environmental reporting, eg ICC/WBCSD Business Charter for Sustainable Development, CERES Principles, and the EU's EMAS. Hence a company will begin the process of environmental reporting if it decides that it is beneficial to implement one of these schemes.
- If a company finds that its competitors are issuing environmental reports it may decide that it is necessary to follow suit in order not to leave itself at a disadvantage.

Company Resistance to Reporting

The UNEP study *Company Environmental Reporting* (UNEP IE, 1994) notes that by the end of 1993, well over 100 companies had issued stand-alone reports and many more had included some degree of environmental information in their annual reports. However it notes that this figure should be compared with the 35,000-plus companies that operate on a transnational basis, and the millions of small- and medium-sized companies that represent the bedrock of the world's economies. As Gray et al (1993) state, 'given the low levels of disclosure, the more interesting questions concern why a company does not disclose more.'

In their survey, Gray et al (1993) found

> *a general resistance to disclosure...The clearly dominant reasons given for non-disclosure were (in rank order): the absence of any demand for the information; the absence of any legal requirement; that the costs would outweigh the benefits; and, somewhat less important, that the organization had never considered it.*

Commenting on the costs involved in disclosing information Gray (1994) states 'I can see very little evidence that would suggest that corporations would voluntarily undertake...significant, systematic reporting that might reflect badly on the organization and/or have negative financial consequences.' This view was also expressed by representatives of Japanese companies at a workshop held in Tokyo (DTTI et al, 1993). Sixty-seven per cent of respondents agreed with the proposition that 'companies will hardly ever release disadvantageous information', while only 8 per cent disagreed (25 per cent were undecided).

Why Report? – the Citizen's Perspective

The previous sections have looked at the reasons for (and against) reporting from the company perspective. This section will look at the question 'Why report?' from outside the company. Why, from the perspective of the citizen, should companies report?

It has been argued that companies should report publicly on their environmental activities because citizens have a right to know about these activities. The activities of companies have a profound effect on the environment in which citizens live and people are entitled to be informed about such activities so as to be able to make fully informed decisions relating to their environment. As Gray et al (1993) put it: 'Information and decision-making must be democratic in the widest sense of the term because it is society as a whole which must make the choices and trade-offs that are essential in the path to sustainability.' Agenda 21, the primary policy document to emerge from the Rio Earth Summit, identifies right to know as a priority issue and calls on the international community, countries and individual companies to adopt it as a matter of environmental policy (DTTI et al, 1993).

Should Environmental Reporting Become Mandatory?

If one accepts that society has the right to a detailed account of companies' impact on the environment and if it is probable that the disclosure of this information will not occur voluntarily then it is necessary for environmental reporting to be made mandatory.

This is the stance taken by Gray (1994), who argues that the first wave of voluntary social and environmental accounting that took place in the seventies had little or no impact on subsequent reporting practices, with, at most, only very marginal increases in the amount of social and environmental information that companies disclosed. He argues that 'with virtually no exceptions, it is only the regulated changes in reporting that actually bring about any widespread change in behaviour or reporting practice.'

UN CTC ISAR is also in favour of mandatory reporting. In 1991 UN CTC ISAR made detailed recommendations as to the types of environmental disclosure that corporations should undertake, with the intention that these be adopted by sovereign governments. These recommendations are shown in Table 10.3. In the Tokyo workshop mentioned previously there was solid support for mandatory reporting with 62 per cent of respondents agreeing with the proposition that 'Voluntary reporting will never be enough. The public needs more information and there needs to be tougher legislation.' Twenty-three per cent disagreed with 15 per cent undecided.

And there is a feeling among many of those involved in the reporting field that environmental reporting *will* become mandatory. As early as 1991 Dr R Brouzes, Director of Environmental Affairs at Alcan Aluminium Ltd, Canada commented that

> *Certain companies have published annual environmental reports for shareholders and a broader community of external stakeholders...I believe it is only a matter of time before the stand alone report to shareholders will be an annual duty of the corporation.*

The *Coming Clean* report (DTTI et al, 1993) is of the view that 'regular, quantified, credible environmental disclosure will become a basic business requirement for corporations, companies and firms of every size for three main reasons:

Table 10.3 Recommendations for environmental financial reporting from UN CTC ISAR 9th session (Gray et al, 1993)

In the directors' report
- environmental issues pertinent to the company and industry;
- environmental policy adopted;
- improvements made since adopting the policy;
- enterprise's environmental emission targets and performance against these;
- response to government legislation;
- material environmental legal issues in which the enterprise is involved;
- effect of environmental protection measures on capital investment and earnings;
- material costs charged to current operations;
- material amounts capitalized in the period.

In the notes to the financial statements
- the accounting policies for recording liabilities and provisions, for setting up catastrophe reserves and for disclosing contingent liabilities;
- $/£ amount of liabilities, provisions and reserves established in the period;
- $/£ amount of contingent liabilities;
- tax effects;
- government grants received in the period.

---

1. the need of shareholders, lenders, insurers and other stakeholders for information which will help them to assess the real present and potential future value of – and risks associated with – the companies they are dealing with;
2. wider stakeholder demands for in-depth information from companies they live near, work for or buy from;
3. the likely demand for data that will help to assess whether particular companies, industries and economies are 'eco-efficient' and, ultimately, sustainable.'

3. WHO IS DOING WHAT AND HOW?

In response to the question 'Who is producing environmental reports?', the general answer would be – large scale industrial organizations. The vast majority of such organizations tend to be based in North America or Europe, although a small number of Japanese companies have recently established themselves. Environmental reports have been produced by almost every industrial sector. A greater number of reports, however, have been observed from those industries which have been exposed to pressure from environmental groups, particularly the petroleum, gas and chemical sectors. Overall, relatively few organizations have compiled environmental reports, although amongst the largest companies in the western world reporting is more common. This fact has been underlined by a number of surveys. For example, SustainAbility (1994) a UK-based environmental consultancy, observed that less than a quarter of the world's Fortune 100 companies had produced an environmental report. Similar figures were observed by KPMG (1993a) in their 1993 UK survey of environmental reporting among the top 100 British companies.

Since existing reports have been produced by individual organizations in order to meet their own requirements, it comes as no surprise to learn that there are a wide variety in the types and styles of reports currently in circulation. Gray (1994) has attempted to define the voluntary disclosure and reporting of environmental information into one of three categories:

1. **General narrative reports** – perhaps including statements of policy and selected elements of hard quantitative data, these are the most popular forms of environmental reporting;
2. **Non-financial quantitative and qualitative data reports** – which might include such things as emissions statements and / or reports on environmental audits for example;
3. **Financial reporting of environmental information** – which is not yet widespread outside of the US's 'Superfund' Act. While a number of companies may give selected items of financial data, other companies have made attempts to report 'complete environmental accounts'. It is only a matter of time before other parts of the globe follow suit.

A number of companies, particularly in Britain and North America, have previously attempted a 'Compliance with standard' (CWS) approach to environmental reporting. Under this approach a report is produced which details the extent to which organizations have met various performance standards required of them. The standards reported on usually refer to such issues as emissions, spills and dumping. The standards are derived from federal, national and international law, regulatory body consents, and various charters or guidelines set by, for example, trade associations. It can be argued that of the environmental reports currently in circulation, those at the forefront have successfully managed to combine CWS reporting with any of the three approaches outlined by Gray above.

When examining the type of environmental reports that are produced, consideration will also need to be given to the level at which reporting is approached. *Coming Clean* (DTTI et al, 1993) has observed that most organizations have preferred to disclose information on a world-wide or company-wide basis, rather than by process-specific, product-specific or site-by-site reporting. Notable exceptions however do exist. Dow Europe and ICI, for example, have successfully combined company-wide *and* site-by-site reporting. Dow Europe tabulates pollutants to air, water and soil from its individual plants and lists the extent to which they have been reduced or increased in recent years. It reports company-wide figures beside detailed breakdowns of emissions for individual plants. From Dow's report it is possible to calculate, for example, the amount of hazardous waste going to landfill at its Spanish plants, and compare this value with previous years; or to discover the amount of CFCs released by its Danish operations.

An alternative to Gray's classification methodology has been suggested by the *Coming Clean* survey on environmental reporting, and which was later modified by UNEP in 1994 (Figure 10.3). Instead of three categories UNEP suggest that there are five *stages* to environmental reports, with a gradual progression from Stage 1, consisting of green glossies and newsletters, to Stage 5, sustainable development reporting. If current environmental reports are broken down and classified in this manner, the majority of existing reports are only at Stages 1 and 2. A quarter of companies have progressed to Stage 3, while a further 11 per cent are making the transition to Stage 4. At present UNEP estimates that only 5 per cent of environmental reports have actually reached Stage 4, while Stage 5 is largely unoccupied territory.

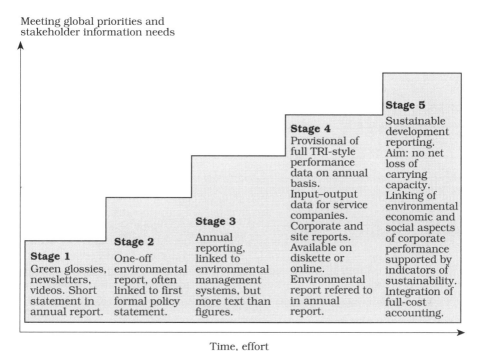

Source: UNEP IE – Company Environmental Reporting (1994)

Figure 10.3 Stages in corporate environmental reporting

The question of 'what is being reported' is a more difficult issue to address. Individual organizations are obviously tailoring their environmental reports to meet their own specific requirements, and thus the content of reports may differ radically. There are, however, a number of general themes which can be examined. For example, KPMG in their International Survey of Environmental Reporting (1993b) analyzed the subject areas of policy statements in environmental reports – they observed that when policy statements were broken down they tended to be dominated by the issues of resource conservation, emission levels, legislative compliance and employee involvement.

Relatively few reports have dealt with the issue of environmental costs. KPMG noted that only 7 per cent of companies in their international survey dealt with the matter, the vast majority of whom were Canadian- or US-based organizations. Where environmental costs have been disclosed they typically centre on the issues of contingent liabilities, future site removal and environmental restoration costs.

The majority of environmental reports publish policy statements and give details of how such policies are to be implemented within their organizations, by setting specific plans and targets. The targets identified in environmental reports commonly refer to: air emissions, effluent discharges, waste management, energy conservation, legislative compliance and employee involvement. Waste management and energy conservation are areas which feature frequently since they offer both direct cost savings and environmental benefits to the organization.

When setting environmental targets organizations may elect to choose either quantitative or qualitative targets (see Chapter 9). In setting quantitative targets companies are demonstrating that they have an environmental management system capable of producing the necessary quantitative data that will enable them to measure progress against such targets. When large-scale surveys are undertaken, however, it is found that only a minority of organizations are prepared to set quantitative targets – KPMG's survey (1993b) put the figure at 36 per cent. This may be a reflection on either the inability of current management systems to measure and track environmental performance, or may indicate a certain unwillingness among organizations to make commitments for fear of not meeting them in the future.

Where quantitative targets are defined it is important that companies also produce corresponding quantitative data concerning their environmental performance. On the issue of environmental performance, however, KPMG commented that 'Quantitative data... is something that most organizations have yet to produce'. Where quantitative data has been presented on environmental performance it generally consists of brief references to investment costs or fines incurred. On the subject of quantitative targets and environmental performance, KPMG concluded:

> *The lack of quantitative data provided overall is probably an indication that companies are still in the early stages with respect to setting up comprehensive environmental management systems that produce regular, quantifiable data with which they manage and measure their performance. No doubt there is also a reluctance or lack of willingness among some companies to address this issue (KPMG 1993b).*

A number of environmental reports have dealt with the subject of 'bad news' – identifying the occasions when a company has been prosecuted, fined or has failed to meet expected standards. The approach however is still relatively rare, accounting for approximately 10 per cent of environmental reports (KPMG 1993b). Yet the disclosure of bad news is important if companies are to gain credibility for their reports, otherwise such reports may often appear biased. Companies need to be 'up-front' in their environmental disclosures if they are to win the confidence of stakeholders. Where bad news has been reported companies have usually taken the opportunity to give details of actions they intend to undertake in order to rectify the situation or ensure future accidents do not recur. The credibility of reports will be significantly enhanced if such a proactive approach were to become more widespread.

Other subjects which are occasionally dealt with in environmental reports include environmental auditing and third party verification techniques. Both issues are important in establishing the credibility of a report particularly where third party verification occurs. The regular auditing of an organization's environmental performance is vital for companies that wish to progress and demonstrate real improvement, while external verification is probably the single most important method of instilling confidence in a report. Despite this importance relatively few reports make specific statements on verification or environmental audits. Approximately one in ten reports refer to auditing, of which only half have been externally assessed, while KPMG (1993a) noted that of the top 100 companies in the UK, only six had produced environmental reports which were independently verified.

Most organizations are not as yet committed to an annual environmental report. Some organizations have specifically stated that they intend to work to longer time scales, Norway's Norsk Hydro, Germany's Henkel, and Italy's Pirelli are all aiming to produce reports on a two to three year cycle. Although yearly reports are not as yet common practice, over two-thirds of the organizations currently producing environmental reports feel that an annual report is the most appropriate (DTTI et al 1993).

A number of surveys have provided recommendations for future environmental reporting. Such recommendations give an indication of the problems with the contents of existing reports. *Coming Clean* (DTTI et al 1993) for example, stated that future reports should:

- focus on areas of greatest environmental impact;
- contain a much higher level of quantification;
- establish benchmark years and then compare performance in subsequent years to these benchmarks; and
- spell out clear targets, at least for the next year.

In a similar manner KPMG's UK survey (1994) concluded that the evaluation of relative performance within or between industrial sectors remained difficult, largely due to a lack of standard reporting mechanisms and of comparable indicators within existing environmental reports.

Environmental Reporting Guidelines

Since environmental reporting is still in its infancy, and few reports have progressed beyond the experimental stage, a number of organizations and associations have developed guidelines and frameworks to help new organizations undertake environmental reporting. The number of guidelines and frameworks available mean that there is a diverse range of options open to any company considering environmental reporting. In order to demonstrate the variety this chapter will briefly examine a number of the reporting initiatives.

PERI

The Public Environmental Reporting Initiative (PERI) is composed of nine leading North American companies – Amoco, Dow Chemicals, Du Point, IBM, Northern Telecom, Philips Petroleum, Polaroid, Rockwell and United Technologies. The PERI guidelines aim to:

- develop a comprehensive and credible framework for environmental reporting; and
- encourage the use of environmental reporting.

As is shown by the nine founding members, PERI is not linked with any industrial associations. The impetus for establishing the guidelines came as a response to stakeholder pressure for companies to endorse the alternative CERES Principles (see Chapter 6). PERI is composed of 'nine components' which are intended to form the core requirements of any comprehensive environmental performance report. Companies are free to select the style and format of their report, an approach which PERI believes will allow sufficient flexibility to accommodate the unique aspects of companies from different industrial sectors. The nine components of the PERI guidelines are; company profile, environmental policy, environmental management, environmental releases, environmental risk management, environmental compliance, product stewardship, employee recognition and stakeholder involvement.

GEMI

The Global Environmental Management Initiative (GEMI) is intended to be an internal management tool designed to evaluate an organization's performance against the 16 Principles defined within the ICC Business Charter. GEMI's Environmental Self-Assessment Programme (ESAP) allows organizations to assess themselves against four performance levels – compliance, system development, integration and total quality. The results of ESAP are to be used within a company and there are no requirements or expectations that self assessments be made public.

CEFIC

The European Chemical Industry Council (CEFIC) adopted its 'Guidelines on Environmental Reporting for the European Chemical Industry' in June 1993. The CEFIC guidelines demonstrate to organizations how they should approach:

- corporate environmental reports;
- site environmental reports; and
- presentations of data in emissions tables.

Member companies are advised to present information on emissions to water and air for a number of key substances, if defined threshold levels have been exceeded. Substances include nitrogen oxides, sulphur dioxide, VOCs, heavy metals and phosphorus. Companies are also requested to provide information on energy, safety, environmental expenditure, community activities, and details of complaints. CEFIC has developed a common structure for reporting which includes details on the organization, products, production processes, company plans and environmental management systems.

WBCSD

The World Business Council for Sustainable Development (WBCSD) is composed of many of the world's leading businesses (including AT&T, BP, ICI, Mitsubishi, Mobil, NEC, Pirelli, Samsung, Shell, Sony, and Texaco among others). It has been a highly influential lobby group for industry although not without its critics (see Welford, 1997, for example).

The WBCSD seeks to encourage enterprises to be more open about their environmental policies, practices and performance. The WBCSD guidelines are not a framework for environmental reporting as such, but rather an information source. The Environmental Reporting Guide gives detailed information under the general headings: Getting Started, Audiences, and Possible Contents. To aid organizations approaching environmental reporting for the first time WBCSD have developed a reporting matrix which lists potential audiences against suggested contents. The matrix is intended to prompt organizations to consider the alternatives available.

ACCA

The Chartered Association of Certified Accountants' 'Introducing Environmental Reporting – Guidelines for Business' is a UK initiative closely linked with the CBI Environment Business Forum. The guidelines are not intended to provide companies with detailed advice, but rather introduce environmental reporting and give direction to other guidance. ACCA have drawn much of their inspiration from PERI and the WBCSD.

Reports may be written in any style or format, as under PERI, although details are provided on 'stand alone' reports, annual reports, and employee newsletters as possible distribution options. It is suggested in the guide that companies may wish to consider disclosing environmental information under the following headings: qualitative (company profile, environmental policy, targets and objectives, community relations), management (EMS, risk management, site practices), quantitative (environmental indicators, energy and natural resources, regulatory compliance, financial indicators), and products (products, processes and contact personnel).

UNEP

In Chapter 5 of 'Company Environmental Reporting' UNEP have identified '50 reporting ingredients' which can be used as a guide when reporting. The 50 ingredients are not in themselves a reporting standard, but rather building blocks which companies can use when constructing their own reports. The ingredients are based on a combination of reporting frameworks and on UNEP's review of actual reporting practice. As such the 50 ingredients are arguably one of the most comprehensive frameworks within which environmental reporting can be developed.

Table 10.4 20 core reporting requirements

Core Reporting Requirements

Management Systems
1. Environmental Policy
2. Environmental Management System
3. Management Responsibility
4. Legal Compliance

Input/Output Inventory
5. Material Use
6. Energy Consumption
7. Water Consumption
8. Health and Safety
9. Accidents and Emergency Response
10. Wastes
11. Air Emissions
12. Water Effluents
13. Product Impacts

Finance
14. Environmental Spending
15. Liabilities

Stakeholder Relations
16. Employees
17. Legislators and Regulators
18. Local Communities
19. Investors
20. Industry Associations

Source: UNEP IE Company Environmental Reporting (1994)

UNEP have further refined their list of 50 ingredients to form 20 'core requirements' (Table 10.4) which are viewed as the minimum requirements for any effective environmental report. The 20 core requirements have also been developed as a suitable framework for SMEs to report under.

WHERE DO WE GO FROM HERE?

As a result of the 1992 United Nations Conference on Environment and Development, (commonly known as the Rio Earth Summit), sustainable development has become an internationally accepted policy goal. If a sustainable society is to be achieved, what role must business play? Companies are crucial in any progress towards sustainability. They account for a large proportion of the world's economic activity, they control much of the world's resources, technology and innovation and in the case of major transnational corporations, they may wield a considerable degree of political influence. Obviously, sustainable development requires sustainable companies. So what might a sustainable company look like?

Sustainable development can be defined as 'improving the quality of human life while living within the carrying capacity of supporting ecosystems' (IUCN/WWF/UNEP 1991). In translating this definition to the level of the company we can say that a sustainable company is one whose activities have a non-negative impact on ecosystem carrying capacity over time. This would mean, for example, that the activities of a company at the end of any year should leave the environment no worse off than it was at the beginning of that year.

Given that we now have a definition of a sustainable company, the question is, how can we judge if a company is moving in this direction? In effect, we are asking how to assess the sustainability (or unsustainability) of a company. The answer is sustainable reporting.

What is sustainable reporting? There is as yet no agreed definition. The whole concept is still new, and any research is at the early experimental stage. Gray (1994), however, has identified two theoretical approaches to sustainable reporting: the 'Inventory' approach and the 'Sustainable Cost' approach. Under the Inventory approach companies would identify, record, monitor and then report on how their activities deplete or enhance natural resources. Those resources under the control of the organization could be identified, and sustainable reporting would distinguish and comment on those areas where changes could be made, substitutes introduced, impacts reduced, and steps taken to mitigate the effects of the organization upon natural resources. Consecutive reports would not only update this process but also monitor progress against these targets.

Reporting through the Sustainable Cost approach requires companies to evaluate and then quantify in financial terms the failure of the organization to operate in a sustainable manner. Thus companies would theoretically calculate over a given period, for example a year, the amount of money the organization would have to spend in order to place the environment back into the position it was one year earlier. This figure, although a notional amount, would provide an indication of the true environmental operating costs of the company.

UNEP IE (1994) adopts an alternative approach to sustainable development reporting. Its report states that;

> *...if nations and world regions are genuinely to move towards environmental sustainability, corporate reporting must become part of industry sector reporting against declared targets – which in turn must become part of national and regional environmental goals.*

As has been mentioned above, sustainable development requires the maintenance of environmental carrying capacity over time. In order to bring about sustainable development it will be necessary to calculate the quantities of substances that can be extracted from and released into the environment without lessening carrying capacity. Under the UNEP approach these quantities will become the basis for national or regional environmental performance targets. These targets will then be disaggregated with performance targets being set for smaller geographical regions and/or industry sectors and eventually targets will have to be set at the level of the individual company. The purpose of the firm's CER will then be to satisfy stakeholders that it is meeting its sustainable development targets. Under this target approach, corporate reporting will need to be standardized in order to allow comparisons between companies and this will require the use of standardized EPIs. TC 207 of the International Organization for Standardization is currently undertaking work to formulate standardized sets of EPIs.

CONCLUSION

This chapter has identified the three categories of environmental disclosure; voluntary, involuntary, and mandatory disclosure, only two of which comprise environmental reporting – ie, the voluntary and mandatory disclosure of information.

There is as yet no legal requirement for companies to report any information through corporate environmental reports (CERs). However, there is a sizeable and increasing body of legislation worldwide requiring companies to disclose information on their environmental performance. While this chapter has demonstrated the benefits of environmental reporting from a company perspective, surveys have shown that corporate environmental reporting is still a rarity among major industrial enterprises. It has been argued that the practice of corporate environmental reporting is unlikely to become widespread as most companies will be unwilling to voluntarily disclose information they feel that may have a negative impact upon them. As this stance conflicts with society's right to know, it has been argued that the environmental disclosure of information through CERs should become mandatory, and there is a considerable body of opinion to suggest that this will occur.

The main focus of CERs to date has been centred on the issues of legislative compliance, resource conservation and emission levels. Since efficient resource management brings direct cost savings, and all companies seek to avoid prosecution by ensuring regulatory compliance, it could be argued that genuine concern for the environment is not a principle motive in encouraging organizations to undertake environmental action.

At first glance, it would appear encouraging that most organizations who are producing environmental reports also include specific targets and objectives within those reports. However, closer inspection reveals that of those targets defined, relatively few are in fact quantitative targets. And even when quantitative targets exist, companies are consistently failing to provide data which will allow assessment of whether targets have been met. In addition, surveys have shown that less than 10 per cent of CERs are verified by third parties, and less than 5 per cent are externally audited. Bearing these considerations in mind the initial picture of corporate environmental reports is no longer quite so impressive.

It is now widely accepted that sustainable development is the framework on which all future environmental policy decisions should be based, and in this chapter we advocate that sustainable development should become the ultimate goal of all companies. To achieve this it is essential that organizations play an active role, and this will require the creation of sustainable development reporting systems. It is clear that current practices are as yet a long way from constituting sustainable development reporting. Unless there is concerted action by regulators at both the national and international level, as well as by companies themselves, sustainable development reports (and thus by implication sustainable development) will not occur in the short- or medium-term future.

REFERENCES

Ball, S & Bell, S (1994) *Environmental Law* Second Edition, Blackstone, London

Deloitte Touche Tohmatsu International, International Institute for Sustainable Development, & SustainAbility Ltd (1993) 'Coming Clean – Corporate Environmental Reporting, Opening Up for Sustainable Development' Deloitte Touche Tohmatsu International, London

Garbutt, J (1995) *Environmental Law – A Practical Handbook* Second Edition, Wiley Chancery, London

Gray, R, Bebbington, J & Walters, D (1993) *Accounting for the Environment* Paul Chapman Publishing Ltd, London

Gray, R (1994) 'Corporate Reporting for Sustainable Development: Accounting for Sustainability in 2000AD' *Environmental Values*, 3: 17–45, The White Horse Press, Cambridge

Gray, S, Radebaugh, L and Roberts, C (1990) 'International perceptions of cost constraints on voluntary information disclosures: A comparative study of UK and USA multinationals' *Journal of International Business*, Fourth Quarter Winter 1990, 597–622

IUCN/UNEP/WWF (1991) *Caring for the Earth: a Strategy for Sustainable Living* Earthscan Publications, London

KPMG (1993a) *UK Survey of Environmental Reporting* KPMG Peat Marwick Thorne, London

KPMG (1993b) *KPMG International Survey of Environmental Reporting* KPMG Peat Marwick Thorne, London

KPMG (1994) *UK Environmental Reporting Survey 199*, KPMG Peat Marwick Thorne, London

SustainAbility (1994) *The 1993 Fortune 100 Survey of Corporate Environmental Reporting* SustainAbility Ltd, London

United Nations Centre for Transnational Corporations Intergovernmental Working Group of Experts on International Standards of Accounting and Reporting (1991) Papers E/C10/AC3/1991/5, 13–14, United Nations, New York

United Nations Environment Programme – Industry and Environment (UNEP IE) (1994) 'Company Environmental Reporting – A Measure of the Progress of Business & Industry Towards Sustainable Development' Technical Report No 24, UNEP, Paris

Vidal, J (1995) *The Guardian*, Saturday 17 June, London

Welford, R J (1997) *Hijacking Environmentalism: Corporate Responses to Sustainable Development* Earthscan, London

Part 3

Wider Applications of the Systems Based Approach

Chapter 11

The EMS in the SME

Donal O'Laoire and Richard Welford

INTRODUCTION

The importance of the SME sector to the world economy is easily recognized. Typically, the sector globally accounts for about 70 per cent of national product although this may vary considerably from country to country. The sector is of relative importance and its status differs in relation to economic classification, whether developed, in transition, newly industrialized, or in developing economies.

Precise definitions of the SME sector differ at regional and national levels and also in relation to the sector and type of industry. Clearly there will be an issue of scale which may be related to the number of employees or turnover. However, we might also examine an SME in terms of where it is located in the supply chain. Typically, most SMEs will be involved in business-to-business activity. More importantly, in the manufacturing sector it will not be unusual for the SME to have a small number of customers who may be other (larger) companies. Thus there is a direct dependence on the financial well-being of the larger partner in the arrangement.

We know that SMEs generally place the environment low on their list of priorities (even if it is a priority at all). Work by Welford (1994) based on survey results in 1992 and 1993 suggested that most SMEs are 'burying their heads in the sand', not recognizing the environmental challenge which faces industry. They assume that this is another passing phase, that their environmental performance has a negligible impact on the world and that environmental issues are an unnecessary annoyance. Moreover, many think that their competitors will also do nothing and that even where consumers are demonstrating environmental awareness, they are unwilling to pay the perceived higher prices necessitated by environmentally superior products.

Moreover, even where SMEs are proactive, their view is often that the use of an externally certified environmental management system such as ISO14001 is not entirely relevant or within the financial resources of the company. Experience of small firms having to put quality systems in place such as ISO 9000, simply because larger partners have written it into contracts, suggests that many SMEs spend an excessive amount of money employing consultants simply to write documentation for systems which already existed, however informally.

In a survey on small firms and the environment (British Chamber of Commerce, 1994), it was legislation rather than any other factor which was found to be the driving force for environmental management in the SME. Nevertheless, an increasing interest in environmental management systems was reported with 11 per cent of respondents considering the implementation of such an EMS standard.

ENVIRONMENTAL MANAGEMENT SYSTEMS

It is certainly not being suggested that the environmental management system approach is inappropriate to the SME, rather that it must be tailored to the scale and financial resources of the business. This means that formal auditing and third party accreditation procedures may be inappropriate and it is the aim of this chapter to demonstrate how small businesses can achieve environmental protection through the use of more flexible systems and other forms of accreditation. We also demonstrate how small businesses can use larger customers to their advantage.

Moreover, improved environmental performance is likely to be increasingly required to gain market access. In particular, those companies on the periphery in any economy (SMEs in Ireland on the periphery of the Single Market, for example) may be able to use an environmental profile to their advantage. Increasingly, intra-industry trade will be predicated on the attainment of standards such as ISO 9000 and ISO 14001, particularly in a world which is seeing a decline in internalization of operations and an increase in contracting and sub-contracting activities.

The key to implementing an environmental management system in an SME is no different to that in larger firms. But since communications and the whole organization of the system are central and have to be transparent and clearly understood, the small size of the enterprise can make this process easier. Moreover, since we have identified several benefits of participatory arrangements and of teamwork earlier in this book, the SME needs to place these firmly within the design of the system.

The achievement of environmentally friendly production requires continual monitoring at all stages of the production and servicing process. While the working of this system may be a task for management, the system itself relies on the compliance and awareness of all members of the firm, whatever their status might be. Within the small organization, gaps which can occur because of a lack of commitment by only one person will be more serious in relative terms than in the large firm. Clear communication flows are therefore needed and workers need to recognize that it is better to highlight a mistake or error than to cover it up in case it gets them into trouble.

Environmental reviews and environmental audits are also clearly part of the EMS. The SME is less likely to have the expertise to undertake these in-house and is less likely to have sufficient money to bring in a team of consultants. Nevertheless there are a number of sources of help and advice to which the SME can turn when some sort of environmental assessment is needed. Some local authorities may be willing to help in the process and in many areas organizations such as the Groundwork Trust will help SMEs carry out environmental reviews at very small, or sometimes no charge (see Chapter 12). Businesses in the same area can often get together, work cooperatively and spread costs and it is always worth tying into local initiatives such as Business and Environment Forums and linking up with sources of local expertise such as universities.

When it comes to energy audits and the assessment of possible new systems, many regional electricity companies offer a free (or at least very cheap) service which will assess the SME's needs and offer advice on possible actions. Local regulators are also likely to be helpful if approached for advice. Local authority departments responsible for registrations under the Environmental Protection Act, regional waste management regulators, local water companies and the regional offices of the Environment Agency will all be a source of help and advice although they are will not undertake a full review for any business.

At the centre of an EMS has to be commitment on the part of all workers. This is worth repeating time and time again because gaps in an EMS system allow inefficiency to leak in and waste and pollution to leak out. The maintenance of that commitment cannot be taken for granted though and it is through a reward system based on the environmental performance of the firm that the commitment can be held and enhanced.

A major opportunity to address the specific issues of environmental improvements in the SME is therefore provided by the publication of ISO 14001. That standard, which addresses the needs of the SME manager in a way which previous standards have neglected, sets out to provide some practical suggestions for implementing the EMS in a way more appropriate to the SME. In the rest of this chapter, we lay out some of the issues to be addressed, point towards the sort of advice which is provided by environmental management systems standards and provide some practical suggestions for implementing and recognizing the EMS in the SME.

GETTING STARTED

Companies in the SME sector may have different views on the relevance of independent certification of systematic environmental management for their business. This assessment will reflect the company's own relative position and assessment of its needs. This assessment, or perception, may include considerations such as:

- The company may be small and have limited managerial, financial and time resources.
- The company may be inhibited by the perceived cost of going down the environmental management road.
- The company may consider itself to be in compliance with the requirements stipulated in the ISO 14001 EMS specification in a limited range

of activities.
- The company may feel that its technical, pollution, management equipment are adequate.
- The company may entrust its waste disposal to a professional agency.
- The company may have one or two major customers in a closed supply circuit.
- The company simply has not got the time to assess or understand the situation.

It is suggested therefore that for many SMEs, a starting point might be a staged adoption of ISO 14001 Environmental Management Principles. Environmental Management Principles are grounded in awareness and it will be necessary as a first step, for companies to become aware of a number of key issues:

- Awareness of the legal and regulatory requirements associated with their operation.
- Awareness of the environmental aspects of their operation.
- Awareness of the direct, indirect, and potential financial costs and benefits associated with these environmental aspects.
- Awareness of the growing pressures from their customers to demonstrate and give assurance of environmental integrity to the market.
- Awareness of what competitors are achieving or implementing in relation to environmental management.

Awareness in these areas will provide a basis on which to adopt good management practices appropriate to the scale and position of the SME in the production, supply and distribution chain. These good management practices could, in themselves, provide customer assurance to some companies by actively communicating with, and agreeing Codes of Practice with their main customers. This approach may meet the needs of enterprises in the business-to-business chain or companies in the local services and retail sector. It may, in any case, provide a good grounding to move towards a formalized and recognized EMS. SMEs that commit themselves to a staged implementation certification of environmental management systems should adhere to the crucial elements of ISO 14001, but that these crucial elements should be applied flexibly, taking into account the particular characteristics of the SMEs.

MANAGEMENT AND MANAGEMENT STRUCTURE

The SME's environmental management system should directly reflect the general management system within the company. It is not the intention of any standard to impose new burdens on the company. EMSs should use the same general management techniques of analysis, planning and implementing in approaching environmental management.

By taking this approach, companies are not being asked to engage a new resource but to refocus the existing capacity. It may be the case that adoption of environmental management in a company may be the catalyst to examine objectively the general management system to the benefit of the company. Normally, however, the SME manager will maximize resource efficiency by using existing organizational structures, procedures and recording systems, which can be adapted to incorporate an environmental dimension.

Moreover, we should realize that in an SME some of the central principles of the management systems approach may be present naturally. By this, we mean that teamwork, a close cooperation between management and workers, participation, good communications links and open planning and organizational arrangements might be a natural outcome of the small size of the organization. Documenting this may therefore be a relatively easy task and allow everyone in the organization to see his or her place more clearly.

The SME manager should consider the review as a catalyst to examine the effectiveness and efficiency of the operation. The SME should also consider:

- employee practices, procedures and training;
- administrative practices and procedures;
- the financial costs of present inputs, procedures and practices;
- product and process specification demanded (or anticipated) by the SME customer base.

Environmental management of the SME should be rooted in competitive advantage, driven by efficient production and provision of goods and services of environmental integrity to an increasingly discerning market.

The objectives and targets set by the SME manager must consider all of the above. They should, in the first instance, be realistic and attainable, and consistent with the resources available. They must demonstrate a commitment by the SME towards improvement of environmental performance to a stated standard. It should be emphasized to the SME manager that continual gradual improvement towards stated targets, consistent with the resources available to attain this, is acceptable.

INFORMATION AND ANALYSIS

Central to the development of an EMS is the need to gather information about environmental impacts and impact mechanisms. Analysis is, in turn, the process of using that information about the environmental status of the SME with the aim of identifying appropriate action to be undertaken to reduce negative environmental impacts. As part of this process and in order to establish and maintain an EMS, a continuous status review is required. The minimum requirements of the ISO 14001 specification demand an understanding of:

- the relevant legal requirements relating to the activities of the organization;
- the environmental aspects of the operation (in some cases, the SME

should be in a position to provide assurance to its stakeholders in relation to its regulatory requirements); and (as a minimum)
- to show familiarity with or have access to legal data relevant to activities of the organization.

Common sense and social responsibility should be the guiding principles in demonstrating an understanding of the environmental aspects of the organization. In the majority of cases, the SME manager will be capable of compiling a register of environmental aspects without external assessment. It is also recommended that the SME manager should establish the financial costs and benefits of energy, packaging, waste, effluent management, etc in order to give focus and prioritization to the potential financial benefits of proactive environmental management. This exercise will help the SME manager to restate the environment in traditional business language. Above all, the SME manager should view proactive environmental management as a tool to maintain or reduce operational costs and a means to secure or enhance market access.

Within the information gathering stage the SME will have to identify its most important environmental aspects. These will include:

- the identification of the requirements of environmental legislation pertaining to the SME;
- the identification of key environmental effects of the SME's operation. This should consider various elements that could have greatest impact on the environment, taking into account the characteristics of the product and the industrial sector in which the SME is engaged;
- the investigation of threats and opportunities pertaining to the SME's environmental performance;
- the identification of SME contributor activities central to environmental performance in order to prioritize the risk inherent in various elements of the SME's operation.

In order to establish these environmental aspects, the SME may utilize the following support structures:

- results of the activities and the experience of other organizations (see below):
- organizations representative of industrial sectors or standardization bodies can be encouraged to prepare and disseminate reference manuals to define how the SME sector can establish its environmental aspects effectively; and
- local sources of information including local authorities and universities.

An important part of the information and analysis which the SME will have to undertake will include the evaluation of environmental risk. Even though the SME may have an emergency response action plan in place in relation to fire, it may not be adequate to address emergency spills or impacts which have a negative impact on air, water, or ground. In the first instance the SME therefore needs to establish:

1. the areas in the company's or organization's processes or activities which could precipitate an emergency or are vulnerable to the impacts of a spill;
2. the nature and scope of risks associated with potential spills or emergencies;
3. the response capability of the organization;
4. the compatibility of the response capability with national or local emergency response planning; and
5. notification and communication requirements to third parties.

EVALUATION OF COSTS

In establishing the present costs and predicted savings with respect to energy, packaging, waste, effluent management etc, the SME manager should focus attention on the potential financial benefits that could result from systemized environmental management. In so doing, the costs associated with the implementation of EMS also needs to be estimated to provide the beginnings of a cost benefit analysis. The SME manager should consider all the costs of installation of pollution prevention facilities, human resources, training, organization, documentation, measures and certification.

In addition, in evaluating the effects of non-implementation of environmental management, the SME manager will need to identify the potential drawbacks of not introducing environmental management strategies, such as market exclusion, customer damage claims, reduction of turnover, increased insurance costs, possible legal costs and fines. Once again, in evaluating the effects of these drawbacks, the SME manager will need to compare them with the cost of establishing an EMS.

PLANNING AND IMPLEMENTATION

Planning is the process during which information is used, objectives set, and resources committed. The ISO 14001 specification requires evidence of the management programme which defines objectives and targets set in relation to company environmental policy. This programme should also specify the guiding principles by which the firm will operate. A measurement of the adequacy of the management programme will be its consistency with good and proactive management practices.

Although environmental management will be the responsibility of all staff in the SME, it is recommended that a 'responsible person' is appointed for the internal direction and external communication with respect to environmental affairs. Typically, this person might be the owner/manager, the operational manager or, in somewhat larger firms, the quality manager.

The important point to recognize in the SME is that planning will always be flexible and this should be acknowledged in documentation. Strategic planning is a difficult concept for the SME. The SME manager will be centrally concerned with the short term. The SME may perceive that strategy is the domain of larger companies and other forces outside the small company's control. However, there will be little need for long-term strategic plans which are often inappropriate to the SME. Moreover, documentation supporting planning arrangements can be quite minimal, recognizing the changing nature of markets in which SMEs often find themselves.

Implementation is the process of implementing, controlling, measuring, and reassessing the system. The implementation of the EMS will require proper organization and the establishment of procedures, the recording of activities and monitoring programmes consistent with the stated objectives. The organizational structure, the procedures and recording systems should parallel established systems, such as the production system, and should seek to make the work of those involved more effective. The implementation process also requires training and communication procedures.

The ISO 14001 specification for management programmes concerns itself with the following:

- objectives and targets;
- resources, responsibility, timing and priority;
- guiding principles; and
- the environmental manual.

With respect to these elements, the requirement for the SME may be quite basic. Therefore, a measurement of the adequacy of the management programme will be its consistency with good and proactive management practices. Implementation of the system concerns itself with implementing and controlling tasks designed to achieve the stated objectives and targets.

The SME manager should ensure that environmental performance is regularly monitored by:

- establishing a checklist of operational control points which require measurements;
- establishing a regular monitoring and measuring programme;
- establishing target performance measures; and
- establishing regular calibration and testing of measuring and monitoring equipment and systems.

The SME manager should adopt an attitude of continual improvement by:

- initiating periodic reviews of the EMS;
- involving all staff in the review process and subsequent follow-up action; and
- establishing a procedure to identify areas for corrective and preventative action.

RESOURCES AND SOURCES OF HELP AND ADVICE

We have suggested that the SME will have limited resources to implement an EMS. However, there is much that can be done at minimal cost and in some cases there may be grant aid available. In the first instance the SME can look to a number of agencies for help in the review process:

- The local authority in relation to laws and permits and, in some cases, for grant aid to undertake initial environmental reviews.
- Local or regional libraries and local authority information centres for other environmental information and links with voluntary groups and Green Business Forums.
- SME organizations and trade associations for information on how other companies have achieved environmental improvement.
- Collaboration with larger customer firms which will be particularly relevant for small companies who have a limited number of dedicated larger industry customers.
- Other SMEs on a sectoral supply chain or local basis to define and address common issues, to share know-how, to facilitate technical development, to use facilities jointly, to draw up the EMS manual by industry and to establish a system to study the EMS for the SME.
- Other SMEs to collectively engage in consultancy on a local or area basis.
- Universities and other research centres to support production, innovation, and clean technologies.
- Regulators who are often happier in helping companies comply with the law and best practice than engaging in litigation.

CERTIFICATION AND ACCREDITATION OPTIONS FOR THE SME SECTOR

For the SME a full accreditation may not be appropriate or may be financially difficult. We therefore need to finds ways of recognizing the environmental activities in the SME which, despite not being wholly consistent with a recognized standard, will nevertheless be contributing to environmental improvement.

Depending on the commercial and trading profile of the small- and medium-sized enterprise, there are three options which the SME could consider:

1. **Self-Declaration:** This provides for companies to make a self-determination and declaration of conformance with the standard. Typically the motivation, in this approach, is adaptation of good management practices that will bring the benefits of efficiencies and market security in the company. In many cases, this self-declaration may meet the needs of individual companies in the SME sector. Typically these companies would be at the smaller end of the SME spectrum.

   At this level we must rely on the market to deal with those companies who may be tempted to dishonestly recognize themselves. Such actions are likely to incur the wrath of customers who themselves may be attempting to improve their environmental performance. Lying about one's environmental performance will therefore be worse then doing nothing.

2. **Second Party Recognition:** Many SMEs will typically be involved in business-to-business activity, supplying in-process products and parts, as well as finished products, which are governed by particular policies and specifications. In cases where the SME is a dedicated supplier, or has a limited number of large customers, the SME may implement environmental management principles that could be agreed or accepted by the SME customer or customers as evidence of good environmental management practices.

   In this case, the enterprise shall have established an EMS adopting the key elements of ISO 14001 which will be verified objectively by the customer base or by other stakeholders. This therefore presents an opportunity for using the power and influence of major customers.

3. **Third Party Certification:** While the adaptation of environmental management principles may be adequate in some cases, the SME sector may eventually be required to provide third party independent certification of EMSs. This will typically come from requirements demanded by the customer base.

   However, third party certification for the SME may not necessarily have to involve certification by the standard setter itself. A respected consultancy firm, trade association, group of independent managers or academics, or a local authority might consider the introduction of some sort of environmental seal of approval consistent with ISO 14001.

CONCLUSIONS

We conclude by suggesting that the adoption of environmental management systems in the SME, consistent with standards such as ISO 14001 may not be as daunting a task as many SME managers may think. Moreover, the systematic approach inherent in such systems brings about a number of benefits to the SME. The SME manager needs to undertake a cost benefit analysis of the implementation of the SME with particular emphasis placed on the costs of *not* introducing environmental improvement strategies.

We have suggested that there are many support structures and sources of advice which may be freely available to the SME and that full compatibility with the requirements of the standards are not always necessary. However, an approach consistent with the broad aims of ISO 14001 will enable the firm to look towards some sort of accreditation. We suggest that this may not require full certification to the standard but that first-, second- or third-party recognition may provide a useful stating point and bring tangible benefits to the SME with limited resources.

The development of environmental networks amongst small businesses, voluntary organizations and the public sector will enable controlled growth to occur. Ultimately what we do with our environment affects us all and future generations. If the environment is important then we should recognize that the systems and processes used in businesses are also important. It has been suggested here that collaborative arrangements, multi-sector networking and participative strategies and systems associated with environmental management meet the aims and objectives of a developing economy to the extent that this provides us with a model for the promotion and development of industry. There is a need for small businesses to be given incentives to undertake environmental change. Some of these incentives are provided by the legislative framework and a need to survive in a more competitive and environmentally-aware marketplace. In addition, larger firms will push environmental improvement along the supply chain. But there is still a need to convince small businesses that environmental improvements will reduce costs in the long run and this can only be achieved by demonstration of best practice. There is a clear role here for government and local authorities in supporting innovative developments and providing a forum where information can be exchanged.

Whether an environmental management system is ultimately successful may depend in part on factors outside the control of the firm. But apart from the existence of a growing legislative framework aimed at directing firms, the most significant determinants of success will be a range of internal factors including commitment, the appropriateness of the organization of the system and the success of the company in measuring and assessing its environmental performance. There also has to be a good reason for instituting the EMS and this needs to be thoroughly explained and discussed with everyone involved in the firm including workers, shareholders and customers. Over time the aim must be to develop a positive culture surrounding environmental management and its constituent parts. Here there is a very important role for managers.

REFERENCES

British Chamber of Commerce (1994) 'Small Business Survey 7 – Environment' Association of British Chambers of Commerce, London

Welford, R J (1994) 'Barriers to the Improvement of Environmental Performance: the Case of the SME Sector' in *Cases in Environmental Management and Business Strategy* (Welford, R J) Pitman Publishing, London

Chapter 12

Local Economic Development and Environmental Management: A Systems Approach

Richard Welford

INTRODUCTION

The purpose of this chapter is to discuss the sorts of initiatives which can be taken in the local economy which can not only improve regional environmental performance but, by involving businesses, can also aid the development of better environmental performance at the firm level. The main thrust of this chapter is therefore to show how the company based environmental management systems discussed earlier in this book and a regional environmental management system (REMS) can be compatible. It will be argued that there is a direct relationship between environmental quality and the industrial development and economic activities within an area. Using a systems-based methodology, it is argued that a key strategy for environmental management within businesses will involve cooperating with stakeholders at the local level in order to achieve the integration of economic and environmental objectives.

European Union environmental policies on land, water and air pollution have important consequences for planning and use of the EU's land area. In the EU's *Europe 2000* project (Commission of the European Communities, 1991), the issue of the linkage between economic development and the environment is highlighted particularly because quality of life is becoming an important factor in the ability of regions and cities to attract new inward investment. There is a need therefore for regional development policies to reach the right balance between protection of the physical environment and economic growth. Once again, this requires a strategy at the regional level which links the interests of communities and businesses.

The original Treaty of Rome did not give the EU explicit powers to legislate on environmental matters but this was amended by the adoption of the Single European Act 1986, which now provides a firm legal basis for Community legislation on the environment. One of the provisions requires that environmental protection be a component of all other policies based on the premise that measures in the sphere of other policies will normally have a positive or negative impact on the environment. This is an important provision as it establishes a requirement that environmental protection must form an essential component of all Community policies, including economic development policies. This emphasis on the integration of environmental policy is further stressed in the Maastricht Treaty (Article 130r2), within the Fifth Environmental Action Programme and is the central aim of Agenda 21, the most substantial result to come out of the Rio Summit in 1992.

The EU's Fifth Environment Programme has as a major theme the promotion of information and education of the Community's citizens towards the protection of the environment, and the direct involvement of the Community in achieving environmental protection through the increased use of voluntary agreements, codes of conduct and economic incentives.

REGIONAL ENVIRONMENTAL MANAGEMENT

The roots of the regional environmental management approach are to be found within the concept of bioregionalism. Sale (1974) argues that a bioregion is any area of which the boundaries are determined by natural order rather than by human dictates. More importantly, the bioregional model puts an emphasis on local activity, on local development and on the protection of the environment. It stresses the importance of local economy, of the local employment and the development of local trading networks which are less reliant on traditional forms of mass transportation.

The definition of a region used here is therefore based on the notion of a bioregion. Although the modern bioregion may not have such strict natural boundaries as Sale (1974) might have envisaged, it is necessary that the region is sufficiently small and suficiently well defined that local environmental performance can be measured and assessed. It might be an urban or rural area. However, it needs to be of a such a size that the commitment of industry within the area can be channelled into action and it needs to be sufficiently small to allow every participant industry to feel important enough to make an effort towards environmental improvement.

The thing which links these possibly disparate regions is the method by which the environment of the region can be improved. The underlying approach is to develop a plan for the region which will, over time, lead to the development of a comparative advantage based on systems-based, integrated environmental management, at both company and regional levels. This will be referred to as the conversion plan. The REMS concept, in principle, is that commercial and industrial viability in the 1990s and beyond is synonymous with quality at every level including environmental quality. Rather than regarding new environmental control and legislation as a negative factor and a cost, the thrust is to turn apparent constraint into advantage. The REMS concept may also include a 'regional branding' of the area as one renowned for integrated environmental management and in turn where economic benefits accrue from both regional and company level environmental management strategies. This is consistent with the approach of the EU's Fifth Environmental Action Programme when it suggests that local and regional authorities can play a decisive role 'in creating the necessary conditions to enable individuals and private enterprises to play their respective roles' while ensuring 'the sustainable use of resources necessary for that development to take place and prosper' (Fleming, 1992, p 4).

The development of the region must be based on high environmental and product quality at every stage of the production process and at every step in the production chain which will be integrated as far as possible within the region. At the product level, an emphasis on 'cradle to grave' responsibility and integrated supply chains leads to an increased control of the production cycle from primary production right through to direct marketing and final sale. One specific aim might be to encourage different production steps to take place within the same region. This would include the key EU objective of dealing with the disposal and treatment of waste within the region in which it was created.

THE SYSTEMS BASED APPROACH

Integrated preventative action encourages actions to be taken to protect the environment at an early stage, requiring environmental management to go beyond the question of repairing damages, to stopping degradation from occurring in the first place. The 'polluter pays' principle must also be seen as an important instrument enabling the market to be adjusted to reflect the true costs of the production of goods and services. The principle is becoming adopted by the EU and slowly by Member States' governments. Pressures for regulatory compliance will be met, in the main, through the initiation of continuous and sophisticated monitoring systems, waste minimization, more effective investments in process technology, and research and development. As these costs, and those associated with the fiscal instruments of environmental policies, begin to impinge more heavily on an organization's operating and capital costs, evidence of good practice will become a precondition for access to the wider investment community. These further pressures are likely to spill over into other stakeholder relationships.

These trends confirm that industry will need to adopt a more strategic and systems-based view of environmental problems. In tandem with regional and local economic initiatives, it needs to move away from short-termism to problem solving and towards the development of preemptive control strategies, striking a balance between regulation and the need to turn those regulations into competitive advantage. The development of a REMS can help significantly here. Not only does it allow for a cooperative environmental effort on the part of firms in the region which can lead to synergy in research and development, waste management and energy efficiency but a significant advantage can also be derived from a common marketing approach. A regional conversion plan embedded within the systems-based approach aims at focusing the marketing instrument not only on the company, but also on the region in which the company is based. The region can develop a competitive advantage by way of an integrated proactive environmental policy and by way of an integrated proactive REMS. In other words, the product will be produced to the highest environmental standards in a geographical region where the quality of the environment is maintained through an efficient REMS.

THE REGIONAL ENVIRONMENTAL MANGEMENT SYSTEM (REMS)

There are inherent risks in treating economic forces and the environment as if they were separate and non-interacting elements. Economic policy which neglects to take into consideration environmental risks and damage is not sustainable. This is exemplified in so many semi-rural areas where economic development has resulted in the exploitation of the natural environment, leaving rivers biologically dead and parts of the landscape aesthetically degraded and sometimes contaminated.

One traditional starting point for dealing with this problem is that taken by environmental economists who argue that an economic value should be put on natural assets and that these costs should be internalized (see, for example, Pearce & Turner 1990). Conceptually, there seems to be no quarrel with the fact that long-term economic benefits accrue from environmental management. When a landscape loses its productivity, standards of living are under negative pressure; when a landscape loses its aesthetic appeal, property values diminish. However a significant tension between economics and environmental management often arises around short-term issues because of the difficulty of accurately valuing natural assets and problems associated with the ownership of those assets. Even where prices can be identified it is often difficult to get these accepted by the parties involved in a development (or perhaps more importantly their lawyers).

A full cost accounting option which would internalize all environmental costs remains speculative and highly controversial, and there are many ecologists and environmental managers who doubt both the wisdom and practicality of attempting to reconcile all ecological impacts with conventional financial indicators. It is not possible to make realistic financial estimates of the intrinsic value of numerous important ecological assets, nor is it possible to predict what value would be placed on these assets by future generations. It is therefore impossible to envisage all key indices of sustainability emerging from cost accountancy.

Where a region is already polluted or environmentally damaged the most common approach to tackling problems seems to be to deal with specific point sources of pollution using regulatory controls. In addition, over time individual impact assessments can mitigate environmental damage, but they do not necessarily alter the larger picture. The effect of this ad hoc approach on the regional environment can often be seen as 'two steps forward, one step back'. Because of the non-integrated and non-coordinated approach, what is beneficial or, more often, 'not harmful' for one industry, may well be harmful to another.

The environment responds as a whole, when stressed at a particular point but the traditional piecemeal approach to environmental management does not provide any information about how the whole system reacts. There is therefore a need to develop a more integrated REMS which is capable of exploring the synergistic effect of applying environmental management policies to all sectors of activity. This change from a piecemeal to a holistic approach can be seen as an important part of a sustainable development approach. The concept of sustainable development recognizes that there is an interdependence between the economy and the environment, not only because the way we manage the economy has an impact on the environment, but also because environmental quality has an impact on the performance of the economy.

Central to the development of a REMS is the cooperation and commitment of regional and local resources facilitated through partnerships between individuals, businesses, public sector institutions and other agencies. A regional strategy of environmental management is required which promotes and stimulates community implemented development. It is particularly important therefore to involve the business sector and to make it clear that there are significant benefits to that sector becoming involved. This process must begin through the provision of information, through education and training, and subsequently the provision of support, advice, and capital for local initiatives. Any EMS starts with, and depends strongly upon, the development of understanding and commitment from all people involved and the REMS is no exception.

There is also a need to have a clear policy for the region which integrates both regional objectives and industrial aspirations. Such policies are already in place where local authorities have followed Friends of the Earth's advice in introducing a declaration of commitment to environmental protection and policy development in the areas of recycling, energy, transport and planning, environmental protection and enhancement, health, and the monitoring and minimization of pollution. Some authorities have also introduced regular environmental audits and invited public and industrial participation.

However, the REMS policy needs to go beyond this and fully integrate the needs of the region, industry and the public into a plan which binds them together with the objective of significantly improving all aspects of the region's environmental performance.

The implementation of the REMS will help to give the particular region a comparative edge, and lead to more sustainable economic growth and development. The environmental quality driven, market-led and proactive approach is increasingly used at the company level, but relatively new at a regional level. As a result of the implementation of the REMS, the area can be promoted as a 'green region' and a number of companies within the region may be able to take advantage of this 'environmental labelling' of the area. The message coming from the companies operating in the region must clearly communicate that the product comes from an area which is managed in an environmentally superior way and where high threshold environmental criteria have been established.

Within the REMS, 'codes of conduct' relating to environmental performance and procedures can be established. These might include targets to reduce emissions, a protocol for handling waste in the region and a commitment on the part of all firms to introduce internal environmental management systems, for example. All institutions and companies in the region would be expected to adhere to these codes over time. Success will depend on commitment of all involved, but there will also have to be incentives provided by the local authority. Because the aim of the REMS would be to go beyond legislation then there will be seldom a 'stick' to go along with the 'carrot'. This is why businesses in an area will have to be convinced of the benefits of being involved in such a regional scheme.

Unlike existing labelling schemes, the focus of increased marketability of products produced within the REMS will not only be on the environmental impact of the product, but will also focus on the environmental performance of the company (possibly becoming accredited via ISO 14001 or the EU EMAS), and on the environmental status of the region where the product is produced. As a result of the REMS, the range of products which are produced in a way which is least harmful for the environment, will expand. 'Green products' will not only be defined in terms of price and performance, but products will convey real protection for the environment.

THE BENEFITS OF A REGIONAL ENVIRONMENTAL MANAGEMENT SYSTEM

Regional management centres around ecological improvement through environmental rehabilitation, and prevention of further environmental degradation through the introduction of specific management and control systems. The REMS goes further than that because it not only introduces environmental management on a regional scale, but actively uses it as a tool to enhance the economic prospects of the region by integrating environmental, economic and social factors in the REMS. Regional management involving such an integrated approach, whereby all developments and all economic activities are seen as part of a larger structure, will have a number of general beneficial effects.

A conversion plan development team, with representatives from local communities and industries, and local government will set environmental targets and protocols at all levels. Targets will be continuously reassessed and every person in the community will have their own environmental responsibility. As a result of this integrated approach, different companies are more likely to cooperate in dealing with pollution and other environmental problems thereby potentially reducing costs. The Landskrona project in Sweden and the Prisma project in the Netherlands are well known examples which demonstrated that such a strategy can work, and that the environmental problems of companies, even if they operate in different industries, are often quite similar (Van Berkel et al, 1991).

Both the region as an entity, as well as the individual companies within that region, may benefit from an increased marketability. Possibilities exist for marketing the region as a whole, bringing generic benefits to companies operating within it. It must be clear that the product comes from a region in which high threshold environmental criteria have been established. New investors may be attracted to the area, because of its more efficient management system.

The landscape and countryside will be better managed and preserved.

Increased environmental planning in the REMS could lead to innovative design and management and to an ecologically sound, socio economic structure. In turn, a coordinated, cooperative and active approach to environmental rehabilitation can be undertaken, leading to a cleaner, healthier and safer environment. Moreover, a programme aimed at prevention of further environmental damage will integrate wider aspects of economic development and improve quality of life. The REMS is also likely to involve making the most of space, landscape, cultural and craft traditions, architectural and industrial heritage.

Most of the synergistic effects of the REMS will only occur if all parties involved not only understand the conversion concept, but are also willing to cooperate and actively strive towards its success. The main strength of the REMS lies in the integrative approach towards environmental, economic and social factors.

CONVERSION PLAN DEVELOPMENT AND IMPLEMENTATION STRATEGIES

The goals for economic development inherent in the conversion plan for the REMS will be achieved through the development of regional comparative advantage based on self-imposed market-led codes of practice that ensure quality and integrated environmental management. An overview of the steps involved in the development of the REMS is given in Figure 12.1. Both the company-based EMS and the REMS build a strategic link between business objectives and environmental pressures. The two can no longer be seen as separate and the particular objectives of businesses and environment improvement have to be seen as consistent, which has not traditionally been the case. Moreover, the development of the REMS as expounded here is deliberately in line with company-based EMS standards such as ISO 14001 and the EMAS.

The REMS requires a good source of up to date information about its starting point and its on-going performance. There is a need, as far as possible, to undertake an initial review of the region which will act as a benchmark for future measurement. Using the same sort of approach adopted by firms with EMS there is subsequently a need to audit regularly environmental performance and the REMS itself.

One possibility is to develop an interactive computerized database to create an environmental quality model (EQM) for the region. The model could be based on Geographical Information Systems (GIS) modelling and it would also act as a database for environmental and socioeconomic data. It would allow accurate criteria to be formulated and tested, as well as prediction of the effects of mediation work or of new development. Such a system would allow traditionally difficult factors such as land use and climate to be included in decision making, and can be used to identify existing and potential diffuse pollution sources. The model could be fully interactive, providing the holistic environmental quality control capability required by the REMS. But then the conversion plan needs to entail much more than 'just' an EMS. Environmental, economic, and social factors are included in the REMS and its conversion plan.

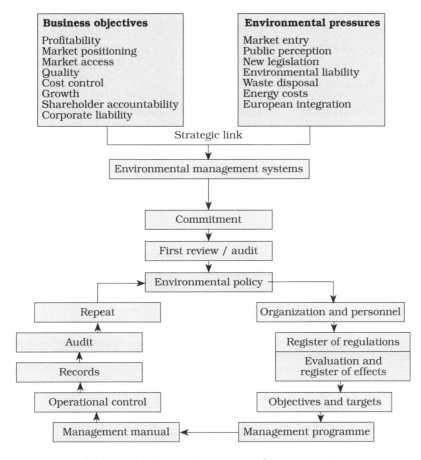

Figure 12.1 Development of the REMS

The REMS should therefore be regarded as a management tool, aimed at facilitating implementation of the regional conversion plan, and comparable to the function of the EMS at the company level. It should facilitate environmental rehabilitation and protection by integrating economic, social and environmental factors, emphasizing local industry and local interests. Instrumental to the development of the REMS will be a conversion plan development team. Specific tasks for this team can be identified in the following ten point strategy:

1. Develop a regional environmental information system, including an environmental monitoring system.
2. Conduct an extensive environmental and socioeconomic study in the area, with emphasis on topics such as migration patterns, effects of infrastructural developments, employment, and the relative importance of the different economic sectors.

3. Extend contacts and communication with local communities and industry.
4. Develop internal strategies to promote information and education of all residents of the area towards environmental protection and the benefits and implications of the REMS and to stimulate community involvement and environmental awareness.
5. Design a template and model for processes and protocols within the area, resulting in improved communications and increased organizational control.
6. Outline a regional environmental policy, with specific standards and targets, and to develop an environmental quality model (EQM).
7. Conduct a detailed environmental quality survey and to identify and prioritize areas for environmental rehabilitation and development.
8. Stimulate and coordinate further development and implementation of company EMS.
9. Identify and prioritize areas for economic investment and growth, and new economic opportunities.
10. Develop strategies to promote and market the area externally and to develop a scheme that gives recognition to 'green companies' within the region.

We know that environmental development can best be established when there is a sense of cooperation and commitment from all parties involved (see Welford, 1992). It is suggested, therefore, that for the development of a conversion plan, representatives of both local communities and industrial sectors are brought together in a development committee and not only help develop, but also ensure broad-based support for the final conversion plan.

COSTING THE CONVERSION PLAN

The REMS ensures an efficient use of existing funds from local, national and EU sources. Furthermore, it may often be the case that several new sources of funds may be applied for in order to develop parts of the conversion plan. The setting up of a company EMS is a relatively low cost exercise. The benefits of a company EMS have been outlined in detail by Welford (1992); and by research in the US, with its high environmental standards and stringent laws, showed that costs of pollution control add up to a mere average of 0.54 per cent of a company's overall costs (Dodwell 1992). Total environmental expenditures are on average 2.4 per cent of turnover (Winsemius and Guntram, 1992). Over a period, instalment of a company EMS will pay for itself several times over. Therefore, expenditure to install company EMSs should have a short payback period and can be self-financing.

As far as the costs of the plan itself are concerned these will depend on the amount of expertise, in the shape of consultants, needs to be introduced into the region and the size of the project itself. Infrastructural investment is clearly required to address the issues of emissions and effluent management and rehabilitation but expenditure of this kind is likely to take place anyway. An additional benefit of the REMS is that such expenditure is likely to be made in a more integrated and systematic way. In addition there may be a need to provide incentives to firms to undertake their own environmental improvements and this can be achieved if money can be found for small grant provision. The initial review of the region may be costly but it is invaluable in identifying priorities for action. In many cases however, local authorities have already started on the process and there are growing sources of regional environmental information.

Expenditure on the REMS needs to be seen as an investment good rather than a consumption good. It should be clear that any such investment will bring returns via improvements in the regional environment and new opportunities for businesses operating within that region. In turn, the increased wealth-generating potential in the region can mean that the project can ultimately pay for itself.

The conversion plan outlined here is concerned with the competitiveness of the region. In this context, the conversion plan framework offers an opportunity to seek funding under EU R&D support programmes and other programmes, such as PRISMA, which are dedicated to levelling competitive disadvantages. The conversion plan addresses the issue of integrated development and, in this context, DGXXII of the European Commission, as the coordinator of structural funds, may find research and experimental opportunities within the region.

CONCLUSIONS

It has been argued that there are benefits relating to the introduction of REMSs, which integrate environmental, economic and social factors. A REMS will only work if it is developed by people that have an interest in the region and central to this is the participation, cooperation and commitment of businesses in the area. Coherent strategies and systems for environmental and developmental management, whether at the company level or at a regional level, have synergetic benefits to businesses within it and to the local community and the environment. Changes in regional management must be designed and developed by people from within the region, supported by professional staff, and a central place in the management framework needs to be taken by representatives from local communities and industry. The role of local government is to provide linkage in the REMS.

Industry itself can benefit greatly by the additional help which will be provided by firms working together cooperatively with the support of a regional team. The REMS will complement the firm's own internal EMS and further add to the firm's competitive advantage if the region can attract a 'green label'. To a large extent the future of the environment and of the planet requires more cooperation and the concept of the REMS extends much of the best practice discussed by a wide range of practitioners. A key concept of environmentalists has long been: local action, global impact. At the centre of this concept is the need for increased cooperation and the REMS extends what firms alone can do towards achieving this important objective.

REFERENCES

Commission of the European Communities (1991) 'Europe 2000: Outlook for the development of the Community's territory' Communication from the Commission to the Council and the European Parliament, Brussels

Dodwell, D, (1992) 'Environment better served by free trade carrot than protectionist stick' *The Financial Times*, 13 May

Fleming, D (1992) 'The Fifth EC Environmental Action Programme' *European Environment*, Special Supplement

Pearce, D W & Turner, R K, (1990) *Economics of natural resources and the environment* Harvester Wheatsheaf, UK

Sale, K (1985) *Dwellers in the Land: the Bioregional Vision* Sierra Club, San Francisco

Van Berkel, R et al (1991) 'Business examples with waste prevention: ten case studies from the Dutch PRISMA project' in *Prepare for Tomorrow* Ministry for Economic Affairs, the Netherlands

Welford, R J (1992) 'Linking Quality and the Environment, A Strategy for the Implementation of Environmental Management Systems' *Business Strategy and the Environment*, 1, 1, 25–34

Winsemius, P and Guntram, U (1992) 'Responding to the environmental challenge' *Business Horizons*, 2, 38–45

Chapter 13

The Role of Environmental Management Systems in Local Government

Alan Netherwood and Mark Shayler

INTRODUCTION

The environmental functions and responsibilities of local government are varied, and have traditionally been managed separately by different service and administrative departments. However, added emphasis has been placed on local authorities in recent years to help deliver sustainable development within the local community by the Rio Earth Summit, Local Agenda 21 and the EU Fifth Environmental Action Programme. These have led to many local authorities adopting broad environmental strategies which bring these functions and responsibilities together.

However, a major problem has arisen in local authorities' attempts to coordinate these functions. Environmental management systems have a role to play in this new agenda for local government in terms of the coordination of environmental management initiatives, and in terms of facilitating improved environmental performance within the local community. Local authorities are using environmental management systems in two ways. Firstly, they are being used to manage the environmental impact of the authority and its component parts and to this end the EU EMAS has been adapted specifically for use in local government. Secondly, local authorities are encouraging small- and medium-sized businesses in this area to improve their own environmental performance by carrying out environmental reviews and adopting the principles of EMS. However in many cases, in order to overcome cultural inertia, this encouragement is often piecemeal and places emphasis upon the positive cost implications of environmental action. This chapter will examine both of these functions in detail.

THE ENVIRONMENTAL ROLE OF LOCAL GOVERNMENT

The Association of County Councils (1990) gives a summary of the environmental functions of local government, and describes these functions in five main areas:

1. **Prevention:** ie in transport management, development control, land use and emergency planning.
2. **Regulation and control:** ie through land use planning, waste disposal, recycling and pollution control.
3. **Restoration, conservation and enhancement:** ie in terms of road management, traffic calming, transport facilities, rural strategies and nature conservation.
4. **Monitoring and coordination:** ie monitoring within a specific spatial unit, in its function as an enabling body and as a coordinator between central, county and district government.
5. **Organizational:** ie in maximizing the authority's environmental performance in terms of the organization and in terms of the services it provides.

Peattie and Hall (1994) point out that as a service provider local authorities have a responsibility to provide for the welfare of the community. In environmental terms this includes the prevention of damaging activities and the removal of substances such as waste, which harm the environment. They also suggest that as a guardian and planner, local government exercises development control, protects the countryside and the urban environment and uses statutory powers to prevent environmental degradation. As a facilitator, a local authority can enable liaison between regulatory bodies, pressure groups and business with respect to environmental management. Local authorities are also landowners and employers, and have many direct impacts on the environment in terms of energy, transport, housing and waste issues. They also act as an educator, having influence over schools, providing advisory teachers on environmental issues, establishing environmental centres and educating staff about environmental issues.

Therefore local authorities have a wide range of environmental responsibilities in managing their own impact as an organization, monitoring the impacts caused through their policies and services to the local community, in their role of managing the local environment through planning control, and in their role as an enabler and facilitator.

Environmental Management in Local Government

Since the 1980s a number of environmental initiatives have been developed in the UK to enable authorities to monitor and manage their environmental performance. In 1988, Friends of the Earth published an 'Environmental Charter for Local Government' which aimed to encourage local government to take a wider approach to environmental issues and to develop policies to improve environmental information for the public, report on the state of the environment, and monitor their own impacts upon the local, national and global environment.

This charter required:

- the establishment of an environmental forum or committee for the local community;
- the carrying out of an environmental audit;
- consultation with the community regarding environmental issues;
- the drawing up of a charter for the environment;
- the development of an environmental strategy, including action plans and target dates, and facilities for the monitoring and review of environmental performance; and
- the establishment of a working group or committee to coordinate and develop environmental activity.

It was suggested in this document that a number of tools should be used to meet these requirements.

Environmental Charters

These generally contain the following types of principles and commitments:

- Achieving a more sustainable future.
- A reduction in local and global pollution.
- The conservation and sustainable use of natural resources.
- The improvement of the quality of the local environment.
- The provision of recycling and waste disposal facilities.
- An improvement in transport planning.
- Conservation management.
- Public health.
- Planning policy development for the environment.
- Internal and external environmental education.
- Public information.
- Promotion of economic development with regard to the environment.

State of Environment Reports

These are an appraisal of the local authority area in terms of its environmental condition. Hams et al (1994) describe it as a review and analysis of scientifically based information on the natural processes and human activities in the county or district and their effect and implications for the environmental resources, health of humans, ecosystems and economy of the area. This description of the condition of the local environment should provide the basis of policy and target formulation for the internal and external activities of the authority.

Internal audits

Internal audits are similar to environmental reviews, in that they are a systematic and objective evaluation of the environmental performance of the local authority. Internal audits are the measurement and appraisal of the local authorities' impacts upon the environment in terms of both direct impacts of the organization from their activities and policies and service impacts resulting from their various functions.

The Friends of the Earth Environmental Charter (1988) provided a great stimulus for local government to begin organizational environmental management. By 1992 three-quarters of British local authorities had either developed cross-departmental plans addressing environmental issues through Green Charters, carried out some form of internal audit or developed state of the environment reports (Raemakers & Wilson 1992, 1993). Environmental fora were also developed by a number of local authorities involving consultation and liaison with representatives from all sectors of the community, and other initiatives such as green business clubs coordinated by local authorities were set up for local business communities.

Internal audits and other environmental initiatives had developed independently within UK local government, with no widely agreed standards or procedures. However, *Environmental Practice in Local Government* published by the Local Government Management Board (LGMB, 1992) attempted to assist local authorities in identifying environmental best practice regarding strategies and management systems, internal audits, education, training, finance, energy, design, planning, transport, landscape, waste, health, purchasing and state of environment reports, through the use of case study material.

Even though a great deal of progress had been made in these areas of environmental management, local authorities are still faced with the same problem as organizations in other sectors in finding a suitable framework to implement environmental policy and coordinate environmental management activities. According to Netherwood (1995) the problem of policy implementation is exacerbated in local government because of the difficulties in implementing environmental management across such large organizations, who have a number of departments with varying functions, especially with the added barriers of devolved financial management and compulsory competitive tendering. Many local authorities, like other organizations, found problems in translating the findings and recommendations of their internal audits into environmental responsibilities and action within their organizational structures. Logically, local government began to look at the developing concept of EMS to solve this problem.

An Initial Statement by UK Local Government on Agenda 21 UK identified the development of EMS within local authorities as one of the five tools of policy making for sustainable development (LGMB 1993b). Similarly the EU Fifth Environmental Action Programme (1992) identified the role of EMS in facilitating policy integration, measurement and monitoring, environmental training, target setting and the use of environmental indicators within local government.

Subsequently, both the LGMB and individual local authorities have turned to the voluntary environmental management standards to provide a more strategic methodology for assessing environmental impacts, coordinating environmental activity and implementing environmental policy .

The EU Eco-management and Audit Scheme for Local Government

A great deal of progress has been made in the adaptation of EMAS to local government within the UK. The LGMB (1993c) published *A Guide to the Eco-Management and Audit Scheme for UK Local Government* after a central and local government funded pilot project was carried out. The guide is intended to provide advice on how to set up an EMS within a local authority, and its main aims are to enable the authority to achieve the following:

- Development of environmental policies, programmes and management systems within participating authorities.
- Periodic evaluation of these policies, programmes and management systems.
- Provision of information on environmental performance to the public.

There are, however, a number of fundamental differences between the original EMAS regulation and EMAS for local government. Firstly, instead of being site-based, EMAS for local government considers the 'operational unit' as the department, division or service functions of local authorities, for example social services or planning, which may exist on different sites across the authority.

Because of this difference, there is a requirement for a Corporate Overview and Coordination System for the whole local authority to ensure that operational units have adequate resource commitments to environmental management and to facilitate a standard organizational approach to EMAS. There is also a need for a corporate commitment to registration with EMAS in the long term, through a corporate environmental policy.

There are also differences in the scope of impacts reviewed by the scheme. The local government EMAS focuses upon *direct* effects (eg energy, waste, transport, resource consumption, pollution etc) which may have been covered already by an internal audit. EMAS also considers *service* effects which have a larger potential effect upon the environment (eg planning activities such as development control, transport policy, land use policy, nature conservation and economic development). This review of service effects within EMAS, especially regarding the strategic planning and development responsibilities of some local authority departments, are directly relevant to recent initiatives in the environmental appraisal of development plans (LGMB 1993a).

EMAS for local government is also intended to be adaptable. Some authorities will seek formal registration, whereas others will use EMAS as a framework or toolbox for environmental management, enabling different environmental issues to be investigated and different stages of the environmental management system to be tackled independently. LGMB's guide (1993c) consists of a systematic progressive tour through the EMAS process, with separate guidance notes on the environmental effects of authority services and simple worksheets to provide the majority of information required for registration.

A pilot programme was carried out to test the draft EMAS in seven local authorities, which presented a cross section in terms of tiers (ie county, district and metropolitan) and location (ie urban and rural). These authorities were at different stages of implementing environmental management and according to Taylor (1994) tested different aspects of the EMS process, at both corporate and unit levels. Four tested the management system component of EMAS for operational units as diverse as housing, economic development and client and committee services. The pilot programme resulted in four of the seven participants expressing interest in completing the EMAS process and seeking validation, two remaining undecided about the use of EMAS and one deciding that the EMAS process was unsuitable for their environmental management needs.

Many local authorities are testing EMAS within their operational units. Lancashire County Council (LCC) have tested EMAS as part of a review of their greening strategy. LCC had already carried out an internal audit and developed a Better Environmental Practices Strategy (BEPS). However, activity was confined to certain departments, and the information collection and procedure for environmental management differed across departments. LCC is therefore hoping to use EMAS as a basis for a more structured approach to environmental management across the authority. By carrying out a pilot project for EMAS in two operational units of the authority (Planning and Social Services), information is being gathered on the resource costs of carrying out the EMAS procedure in different types of departments and the type of information and performance indicators that are needed. This information will be used to assess the applicability of EMAS registration for the whole authority and the use of EMAS methodologies in BEPS (Lancashire County Council 1994, Netherwood 1995).

Taylor (1994) suggests that the benefit of the local government EMAS will enable authorities to set environmental priorities more systematically, turn policy into action, mesh the environment into day to day management, motivate staff and members, and deal more effectively with the environmental impacts of compulsory competitive tendering and contract management. He suggests that the corporate nature of the scheme will get over the problems of isolation and lack of influence that many environmental officers and green teams experience in local government, and that EMAS will achieve a clearer structure and rationale for participation in environmental management throughout the organization.

Taylor (1994) also discusses a number of potential problems with EMAS which were highlighted by the pilot scheme. Firstly there were reservations about the amount of detail needed for the EMAS process and secondly, the participants found problems with the time commitments involved. The third area of concern was the financial commitments necessary to complete the process and the fourth and perhaps most important reservations were those concerned with the coordination of the process and the likelihood of gaining a corporate commitment to EMAS. Taylor argues that the detail needed for EMAS is only equivalent to the detail needed for customer care and quality and that time can actually be saved through efficient documentation. He also suggests that resources can be saved through linking EMAS into existing training courses and by initially applying EMAS into the most environmentally problematic departments. Taylor admits that financing EMAS will be a problem and that cultural changes within the organization will be difficult without corporate support

Hereford City Council and Kingswood Borough Council have both been involved in the application of an EMS to their operations, carrying out initial appraisals of environmental effects and developing environmental policies (*Local Government News*, 1993). Wright (1994) suggests that like the EMS standards for industry, there is a fundamental difference between EMAS for local government and the application of ISO 14001 to local authorities, in that EMAS requires a published environmental statement. There is a legal requirement for local government under the EU Regulation for Environmental Information (EU 90/313/EEC) to provide environmental information on its performance, activities and the local environment, so it could be argued that due to this requirement for external reporting, many local authorities will favour EMAS over ISO 14001.

Wright suggests that because the original EMAS was not drawn up for local government the scheme is flawed because no provision was made for public consultation and participation at the environmental statement stage. He suggests that future amendments to the scheme should involve the community in a similar fashion to Environment City and Local Agenda 21, with perhaps a local commission made up of representatives from community groups to validate the authority's environmental statement.

EMAS was formally adopted by the UK Department of Environment in April 1995. However, its relevance and effectiveness will only be seen when pilot studies are carried out within operational units and the schemes are applied across whole local authorities.

The Future Role of EMS in Local Government

Even though there has been a great deal of activity in environmental management in local authorities, local government reorganization in the UK has meant that many councils are unwilling or unable to allocate resources to EMS initiatives (Netherwood 1995). However, even in these adverse circumstances the EMS approach in local authorities is still being developed.

Criticisms could be made of the potential effectiveness of EMAS for local government and ISO 14001 in ensuring major improvements in environmental performance due to the fact that it is an internal process and that targets, objectives and commitments are set by the authority itself. However, external verification of the environmental statement and the cultural emphasis within local government on public accountability may mean local authorities will be more honest and challenging in terms of their environmental commitments, objectives and performance than organizations in other sectors.

One advantage of the EMAS process to local government is that it can use the findings of State of Environment reports to provide the basis for environment policy, objectives and targets and can also link the findings of other initiatives such as the environmental appraisal of development plans (LGMB 1993a) into the EMS process. In this respect it not only provides a broad framework for the traditional environmental management functions of local authorities to be brought together, but will also enable the integration of these newer initiatives into the broad environmental strategy, ensuring that these initiatives are not isolated and that all environmental activity within the authority is coordinated and working towards the same goals.

Obviously the common factors which inhibit the development of an effective EMS will be exacerbated in local authorities due to their size, varying functions, vertical management structures and fragmented financial management arrangements. However if an adequate environmental management structure is developed to facilitate effective communications and allocation of responsibilities, and environmental training is integrated into the organization to ensure a feeling of ownership among personnel, then many of these barriers will be eliminated. Hill and Smith (1994) suggest that many of the existing management functions and structures already exist to facilitate effective environmental management within local authorities and that a great deal of existing policy can act as a basis for adopting environmental management practices.

However, the key to the development of an appropriate management structure and a successful EMS within a local authority is a corporate commitment to the EMS which should ensure the adequate allocation of human and financial resources to the process and adequate status for environmental management within the organization. Hill and Smith (1994) suggest that this commitment needs to be political as well as managerial, and that in order for an EMS to be successful, the local authority will need to adopt sustainable and integrated environmental management as one of its core values and as an essential priority for the whole organization. Obviously this will result in some major policy conflicts related to the authority's service effects, for example between transport planning, economic development and environmental conservation.

BEYOND THE WALLS OF THE LOCAL AUTHORITY – LOCAL ECONOMIC POLICY AND THE ENVIRONMENT

While much attention has been spent on managing the environmental impact of the internal functioning of the local authority or providing an audit of sections of a local authority, little progress has been made in ensuring that the functions of a local authority help deliver sustainability. Environmental issues currently have a very high priority in many local authorities. This new strategic focus was brought to a head by the requirement to prepare a local Agenda 21 by 1996 (LGMB 1993b). Sustainability – the goal of virtually all these policies – is, however, a much wider economic problem. It encompasses the activities of households in the locality and also businesses and other centres of employment. A number of authorities have endeavoured to demonstrate the benefits of environmental management to the local community.

The last decade, however, has seen a rapid erosion in the powers of local authorities to intervene in the local economy to achieve wider economic, social or environmental goals. In the early 1980s many local authorities pursued a direct method of intervention such as equity participation in local businesses to influence investment and management policy. However, during the latter half of the 1980s a series of statutes removed these powers, culminating in Part V of the 1989 Local Government & Housing Act which stopped direct local authority involvement in investment companies such as Enterprise Boards. In recent years these legal restrictions on local authorities have been paralleled by the growth of new local economic development agencies such as Urban Development Corporations and more recently, and more pertinently in relation to business support, the Training and Enterprise Councils.

Increasingly the Training and Enterprise Councils have become the leading body in business support in a locality. Their position is strengthened by their role as the main conduit for central government funding for local economic development. Many local authority economic development units now operate in close partnership with Training and Enterprise Councils to deliver economic development programmes. Often local authorities find themselves delivering business support contracts for Training and Enterprise Councils, bodies with very different aims to those of the local authority. These partnerships will, in future, be framed in the context of the Department of Trade and Industry's 'Business Link' - the one-stop shop for business information and advice.

In order to achieve its wider aims in relation to the business community, including the goal of sustainability via environmental management, local authorities have to work through a range of instruments and organizations. The following section concentrates an increasingly common theme of recent industrial policy - competitiveness - and examines its relationship with environmental management and sustainability at the local level. This relationship provides the framework for the development of common goals and benefits.

Competitiveness

In common with sustainability there are a number of definitions of competitiveness. In relation to firms it means, in the words of the DTI, its ability to 'produce the right goods, and services of the right quality, at the right price, at the right time' (HM Government 1994b). However, the concept has also been applied to areas, usually nations, and the most commonly accepted definition is that of the Organization for Economic Co-operation and Development, which defines national competitiveness as:

> *...the degree to which it can, under free and fair market conditions, produce goods and services which meet the test of... markets, while simultaneously maintaining and expanding the real incomes of its people over the long-term.*
> *(HM Government 1994a)*

Much of the interest in this idea can be traced back to the work of Porter (1990). He argues that nations can achieve increased economic growth through improved competitiveness. Many of the principles he outlines can be translated relatively easily to the local level. Substituting 'city' for 'nation' the central role of local agencies in promoting competitiveness is clear in the following passage from Porter:

> *There are striking differences in the patterns of competitiveness in every nation [city]; no nation [city] can or will be competitive in every or even most industries; ultimately, nations [cities] succeed in particular industries because their home environment is the most forward-looking, dynamic and challenging.*

This emphasis on the competitiveness of cities and regions has been recently underlined by both European Union and national government policy statements. The so-called Delors' White Paper (Commission of the European Communities, 1993) embraces improved competitiveness as the key to economic growth and job creation in the European Union. Interestingly it harnesses this policy with the objective of 'promoting a sustainable development of industry'. The European Union policy document was followed by the Government's own document 'Competitiveness – helping business to win' (HM Government 1994b). Environmental issues are raised in this document but sustainability is not given a prominent place.

These documents are important influences on local economic policy. An increasing share of economic funding, especially in the cities and peripheral areas, is obtained through European funds. The Community Support Framework for Yorkshire and Humberside, for example, (which is the Government's strategy for employing European funds in the region) gives prominence to both competitiveness and sustainability in its business support priority, stating that 'it is also important to ensure that economic development activity is sustainable in environmental as well as economic terms' (HM Government, 1994a).

The Government White Paper will establish guidelines for much local economic intervention especially through the Training and Enterprise Councils and Business Links which will be the government's preferred mechanism for delivering business support.

Although it has to acknowledge government and EU policy statements, a local authority can still achieve wider local policy aims, for example environmental management within SMEs, through intervention in the business community despite the multiplicity of aims and organizations it has to work through, or in partnership with.

ENCOURAGING ENVIRONMENTAL ACTION IN SMALL- AND MEDIUM-SIZED FIRMS – THE ROLE OF THE LOCAL AUTHORITY

Small- and medium-sized enterprises (SMEs) are essential to the local economy of many of the regions in the UK. In Bradford district, for example, 94 per cent of firms employ less than 50 people. There are over 10,000 small firms in the district and they account for about 75 per cent of local jobs. The SME sector contains the potential stars of the economy of tomorrow with the potential of rapid job growth.

In the same way that the cumulative impact of SMEs in terms of employment is large, so too is their cumulative impact in terms of environmental degradation. This is particularly important as many SMEs perceive their business to have little, if any, environmental impact at all. Larger firms are more aware of the level of their environmental impact and are more able to take action to reduce it, given the level of resources to which they have access. SMEs, on the other hand, face a number of other problems which exacerbate the pressures for environmental action. For example they generally have limited access to finances, environmental information and expertise, and they face the same time pressures. In addition SMEs face a number of other business demands and often have to comply with short pay-back periods, particularly in times of recession. Hence encouraging environmental management within this sector is particularly important in order to manage environmental improvement in a cost effective way.

A number of initiatives have been developed in the Bradford area that cater specifically for SMEs who wish to begin a programme of environmental management. The first initiative to be developed was the Bradford Business and Environment Forum established in 1992 by the University of Bradford Management Centre and the Economic Initiatives Division (EID) of Bradford Metropolitan Council. It was one of the first cooperative business and environment clubs to be established in the region. The forum focuses on the potential opportunities of environmental action, as well as the more negative aspects of compliance and liability. Over 500 local firms have used the forum to date.

Closely linked to these clubs are the University of Bradford's technology exchange clubs (particularly the Environmental Technology Transfer Club) and the Excellence Club which is organized by the Economic Initiatives Division of Bradford Council which promotes business excellence (through raising awareness of new production and management techniques such as Just-in-Time, Total Quality Management and so on) in the Bradford area.

Although the Bradford Business and Environment Forum has been successful in terms of attracting a large number of businesses to its events it became apparent that SMEs were not being involved to the degree that was hoped. Research commissioned by the regional office of the Department of Trade & Industry and conducted by the University of Bradford found that SME owner/managers required 'hands-on' assistance in improving their environmental management.

In order to address these issues a funding bid was drawn up under the European Union's RETEX programme, a fund for areas with declining textile industries, in order to establish a project of practical assistance particularly aimed at providing environmental management assistance for local SMEs. The project consisted of two strands: a package of practical assistance; and an environmental information scheme supported by the West Yorkshire Business Information Centre. The EID was successful in gaining funding in late 1993. Additional funding was secured from Bradford City Challenge Ltd and via a bid under the European Objective Two programme for Bradford. The following section describes the operation of this scheme.

The Business and Environment support team meets the demand for environmental help among local SMEs. The team has been established at an opportune time as many SMEs are beginning to feel pressure to initiate environmental improvements from others in the supply chain. Other firms need assistance due to attention from the regulators, while others are interested in improving their bottom line via environmental management. The support team consists of two parts.

The Environmental Information Service

An Environmental Information Officer was recruited in order to deal with the increasing number of queries regarding the environmental problems of local firms. The Environmental Information Officer provides a range of information on environmental legislation and standards, funding opportunities, potential new environmental markets and other environmental issues. The officer is based at the West Yorkshire European Business Information Centre within the EID, therefore the links with the general business information officer and the technology information unit are well developed.

Practical Environmental Management Support

In order to provide an on-site, practical environmental support an Environmental Business Support Officer was employed. The package of support subsequently developed aims to provide hands-on assistance to local firms who wish to improve their environmental performance. Assistance available to local SMEs includes all aspects of environmental management:

- Base-line environmental reviews;
- Assistance with environmental management systems;
- Full environmental audits;
- Energy efficiency audits;
- Interpretation of audits and development of environmental policies;
- Environmental training;
- Contaminated land studies.

Many items on this list are essentially piecemeal and only make up a small part of an environmental management system (ie energy efficiency audits). However, by picking the 'low hanging fruit' first the EID are able to demonstrate the benefits of environmental management and this will often lead on to the development of a full environmental management system. Each of these items, and other related work, carry an environmental management grant of 50 per cent.

The scheme has been successful with a high grant take-up and SME assistance rate. At the same time similar schemes in other areas have been less successful as they have been too prescriptive. For example schemes in Leeds and Wakefield have offered businesses a set 'menu' of assistance at a set price. While this may be attractive to certain firms others may wish to take environmental improvement at a slower pace, possibly due to financial constraints. For example, it appears that those firms able to afford such assistance are those that could afford to make this sort of environmental improvement regardless of financial assistance. It also appears that it is the larger, cleaner firms that are attracted by such schemes rather than those firms that are more polluting or who use a larger amount of natural resources. Therefore, Bradford's Business and Environment Support Team provide whatever a firm wants. This may simply be a short energy efficiency audit or a desk-based contaminated land audit. While this piecemeal, small scale approach may be frustrating for the more altruistic officer it does help convince firms of the financial benefits of action. It could be argued that it is better for a lot of firms to do a little, than only one or two firms to do a lot.

Other local authorities have also initiated schemes that have met with considerable success. A partnership between the University of Hull and the local authority has resulted in a package of environmental support for SMEs. This includes an introductory training course on environmental policies and environmental management, grant aid for environmental management initiatives, a green business club, a directory of local environmental technology, and a practical exemplar programme of visits to local firms displaying good environmental practice.

Coventry City Council offers an environmental assistance package provided by the council's own staff. This differs from other local authorities who provide advice but do not perform environmental management tasks, despite being qualified to do so. This is due to the implications of public indemnity issues surrounding such a service. Instead other authorities rely on external consultants to provide such assistance. By using internal consultants Coventry is able to reduce dependency on external funding as they can make some heavily subsidised charges; however, the potential implications of public indemnity problems have dissuaded other authorities from following suit.

Key Aspects of Local Authority Schemes for Environmental Improvement in Business

The success of any local environment improvement initiative relies on a number of key factors. Firstly, it is important to recognize the role of the local authority as a facilitator, both in terms of linking businesses to experts and financial assistance, and in terms of communication between the regulation and business support arms of the council. Given the development of local economic intervention outlined earlier, this is now a crucial role for the local authority.

Secondly it is vital to make full use of existing business support networks. Most businesses react more favourably if approached by an economic development unit rather than by the regulatory arms of the local authority (such as planning or pollution control). This link is also important because many conventional business problems are often amenable to environmental solutions (eg high revenue costs due to fuel bills) and these can be identified by mainstream business support officers. The role of Business Links as 'sign posters' should not be underestimated.

Thirdly, it is essential to involve industry at an early stage in terms of gaining support for the initiative and also to ascertain whether the service is providing the most relevant assistance. This can be achieved through the steering group of the Business and Environment Forum which might include representatives of the engineering, chemical, textile, finance and legal sectors as well as the Training & Enterprise Council, Chamber of Commerce and the local university.

Finally it is very useful to involve the regulators and let them know what it happening, ie the local pollution control section, the National Rivers Authority, HMIP and the local water and waste management authority.

CONCLUSIONS

The first half of this chapter outlined the benefits of environmental management and EMSs to local authorities. It is suggested that although the adoption of an EMS will not necessarily result in sustainable management within local government, it is likely that it will be one of the major tools that will be used in the future to provide a central focus for the organization to coordinate and evaluate all those activities which aim to minimize internal, policy and service environmental impacts. In this respect they will be essential in local government's efforts in working towards Local Agenda 21, and considering the wider issues involved in sustainable development.

The role of local government, however, also includes the encouragement of environmental management within small- and medium-sized businesses. In many local authorities this results in SMEs adopting small, piecemeal environmental improvements. This may not translate into the adoption of a formal environmental management system. It may, however, lead to an informal environmental management programme that is affordable and which demonstrates the links between environmental management and cost savings.

A number of local authorities are taking environmental management seriously, both internally and externally. However, there are still some authorities which appear to be paying lip service to the issue, even with the need to develop and implement Local Agenda 21. There are also many authorities which are hampered by a lack of information regarding environmental issues and a lack of both practical and financial support, particularly from central government (Larner and Shayler, 1995). Therefore, despite the actions of a number of committed local authorities, this lack of support will inevitably mean that many authorities will fail to embrace their own responsibilities to local communities regarding environmental improvement, economic development and Local Agenda 21.

REFERENCES

Association of County Councils (1990) County Councils and the Environment, ACC, London

Commission of the European Communities (1993) Growth, Competitiveness, Employment: the challenges and ways forward into the 21st century, [COM (93) 700]

European Union (1992) 'Towards Sustainability: The Fifth Environmental Action Programme' CEC, Brussels

Friends Of The Earth (1988) *The Environmental Charter for Local Government* Friends of the Earth, London

Gibbs, D C (1993) *The Green Local Economy: Building a new local economic environment* Centre for Local Economic Strategies

Hams, T, Jacobs, M, et al (1994) *Greening your Local Authority* Longman, Harlow

Hill, D & Smith, T in Agyeman, J & Evans, B (eds) (1994) *Local Environmental Policies and Strategies* Longman, Harlow

HM Government (1994a) Yorkshire and Humberside Objective 2 Programme 1994–1996: Single Programming Document, Government Office for Yorkshire and Humberside (unpublished)

HM Government (1994b) Competitiveness: Helping businesses to win, Cm 2563, HMSO, London

Lancashire County Council (1994) Better Environmental Practices Strategy, Draft Annual Report, Internal Document, unpublished

Larner, D and Shayler, M (1995) 'Competition and the Environment: Responses of European Cities' Paper given at the first International Sustainable Development Research Conference, Manchester, 27–28 March 1995

Local Government Management Board (1992) *Environmental Practice in Local Government* Second Edition, LGMB, Luton

Local Government Management Board (1993a) *Environmental Appraisal of Development Plans: A good practice guide* HMSO, London

Local Government Management Board (1993b) The UK's report to the UN Commission on Sustainable Development: An Initial Submission by UK Local Government, May 1993, LGMB, Luton

Local Government Management Board (1993c) *A Guide to the Eco-Management and Audit Scheme for Local Government* HMSO, London

Local Government News (1993) Councils and BS7750, April 1993, 3

Netherwood, A M (1995) 'Environmental Management Systems: Methodologies and Organizational Impacts', PhD Thesis, University of Central Lancashire, Preston, unpublished

Peattie, K & Hall, G (1994) 'The Greening of Local Government: A Survey' Local Government Studies 20 (3) Frank Cass, London

Porter, M (1990) *The Competitive Advantage of Nations* Macmillan, London

Raemakers, J & Wilson, E (1992) Index to Local Authority Green Plans, Edinburgh College of Art, School of Planning and Housing, Research Paper 44

Raemakers, J & Wilson, E (1993) 'Local authority green plan machine rolls on' *Planning*, 1004

Taylor, D (1994) Piloting the EC Eco-Management and Audit Regulation in Local Authorities, Third Annual Membership Conference of the Institute of Environmental Assessment, York, UK, 20–21 September 1994

Welford R J (1994) *Cases in Environmental Management and Business Strategy* Pitman Publishing, London

Wright, G (1994) 'Improving the Environmental Performance of Local Government' *Eco-management and Auditing*, 1, 2

Chapter 14

Beyond Environmentalism and Towards the Sustainable Organization

Richard Welford and David Jones

SUSTAINABLE DEVELOPMENT

Earlier chapters in this book have identified that the continuing ability of the environment to supply raw materials and assimilate waste while maintaining biodiversity and a quality of life is being increasingly undermined. If growth and development are to take new responsible paths we therefore have to find a way of doing it that will not further degrade the environment in which we live. In its simplest form, sustainable development is defined as development that meets the needs of the present generation without compromising the ability of future generations to meet their own needs (World Commission on Environment and Development, 1987). Such a simple statement has profound implications. It implies that, as a minimum, all human activity must refrain from causing any degree of permanent damage through its consumption of environmental resources now and into the future.

As an ultimate objective, the concept of sustainable development is immensely valuable. However, strategies are needed to translate conceptual theories of what sustainable development means into practical ways of achieving it over time within the corporate context. According to Welford (1995) this requires a more radical assessment of corporate environmental strategy than we have seen to date. We must accept that sustainability is not something that will be achieved overnight, but in the longer term, individual businesses need to look towards new types of activity, development and growth. This, in turn, requires them to look at their own ethics, their objectives and their own forms of organization, corporate culture and communication.

In Chapter 1 we argued that sustainable development stresses the trade-off between continuous economic growth and the sustainability of the environment. Over time, through greater and greater exploitation, growth causes pollution and atmospheric damage, disrupts traditional ways of living (particularly in the developing world), destroys ecosystems and feeds more and more power into international oligopolistic industrial structures which cannot respond to local needs. The concept of sustainable development stresses the interdependence between economic growth and environmental quality, but it also goes further in demonstrating that the future is uncertain unless we can deal with issues of equity and inequality throughout the whole world. It is possible to make development and environmental protection compatible and to begin to deal with the problems caused by inequity between North and South by following sustainable strategies and by re-orienting those areas of economic activity that are most damaging to the environment and its inhabitants. The Brundtland Report, commissioned by the United Nations to examine long-term environmental strategies, argued that this would require quite radical changes in economic practices throughout the world, however.

A key issue to be tackled is the massive inequality in wealth and standards of living displayed across the world, making sustainable development harder to achieve. Those living in the developing world often aspire to the standards of living of the developed countries and we know from an environmental stance that such aspirations are presently not achievable. Therefore we can see that environmental improvement is inextricably linked to wider issues of global concern. Put simply, we can clearly understand why some people undervalue environmental protection when their immediate problem is finding enough food to eat.

However, equity has also to be tackled at the level of the firm. Flatter forms of industrial organization can empower workers and increase their decision-making powers, increasing democracy in the workplace and a sense of responsibility towards a company's environmental performance. This requires a more socially responsible approach to doing business which values workers as an integral and valuable part of the organization rather than a resource to be hired and fired as external market conditions alter.

THE CORPORATE RESPONSE TO SUSTAINABLE DEVELOPMENT

We have argued that every institution and every individual has a role to play in moving the world towards a sustainable future. In the short term, firms can begin to develop substitutes for non-renewable resources and innovations which reduce waste and use energy more efficiently. They also have a role in processing those materials in a way which brings about environmental improvements. For many products (eg cars and washing machines), the major area of environmental damage occurs in their usage. Firms often have the opportunity of reducing this damage at the design stage and when new products are being developed there is a whole new opportunity for considering both the use and disposal of the product. Industry is also beginning to develop the new technologies and techniques which may help to move the global economy towards sustainability and whilst accepting that the answer will not lie in technology alone, we must continue to do so.

Environmental strategy begins with real commitment on the part of the whole organization. This may mean a change in corporate culture and management has an important role to play. In leading that commitment and laying out the organization's corporate objectives with respect to the environment, management has to be the catalyst for change. Moreover, change has to be on-going and management must be ever mindful of the full range of (often competing) objectives to which it is subject. Management has to find compromise between these objectives if they conflict and design corporate strategies which are operational, consistent and achievable. Change will have to be addressed in a systemic way, dealing with the company as a whole rather than in a compartmentalized way.

Moreover, the company needs also to consider its social impact and this involves a range of ethical considerations. Managers are aware of these issues and research (Welford, 1994) has indicated that when considering social and environmental impacts on their families they are keen to see a whole range of higher standards being adopted by industry and governments. However, this concern does not always spill over into the workplace because of competing objectives and other priorities. However, more ethical firms will, in the future, begin to internalize more of the social impacts which it has identified and managers will play a key role in defining these impacts and putting systems in place to improve performance of a more widely-defined kind.

In many ways, no country can see itself as independent and companies must see their operations in a global as well as a local context. The global spread of industrial activity along with the expansion of information systems means that no country or company can insulate itself from its external economic climate. Perhaps most intrusive, however, are the activities of the transnational corporations (TNCs) who bring with them their own corporate cultures, dominate international trade and production and are therefore to be held responsible for significant levels of transnational environmental damage. In the decade between 1980 and 1990 the Worldwatch Institute has estimated that gross world output of goods and services grew from US$4.5 trillion to US$20 trillion, and international trade grew by approximately 4 per cent per year (Brown, 1991).

The rapid evolution of an international economic system has not been matched by international political integration or international laws to regulate that system. The consequence is that many transnational corporations operate above the law, above national boundaries and are able to set their own international economic agenda. Moreover, by creating a situation where many developing countries are dependent on their patronage, employment and technology, they often wield considerable political power as well. This is hardly a scenario which can be reconciled with sustainable development. This is an ethical issue which companies need to begin to consider and act upon.

The enormous expansion of world trade has been a characteristic of the spread of capitalism and fundamental to the internationalization of the industrial system. The central institution which lays out the terms of engagement in the international trade system and which monitors trade centres around the General Agreement of Tariffs and Trade (GATT). The Uruguay round of GATT negotiations on removing trade barriers began in 1986 and was completed in 1993. Environmental considerations were largely ignored during this process, reflecting the sad fact that issues of international trade and environmental management are seen as discrete. Indeed, while at the Rio Summit governments and other agencies made declarations in support of the principles of sustainable development, when involved in the GATT negotiations, they were making decisions which could undermine progress towards sustainability.

GATT has consistently acted in favour of free trade and against environmental protection. It has consistently linked environmental issues to the issue of protectionism and has ignored issues of sustainability. In 1991 the GATT overruled an American ban on imports of tuna fish from Mexico (claimed to be fished in such a way as to kill an unacceptable number of dolphins) on the grounds that such a restriction would violate free trade. Indeed, the GATT view is that restrictions on trade, claimed on environmental grounds, would be more likely to be mere excuses for protectionism, rather than real attempts to reduce environmental damage. One is tempted to ask whatever happened to the precautionary principle?

With these enormous issues in mind, one might ask what a single organization can do about them. It is true that some issues are best tackled at the level of governments and international organizations, but equally we have argued that every institution and every individual has a role to play in a pluralist society to bring about a more sustainable future. The rest of this chapter therefore examines the role which businesses can play in auditing for and measuring their contribution to sustainable development. In line with the key thrust of this book, it is argued that the company must take a systems-based approach to tackling this issue and as part of that there will be a need to extend our auditing methodology.

AUDITING FOR SUSTAINABILITY

We have seen earlier in this book that the notion of auditing is not a new one but its use in strategies associated with environmental protection does not have a long history. The traditional approach to auditing adopted by many firms has tended to stress clearly quantifiable environmental impacts and rarely goes on to incorporate ecological impacts and wider social issues. We need to widen the scope of auditing if our ultimate aim is to move towards sustainability. Table 14.1 outlines five levels of auditing, classified by the central focus of the approach. The most basic approach to auditing is compliance auditing (level 1) where performance is measured as conformance to legislation, regulation and codes of conduct. Up until the early 1990s the majority of environmental audits were usually little more than compliance audits. Standards such as ISO 14001 and EMAS extend the auditing process to systems audits (level 2) where the focus is on implementing and operating an effective environmental management system which provides for continuous improvement and adherence to self-determined environmental performance targets based on clearly defined corporate environmental policies.

Level 3 describes the traditional approaches to environmental auditing described in Chapter 7 which takes a snapshot of the environmental performance of a company at one point in time, usually on one particular site. The main focus is on the direct impact of an organization, site or process on water, land and the air and therefore concentrates on direct pollution effects, contingency planning and health and safety. ISO 14001 and EMAS demand a

Table 14.1 Environmental auditing techniques

	Level 1	*Level 2*	*Level 3*	*Level 4*	*Level 5*
Type of audit	Compliance auditing	Systems auditing	Environmental auditing	Ecological auditing	Auditing for sustainability
Central foci	Legislation	Level 1 plus:	Levels 1 and 2 plus:	Levels 1 to 3 plus:	Levels 1 to 4 plus:
	• Regulations • Voluntary standards • Consents and discharge permits	• Environmental management systems • Self-determined targets and objectives	• Direct environmental impact on water, air; and land • Health and safety • Protection of employees and the community • Contingency planning	• Inter-temporal impact on ecosystems • Life cycle assessment of products • Measurement of indirect ecological impacts • Recognition of need to live in harmony with nature	• Equity and equality • Futurity • Human rights and protection of indigenous populations • Consideration of wider social and ethical issues • Holistic approach
Assessment	Static	Static	Static	Dynamic	Dynamic

clear and complete approach to auditing at levels 1 and 2 and some requirements to consider environmental issues at level 3. In addition, we should
recognize that for these three levels the mode of assessment is essentially
static, focusing on direct, easily measurable impacts and conformity to the law
and management system in place, all at one particular point in time. Each
audit is discrete and repeated periodically in an attempt to provide information
to manage improvement. But such a process does not mimic the more dynamic
nature of ecological processes which are constantly changing.

Going beyond traditional environmental auditing techniques requires a
change in emphasis in a number of ways. At level 4 we ought to introduce the
concept of ecological auditing which has three key features. Firstly, the mode
of assessment must be dynamic, recognizing that ecosystems which change
over time are of central importance and that the environment is a highly
intricate and interlinked process rather than a fixed resource. A dynamic
approach looks at impact well into the future, stressing the cumulative effect
of ecological damage and the long-term effect some impacts have on
ecosystems. It should not be a bounded assessment undertaken at one point
in time.

Secondly, there needs to be an increased emphasis put on life cycle impacts. Life cycle assessment as a tool of analysis forces us to track products from cradle to grave and to put greater emphasis on all the impacts associated with raw materials extraction, processing at every stage, distribution, use of the product and disposal. It makes us focus on the indirect as well as direct impact of any activity.

Thirdly, a wider set of ecological issues need to be addressed. We need to move away from the mentality of health and safety audits where it is human well-being which is paramount, towards valuing all living animals, protecting biodiversity and putting the emphasis on living in harmony with nature. This requires us to move away from short-term planning horizons towards more long-term inter-generational holistic planning. In effect environmental auditing is anthropocentric whereas ecological auditing is founded on a recognition of a need to live in harmony with nature.

According to the Elmwood Institute (Callenbach et al, 1993) an ecological audit is:

> *...an examination and review of a company's operations from the perspective of deep ecology, or the new paradigm. It is motivated by a shift in values within the corporate culture from domination to partnership, from the ideology of economic growth to that of ecological sustainability. It involves a corresponding shift from mechanistic to systemic thinking and accordingly, a new style of management known as systemic management. The result of the ecological audit is an action plan for minimizing the company's environmental impact and making all its operations more ecologically sound.*

The central focus of level 5 auditing is to go back to the key concept of sustainable development and audit for sustainability. This is a holistic approach predicated on a clear world view and an understanding of the need for further 'paradigm shift' in business culture (Commoner 1990, Welford 1995, Wheeler 1993). Organizations auditing for sustainability should be committed to integrating environmental performance to wider issues of global ecology and should make specific reference to the concepts associated with sustainable development. Thus, as a starting point, energy-efficiency should be focused on the need to minimize NO_x, SO_x and CO_2 emissions and avoid nuclear waste. Waste minimization, re-use and recycling should be driven by the need to conserve non-renewable resources. Product design should prioritize the use of renewable resources. Sourcing of raw materials should have no negative impacts on global biodiversity, endangered habitats or human and animal rights. Overall corporate policies should examine the businesses impact on both the developed and underdeveloped world, both now and into the future.

ELEMENTS OF SUSTAINABILITY

We have recognized that there is a need to define measures of sustainability in order to facilitate an auditing methodology at level 5. The first step in this process is to identify some general principles where a sustainable business will want to facilitate improvement. In Chapter 1 we identified three central elements to the sustainable development paradigm: environmental protection, equity and futurity. It has also been argued (in Chapter 8) that the most appropriate measure of environmental protection is through an assessment of life cycle impacts. We also identified in Table 14.1 that an auditing methodology which is more consistent with sustainability must recognize the need to live in harmony with nature and therefore to assess an organization's approach towards biodiversity and animal protection. At level 5 much emphasis was also put on human rights and the protection of indigenous populations. Lastly, we know that a common call associated with sustainable development is 'local action'. This involves local participatory strategies and a re-examination of the whole issue of scale and location.

In summary, therefore we can define seven broad elements of sustainability within which we need to identify more detailed measures:

1. general principles;
2. equity;
3. futurity;
4. biodiversity and animal protection;
5. human rights;
6. local action and scale; and
7. life cycle impacts.

This necessarily implies a very broad definition of sustainable development looking at both environmental and wider social issues. Nevertheless it is argued that only by beginning to deal with these dimensions can we really move towards a sustainable future. It is not being argued that every firm has to be perfect in every element identified. Indeed, for some organizations there may be conflict even within an attempt to deal with these issues. It is argued, however, that companies must be aware of these issues and should respond to them in a positive way over time. We can then move along a path which leads to performance consistent with sustainable development at the level of the firm.

MEASURING SUSTAINABILITY IN BUSINESS

The implementation of sustainable development objectives discussed above and the preparation of meaningful reports on performance requires the support of appropriate measures of performance and information systems (International Institute for Sustainable Development, 1992). Figure 14.1 illustrates the process for managing a business according to sustainable development principles. Stakeholders' concerns and wishes have to be analyzed which feeds into the development of sustainable development

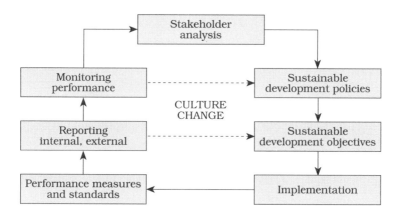

Source: International Institute for Sustainable Development, 1992

Figure 14.1 Recommended management system for sustainable development

policies and in turn into sustainable development objectives. The implementation of these objectives requires measurement of performance and the adoption of appropriate standards. Internal and external reporting on these measures and the on-going monitoring of performance leads back into communication and further analysis of stakeholders. And so the cycle goes on leading to further development of sustainable development policies and objectives which will take the company further and further along the road towards sustainability. But at the centre of the process has to be a culture change programme which develops the values and associated activities of the organization in line with its sustainable development agenda.

A clear distinction, however, needs to be made between measures at the basic eco-efficiency level (which are necessary but not sufficient to attain sustainability) and measures at the wider social and ethical level associated with sustainable development. Clearly, both the wider consequences or impacts of a firm's activities, and the narrower environmental performance of the firm need to be considered (Meima & Ashford, 1994). While traditional environmental auditing procedures deal with static (short-term) and internal performance measures, sustainability criteria demand that we consider longer-term internal and external impacts which move beyond narrow environmental criteria towards wider social and ethical criteria. The challenge which lies ahead is depicted in Figure 14.2. This represents a three dimensional representation of the current situation and suggests that we must widen our measures to include external impacts, futurity and wider social issues. Moving out along all three of these paths is the direction of sustainability. In effect, we can imagine a three dimensional vector which maps out a path towards sustainability. We might not be able to clearly envisage exactly what a sustainable company may look like but this does begin to map out the road down which we should tread.

Given that we have identified the need for an expanded audit methodology and the need to move towards sustainability, by widening the scope of what we measure we are left with the more difficult task of identifying exactly what

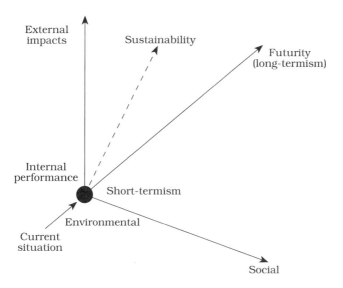

Figure 14.2 3-D representation of measures for sustainability compared to current measures

to measure. We have identified seven elements associated with sustainability in business and they can be translated into key target areas. Our vector towards sustainability is therefore really seven dimensional. In terms of our general principles, Welford (1995) argues that the firm must demonstrate accountability, transparency, and education and learning. For each of these target areas we must now define specific measures. Let us therefore deal with each of the elements of sustainability in turn. A summary table of the discussion in this section can be found in the Appendix.

General Principles

Accountability

The company should demonstrate that it can be held accountable to all its stakeholders. We would expect to see the appointment of non-executive directors and systems put into place which are compatible with the best practice of corporate governance. The internal management structure would be well documented with clear job descriptions, reporting lines and organizational charts. This would be freely available to anyone requesting it. Links would be built up with the local community in order to facilitate consultation and dialogue.

Transparency/Openness

If a company is transparent, open and honest it is less likely to be able to hide environmentally damaging practices and less likely to be accused of doing so by others. Transparency is likely to begin with a wide range of participation arrangements both within the company and beyond. There will be free access to information which is not of a commercially sensitive nature. This will ensure that the company is capable of proving its environmental claims. Part of this information is likely to include documentation on the effects that the organization has on habitats along with their associated impact mechanisms.

As part of a strategy of openness it is likely that there will exist an explicit ethical framework written in terms of corporate values. We need to consider very carefully how we begin to measure values, but by looking at different firms' sustainable development policies, their values or corporate ethics can be compared in terms of the range of issues that they cover.

Lastly, corporate reporting is central to any company working with these ideas. Internal reporting systems that measure performance with regard to sustainability can have a significant effect on corporate culture (International Institute for Sustainable Development, 1992). Regular, third party verified reports covering financial, environmental and social measures will identify the company's achievements and any failure to meet targets set. Measures need to be reported and audited in a common, accountable, transparent and accessible style. The concept of transparency is therefore used to reduce the distance between the organization and external participants, so that society can 'see into' the organization, assess what it is doing with the resources that determine future options and react accordingly (Gray, 1994).

Education and learning

Information availability will not only be important to the achievement of transparency but it is also likely to be at the centre of a company's attempts to improve education and learning both within and external to the organization. Open communications with all stakeholders should try to impart education about the organization and wider issues which will improve everyone's understanding of the sustainable development process. Within the organization we would expect to see clear training records and strategies aimed at two-way learning so that the organization not only imparts education but is a learning organization as well.

Once again, the existence of consultation frameworks and dialogue must be at the heart of sustainability measures. This will include all stakeholders. Moreover, through such a process, the organization can actually become a facilitator of change.

Equity

Empowerment of all stakeholders

Empowerment strategies must be seen as being at the centre of any measures of sustainability. It is by empowerment that we can begin to challenge and change traditional balances of power. Open institutional structures are required in the firm so that any stakeholder has the ability to challenge and question the organization over any issue. Once again, we are looking for two-way processes here with interaction and dialogue shifting the organization on to a more sustainable path.

Participation

The logical next step must be to implement participation measures. Most importantly, we would identify the need for participation within the sustainable enterprise and this would be measured in a number of ways. There is likely to be participation in decision-making as well as financial (profit-sharing) participation and other appropriate non-financial rewards. Essentially we are searching for evidence of an equitable distribution of benefits. Management and workers would be seen to cooperate with each other in order to achieve common goals. The sustainable organization is also likely to have a very wide ownership structure with wider share ownership packages available for employees.

Trading practices

One of the most common criticisms of internationally oriented firms is that they are exploitative of developing world trading partners. The adoption of end price auditing techniques whereby a company declares how the final price of a product is derived (and specifically how much goes to indigenous works in the South) would certainly be in the sprit of achieving increased equity. Moreover we would want to see the company justify that its activities result in an equitable distribution of value added. These issues are clearly linked to the notion of fair trade. Within the issue of international equity the sustainable business needs to put the emphasis on fair trade above free trade. Specifically this will include measures to ensure the maintenance of the welfare of indigenous populations and their lands.

Trading practices in the sustainable organization are also likely to look towards an increase in local sourcing of materials. This will be linked both to a strategy for reducing environmental damage resulting from distribution, but also linked to an attempt to build close links and networks with local communities.

Futurity

Precaution

A sustainable business needs explicit policies and practices which take it beyond the law or beyond simple compliance. This certainly requires the firm to demonstrate due diligence in all its operations and procedures and, again, this must be linked to stakeholder accountability. In effect we require the firm to be anticipative and to have systematic scenario planning and risk assessment procedures. Moreover, this requires the firm to have a long-term planning horizon and to challenge the short-termism so often criticized in business.

Use of non-renewables

Clearly, the sustainable organization will be involved in the phasing out of non-renewable resources and this will mean a new emphasis placed on research into alternatives. Substitution strategies will be linked to closing the cycle of resource use and an emphasis placed on systems which reduce the use of, repair, re-use and recycle resources.

Biodiversity and Animal Protection

Habitat and species conservation

The protection of ecosystems and biodiversity is central to sustainable development. Businesses can be involved in habitat regeneration strategies both locally and often internationally. Partnership and local linkage will be important in achieving this goal. As a start, organizations should report on species and habitats at a local level and through the assessment and identification of their own impacts and improve their own performance in this area. For new sites, processes and products we should expect to see the publication of full environmental impact assessments.

Animal testing

The abandonment of animal testing is part of a wider social ethic for any business. It also reflects an organization's due respect for other living things. As such, businesses should demonstrate that they are in conformance with recognized 'no animal testing' standards and best practice elsewhere.

Human Rights

Employment policies and equal opportunities

A sustainable business might be considered as a business run in a better way. The sustainable business has a particular way of treating its employees. Like much good business practice the starting point here is to have a clear policy on equal opportunities which both creates the feeling that equality of opportunity is important and maps out the procedures by which this will be achieved. Compliance with codes of practice and compliance with legal requirements will be important measures. Employee representation in decisions about employment and appropriate training and education will be central to more participative modes of operation.

Quality of working life

People spend a lot of time at work and part of the wider social ethic of any organization ought to be to try to increase the quality of the time spent at work. This will not only involve the company complying with health and safety legislation but also having wider human resource policies which provide a forum for voicing dissatisfaction without fear of reprisal. Ultimately the sustainable organization will be able to demonstrate that it is moving towards systems which provide for increased levels of industrial democracy.

Women

Women have been relatively undervalued in the workplace and their absence from positions of authority must be seen as a weakness in many organizations. In line with Agenda 21 we need to see much more dialogue with women and policies which empower them and allow them to play a fuller role in any business. Non-discrimination policies will be important in legitimizing the role of women.

Minority groups

Again, minority groups are also under-represented within the decision-making structures of most businesses. As with the case of women, we would want to see increased levels of dialogue, empowerment and non-discrimination procedures.

Indigenous populations

The protection of indigenous populations and their land rights holds a very special place within the ethos of sustainable development. Historically, indigenous populations have been exploited in a number of ways and the sustainable organization will have to demonstrate that it has turned away from any practices which continue this exploitation. In particular, we would expect to see fair wage policies for indigenous workers in place in businesses, an emphasis of purchasing directly from indigenous populations (and not through agencies and third parties who simply extract value added for their own ends) and limited use of child labour (which would have to be justified and supported with educational programmes).

Local Action and Scale

Community linkage

Close relationships with the community within which a business operates have been identified as important. As well as having the traditional dialogue groups and consultative fora, the company should have clear systems to provide an appropriate response to complaints and requests for information (which would not normally be refused).

Appropriate scale

The size of business activity is important. Rather than putting an emphasis on optimum size in terms of how big an organization can grow we might also think about optimum smallness as well (Welford, 1995). It might be argued that much environmental damage has been caused by large-scale production and mass consumption. A justification of the scale of any activity would be a baseline measure of sustainability in a business. Stakeholder involvement will be central to decisions regarding scale and particularly to the decision over whether to internalize or subcontract some operations. Moreover, close links with stakeholders and particularly with the local community raises the question as to whether a certain level of profits might be distributed locally via the support of appropriate local initiatives and projects.

Partnership and cooperation strategies

We keep returning to the need for the sustainable organization to have clear linkage and dialogue with all stakeholders. This will involve support for wider initiatives which can help us move towards sustainability. Moreover, such linkage and participative and cooperative strategies can help to cut down on the duplication of some activities, therefore resulting in a saving of resources.

Appropriate location

The choice over the location of a particular plant or facility can have enormous impacts on the environment. Clearly, inappropriate activities should not take place on or near to sites of environmental importance and, again, there needs to be clear neighbourhood policies and linkages to ensure minimum impact on the local environment. Location will also impact upon distribution networks and sites should be chosen which will minimize the environmental impacts of distribution.

Life Cycle Impacts

Product stewardship

The life cycle of a product begins with the extraction or farming of raw materials and ends with the disposal or reuse of those same raw materials through waste. At every stage of the life cycle of a product businesses should take responsibility for reducing any negative impacts. There is therefore a clear role for product stewardship policies within the business which commit the organization to the management of the whole life cycle. The ultimate aim ought to be to reduce waste and environmental damage at all stages and, where possible, to close the loops which allow that waste to occur.

Life cycle analysis

The starting point therefore has to be a full life cycle assessment of all products which not only identifies environmental damage but also other impacts consistent with the elements of sustainability identified above. Such analysis will be most credible when it is linked to third party verification.

Design

Although an important element within the life cycle assessment, the role of design will be crucial to the sustainable organization. Emphasis should be placed on redesigning products to make them more sustainable and to increase the potential for repair, reuse and recycling though design for disassembly strategies.

Product durability

In most instances, we should be seeking to have longer durability of products. In some circumstances where technology has improved substantially it may be better to replace products before their natural death, but built-in obsolescence and other design factors used to increase sales rather than durability are fundamentally unsustainable. We should expect durability reports for products which give the consumer an expectation about the life of the product and which can be compared with other competing products.

Product justifiability

A detailed debate over needs and wants in any society has no conclusion and it would clearly be wrong to dictate to people what constitutes their needs as opposed to more frivolous wants. Nevertheless through consultation with all stakeholders we should expect a company to be able to justify the design and other characteristics of a product. Moreover, through detailed life cycle assessment and a consideration of the impact of a product on all the elements of sustainability, it should be possible for businesses to publish sustainability audits for each of its products.

MEASUREMENT TECHNIQUES AND REPORTING

Having identified what to measure we must now address the difficult task of how to measure them. Direct environmental impacts such as the emission of chemicals into a local river are relatively easy to measure, although we must also be committed to defining their impact mechanisms and secondary effects. But some of the measures identified above are not capable of being measured in such a direct or quantitative way. We must therefore begin to think about different kinds of measurement techniques, which nevertheless allow us to record progress towards sustainability and which can be built into a corporate reporting strategy. All we really ask of a business therefore is to track improvements over time.

There are three important principles to bear in mind in the measurement process:

1. The judgement as to how far a company is attaining any particular measure of sustainability must be made by a wide range of stakeholders.
2. Absolute measures are less likely to be practical that qualitative measures based on judgement and, where necessary, supported by evidence.
3. It is the direction of change and the speed of change towards sustainability which we are ultimately interested in. We therefore need to track progress along our sustainability vector.

We must recognize that different impacts will be measured in different ways and may have completely different consequences. It is therefore unlikely that we could ever achieve an aggregated score of sustainability. Nevertheless, the use of a set of scales rather than scores may move us forward. This approach provides a set of ideal measures of sustainability at one extreme and opposite measures at the other. Such a scale might be used by a range of stakeholders of a business in an assessment of how far a business has moved. It could provide the organization with a tool to analyze shifts in external assessment by its stakeholders.

For example, let us take our general principles and look specifically at accountability. Our ideal measures are on the right hand side of Table 14.2 and opposites on the left. A scoring scale would be provided for stakeholders to make a judgement about progress. This would identify areas of best practice as well as areas requiring attention. An aggregate score might be calculated for each target area.

We have therefore begun to identify the direction of sustainability for businesses. We have recognized that measures associated with the direction and speed of change are more important than absolutes. Some aggregation of the scores awarded on our scales is possible for each of the seven elements of sustainability, but an aggregated score is less relevant. We can begin to define a vector of change in line with that depicted in Table 14.2. A high score for futurity measures will take us along our futurity axis but this might have to be set against, for example, a low score for equity. Comparison of scores within and between categories will give us an indication of the priorities which the company must examine in its future planning.

Table 14.2 Suggested measurement scales for target areas

• There are no non-executive directors who can be considered as independent	1 2 3 4 5	Independent non-executive directors have been appointed
• Corporate governance has been ignored	1 2 3 4 5	Systems compatible with principles of corporate governance are in place
• There is no readily available documentation of the internal management structure	1 2 3 4 5	The management structure is documented and available for public scrutiny
• There are no links with the local community	1 2 3 4 5	There are clear links and consultative processes with the local community

Ultimately, if corporations are to contribute fully to humanity's attempts to seek a sustainable existence then a strong case can be made for the development of reporting systems which will support the process (Gray, 1994). In order for localities, countries and ultimately the world to move towards sustainability we must recognize the need for all companies to be involved in strategies associated with sustainability and therefore we must consider a move towards mandatory reporting. The problem with the voluntary approach is that it focuses attention and criticism on the small number of companies who stick their heads above the parapet and ignores the majority who are probably the main offenders.

The question then revolves around what do we make it mandatory to report? The sorts of indicators suggested above and the measurement techniques suggested may form the beginnings of a framework of analysis. Ultimately this would allow comparison to be made between companies, the identification of best practice and information, upon which customers could make more informed judgements about products they wish to purchase. There may therefore be a role for benchmarking in this area, in order to allow companies to compare impacts and performance with other companies in the same sector or region.

CONCLUSIONS

We have identified that there is a need to move towards a behaviour of the company which is consistent with sustainable development. This requires identifying the main elements of sustainable development which are most relevant (we have suggested that there are seven), widening the audit methodology and making it more dynamic, and defining measures of sustainability and measurement techniques to facilitate that audit process.

What this chapter represents is perhaps the first attempt at defining just what businesses can do at a practical level to follow strategies consistent with sustainable development. By extending the traditional auditing methodologies and suggesting measures of sustainability in business we can define more clearly the challenge which lies ahead for business and the direction in which it must proceed.

It must be stressed that we are not expecting businesses to adopt these techniques overnight. They may wish to prioritize each of the seven elements according to the importance they attach to each, given the type of business they are involved in. Nevertheless, even though we can never expect any business to achieve a perfect score according to the measures defined here, those measures can be used as a guide for the future development of a business in line with the concept of sustainable development. Beginning to move along the vector which we have outlined is nevertheless imperative if we are to protect the world in which we live for future generations. Business must play its part in securing a sustainable future.

REFERENCES

Brown, L (1991) 'The new world order' in Brown, L et al (1991) *State of the World* Earthscan, London

Callenbach, E, Capra, F et al (1993) *EcoManagement: The Elmwood Guide to Ecological Auditing and Sustainable Business* Berrett-Koehler Publishers, San Francisco

Commoner, B (1990) 'Can Capitalists be Environmentalists?' *Business and Society Review*, 75, 31–35

Gray, R H (1994) 'Corporate Reporting for Sustainable Development: Accounting for Sustainability in 2000AD' *Environmental Values*, The Whitehorse Press, Cambridge

International Institute for Sustainable Development (1992) 'Business Strategy for Sustainable Development: Leadership & Accountability for the '90s', IISD, Manitoba, Canada

Meima, R & Ashford, N A (1994) 'Designing the Sustainable Enterprise: Summary Report of The Second International Research Conference of The Greening of Industry Network' Cambridge, Massachusetts

Welford, R J (1994) *Cases in Environmental Management and Business Strategy* Pitman Publishing, London

Welford, R J (1995) *Environmental Strategy & Sustainable Development: The Corporate Challenge for the Twenty-First Century* Routledge, London

Wheeler, D (1993) 'Auditing for Sustainability: Philosophy and Practice of The Body Shop International' *Environmental, Health & Safety Auditing Handbook* McGraw-Hill

World Commission on Environment and Development, (1987) *Our Common Future* (The Brundtland Report) OUP, Oxford

Appendix to Chapter 14

Elements of sustainability	Key targets	Measures
1. General principles	Accountability	• Appointment of non-executive directors • Systems compatible with principles of corporate governance • Document internal management structure • Links and consultation with local community
	Transparency/ Openness	• Participation arrangements • Freedom of access to information • Documentation of effects on habitats and impact mechanisms • Existence of an explicit ethical framework • Corporate reporting, third party verified
	Education and Learning	• Information availability • Open communication with all stakeholders • Training records • Two-way learning strategies • Consultation framework/dialogue • Facilitator of change
2. Equity	Empowerment of all stakeholders	• Open institutional structures • Ability to challenge and question the organization • Interaction with all stakeholders
	Participation	• Participatory decision-making • Financial participation • Appropriate rewards • Equitable distribution of benefits • Cooperation measures • Open ownership structure
	Trading practices	• End price auditing • Equitable distribution of value-added • Fair trade policy • Welfare of indigenous workers • Local sourcing
3. Futurity	Precaution	• Compliance-plus measures • Evidence of due diligence

		• Stakeholder accountability/linkage • Anticipation • Scenario planning and risk assessment procedures • Long-term planning horizon
	Use of non-renewables	• Phase out of non-renewables • Research into alternatives • Substitution strategies • Reduce, repair, re-use and recycling
4. Biodiversity and animal protection	Habitat and species conservation	• Habitat regeneration and improvement strategies • Partnership and local linkage • Reporting on species and habitats at a local level • Assessment of identification of impacts • Full environmental impact assessments
	Animal testing	• Conformance with recognized standards and best practice elsewhere
5. Human rights	Employment policies and equal opportunities	• Existence of a clear policy on equal opportunities • Codes of practice • Compliance with legal requirements • Employee representation • Training and education
	Quality of working life	• Compliance with health and safety legislation • Human resource management policies • Forum for voicing dissatisfaction • Industrial democracy
	Women	• Dialogue with women • Empowerment policies • Non-discrimination policies
	Minority groups	• Dialogue mechanism • Empowerment policies • Non-discrimination policies
	Indigenous populations	• Fair wage policies • Emphasis on purchasing directly from indigenous populations • Resist/justify use of child labour
6. Local action and scale	Community linkage	• Dialogue groups • Appropriate response to complaints and requests for information • Local contracting, sourcing and purchasing policies

	Appropriate scale	• Optimum smallness
		• Justification of scale
		• Stakeholder involvement
		• Local profit distribution
	Partnership and cooperation strategies	• Linkage and dialogue
		• Support for wider initiatives
		• Avoidance of duplication
	Appropriate location	• Avoidance of sites of environmental importance
		• Neighbour policies and linkage
		• Consideration of distribution networks
7. Life cycle impacts	Product stewardship	• Stewardship policies
		• Management of the whole life cycle
		• Closing loops
	Life cycle analysis	• Full life-cycle analysis of all products
		• Third party verification
	Design	• Redesign
		• Design for disassembly strategies
		• Repair, re-use and recycling
	Product durability	• Longer durability
		• Durability reports
	Product justifiability	• Process of consultation with all stakeholders
		• Design
		• Publication of sustainability audits for each product

List of Acronyms and Abbreviations

ACCA	Chartered Association of Certified Accountants
ATK	available tonne kilometre
BAANC	British Airways Assisting Nature Conservation
BAT	best available technology
BATNEEC	best available technology not entailing excessive costs
BEPS	best environmental practices strategy
BP	British Petroleum
BPEO	best practicable environmental option
BSI	British Standards Institute
CBI	Confederation of British Industry
CCEM	Centre for Corporate Environmental Management
CCPA	Canadian Chemical Producers' Association
CEC	Commission of the European Communities
CEFIC	European Chemical Industry Council
CEN	Comité Européen de Normalisation
CENELEC	European Committee for Electrotechnical Standardization
CER	corporate environmental reports
CERCLA	Comprehensive Environmental Response Compensation and Liability Act (US)
CERES	Coalition of Environmentally Responsible Economies
CFC	chlorofluorocarbon
CIA	Chemical Industry Association
CIMAH	Control of Industrial Major Accidents and Hazards
CSA	Canadian Standards Authority
CWS	compliance with standard
DEA	data envelopment analysis
DMU	decision making unit
EAC	European Accreditation Certification
EC	European Community (now EU)
EDU	Economic Development Unit (of a county council, UK)
EEC	European Economic Community (now EU)
EMAS	eco-management and audit scheme (EU)
EMS	environmental management system(s)
EPA	Environmental Protection Agency (US)
EPCRA	Emergency Planning and Community Right to Know Act (US)
EPI	environmental performance indicator
EQM	environmental quality management
ETSI	European Telecommunications Standards Institute
EU	European Union
EUROPIA	European Petroleum Industry Association
EVABAT	economically viable application of best available technology
GAAP	generally accepted accounting principles
GATT	General Agreement on Tariffs and Trade
GEMI	Global Environmental Management Initiative
GIS	geographic information systems
GNP	gross national product
HMIP	Her Majesty's Inspectorate of Pollution (UK)
ICC	International Chamber of Commerce
IoD	Institute of Directors (UK)

IEC	International Electrotechnical Commission
ISO	International Standards Organization
LCA	life cycle assessment
NACCB	National Accreditation Council for Certification Bodies (UK)
NRTEE	National Round Table on the Environment and the Economy (UK)
PAH	polycyclic aromatic hydrocarbons
PCB	polychlorinated biphenyl
PERI	public environmental reporting initiative
REMS	regional environmental management system(s)
SAGE	Strategic Advisory Group on the Environment (UK)
SARA	Superfund Amendments and Reauthorization Act (US)
SC	Subcommittee (of ISO Technical Committee)
SEA	strategic environmental assessment
SEC	Securities and Exchange Commission (US)
SME	small- or medium-sized enterprise
SWOT	strengths, weaknesses, opportunities and effects
TC	Technical Committee (of the ISO)
TQEM	total quality environmental management
TQM	total quality management
TRI	Toxic Release Inventory (US)
UKAS	United Kingdom Accreditation Service
UNCTC	United Nations Centre for Transnational Corporations Intergovernmental Working Group of Experts on International Standards of Accounting and Reporting
UNDP	United Nations Development Programme
UNEP	United Nations Environmental Programme
VOC	volatile organic compound
WBCSD	World Business Council for Sustainable Development
WG	Working Group (of the ISO)
WICE	World Industry Council for the Environment

Index

ACCA *see* Chartered Association of
     Certified Accounts
Agenda 21 37, 184, 211, 221, 224, 228,
     248
     see also Rio Earth Summit
Allen, 23
animal protection 248, 255
animal testing 248, 255
Ansoff, H I 16, 23
Ashford, N A 149, 150, 155, 171, 244
audits *see* environmental auditing
Azzone, G 168

Ball, S 180
Banks, J Robert 107
Bansal, P 17, 23
Barbier, E B 14
Barrett, S 27
BCSD *see* Business Council for
     Sustainable Development (BCSD)
Beaumont, J R 14, 19, 20, 23, 26
Bell, S 180
Bennett, M 152, 155, 160, 168
Bhopal explosion 9
     see also Union Carbide
biodiversity, protection of 237, 248, 255
biosphere, protection of, CERES
     principles 105
Blanchard, B S 140
Booz, 23
Bostrum, T 16, 17, 23, 27, 29
Buhr, N 29
British Standard for Environmental
     Management Systems (BS 7750)
     64–65
Brouzes, R 184
Brown, L 239
Brundtland Report 3–4, 14, 238
Buhr, N 29
Business Charter for Sustainable
     Development 107–11, 114, 115
aims of 107
commitment to 107–8
common effect, contributing to 109
compliance, assessment of 109
contractors 109
corporate priority 109
criticism of 110–11
customer advice 108

emergency preparedness 109
employee education 108
environmental audits 109, 113
facilities and operations 108
integrated management 108
openness to concerns 109
precautionary approach 108
prior assessment 108
process of improvement 108
products and services 108
research 108
suppliers 108
transfer of technology 109
see also environmental charters;
     International Chamber of
     Commerce (ICC)
Business Council on National Issues,
     environmental charter 113, 164
Business and Environment Forums
     201, 231

Callenbach, E 43, 57, 242
Canadian Chemical Producers
     Association (CCPA), environmental
     charter 113, 115
Carson, Rachel,
     Silent Spring 13
CEFIC, reporting guidelines 190–1
CENELEC 62
Centre for Corporate Environmental
     Management (CCEM),
     Environmental Policy Review
     96–99
CERES principles 103–7, 114, 115
audits 105, 113
benefits of 104
criticism of 106–7
energy conservation 105, 106
environmental restoration 105
Exxon Valdez disaster and 103
informing the public 105
long term commitment 106
management commitment 105
not legally binding 106
protection of the biosphere 105
reduction and disposal of waste 105,
     106
reports 105

OTHER BOOKS ON BUSINESS AND THE ENVIRONMENT FROM EARTHSCAN

Hijacking Environmentalism: Corporate Responses to Sustainable Development

Richard Welford

Hijacking Environmentalism exposes the lack of commitment from business and industry to the challenge of sustainable development. Modernist theories of environmental management have received some attention, but the wider ecological, ethical and social aspects of sustainable development have been ignored. In this provocative text, Welford examines the ways in which senior business executives and their lobby groups have reconstructed the environmental agenda to suit their own purposes, and presents new models of sustainable organizations which might represent an answer to the ideological impasse.

£13.95 paperback ISBN 1 85383 399 1   £32.50 hardback ISBN 1 85383 398 3 224pp

The Earthscan Reader in Business and the Environment

Edited by Richard Welford and Richard Starkey

A selection of the most important and innovative chapters and articles on the interaction of business and the environment. All the main elements of the debate are covered in five clearly structured sections: Perspectives on Business and the Environment; Business Strategy and the Environment; Research, Development and Technology; Techniques for Environmental Improvement; and Business and the Economy. An editorial commentary provides a helpful guide and outlines the issues, and comprehensive lists of sources and recommended further reading are included.

An extremely useful source of reference for students, environmental managers and consultants and those interested in greening the business environment.

£19.95 paperback ISBN 1 85383 301 0   £45.00 hardback ISBN 1 85383 315 0 304pp

Corporate Environmental Management 2: Culture and Organisations

Richard Welford

The first book to address the fundamental role of a company's culture and organization in determining its environmental performance. Part 1 provides an introduction to organizational theory and behaviour. Part 2 demonstrates the link between environmental problems and organizational issues. Problems, challenges, contradictions and complexities are tackled in Part 3, which looks at pragmatic and practical approaches and examines ways in which proactive cultures can be introduced into business.

£15.95 paperback ISBN 1 85383 412 2   £40.00 hardback ISBN 1 85383 417 3 206pp

For information on these and other Earthscan publications, please contact:
120 Pentonville Road
London N1 9JN
Tel: 0171 278 0433   Fax: 0171 278 1142
Email: earthinfo@earthscan.co.uk
Website: http://www.earthscan.co.uk